PUBLISHING

GW00373895

ONLINE RESOURCES INCLUDED

FOR THE FIRST TIME, THIS EXAM KIT COMES WITH
FREE ONLINE ACCESS
TO EXTRA RESOURCES AIMED AT HELPING YOU PASS YOUR EXAMS

IN ADDITION TO THE OFFICIAL QUESTIONS AND ANSWERS IN THIS BOOK, GO ONLINE AND EN-gage WITH:

- Fixed Tests
- Interim Assessments
- Exam paper Guides
- Latest Official ACCA exam questions
- Answers updated to include legislation relevant to next exam
- Frequent and varied new additions to these resources – watch this space!

And you can access all of these extra resources anytime, anywhere using your EN-gage account.

How to access your online resources

If you are a Kaplan Financial tuition, full-time or distance learning student

You will already have an EN-gage account and these extra resources will be available to you online. You do not need to register again, as this process was completed when you enrolled. If having problems accessing online materials, please ask your course administrator.

If you purchased through Kaplan Flexible Learning or via the Kaplan Publishing website

You will automatically receive an e-mail invitation to EN-gage online. Please register your details using this e-mail to gain access to your content. If you do not receive the e-mail or book content, please contact Kaplan Flexible Learning.

If you are already a registered EN-gage user

Go to www.EN-gage.co.uk and log in. Select the 'add a book' feature and enter the ISBN number of this book and the unique pass key at the bottom of this card. Then click 'finished' or 'add another book'. You may add as many books as you have purchased from this screen.

If you are a new EN-gage user

Register at www.EN-gage.co.uk and click on the link contained in the e-mail we sent you to activate your account. Then select the 'add a book' feature, enter the ISBN number of this book and the unique pass key at the bottom of this card. Then click 'finished' or 'add another book'.

Your Code and Information

This code can only be used once for the registration of one book online. This registration will expire when the final sittings for the examinations covered by this book have taken place. Please allow one hour from the time you submitted your book details for us to process your request.

AYW2-2xle-jDT8-QhOl

For technical support, please visit www.EN-gage.co.uk

Paper P1

Professional Accountant

EXAM KIT

PUBLISHING

British Library Cataloguing-in-Publication Data

A catalogue record for this book is available from the British Library.

Published by:
Kaplan Publishing UK
Unit 2 The Business Centre
Molly Millars Lane
Wokingham
Berkshire
RG41 2QZ

ISBN: 978-1-84710-569-1

© Kaplan Financial Limited, November 2008

Printed in the UK by CPI William Clowes Beccles NR34 7TL

Acknowledgements

The past ACCA examination questions are the copyright of the Association of Chartered Certified Accountants. The original answers to the questions from June 1994 onwards were produced by the examiners themselves and have been adapted by Kaplan Publishing.

We are grateful to the Chartered Institute of Management Accountants and the Institute of Chartered Accountants in England and Wales for permission to reproduce past exam questions. The answers have been prepared by Kaplan Publishing.

All rights reserved. No part of this publication may be reproduced, stored in a retrieval system, or transmitted, in any form or by any means, electronic, mechanical, photocopying, recording or otherwise, without the prior written permission of Kaplan Publishing.

KAPLAN PUBLISHING

CONTENTS

To review the real December 2008 exam questions with answers updated in line with legislation that is relevant to your exam sitting, please log on to EN-gage.

You will find a wealth of other resources to help you with your studies on EN-gage and also at www.accaglobal.com/students/.

INDEX TO QUESTIONS AND ANSWERS

ANALYSIS OF PAST PAPERS

Syllabus area	Pilot	Supp Pilot *	Dec 07	Jun 08
A - Governance and responsibility				
1 The scope of governance			Q1	Q1, Q3
2 Agency relationships and theories		Q3	Q4	
3 The board of directors	Q1, Q2		Q1, Q3	Q3
4 Board committees	Q2	Q3		Q3
5 Directors' remuneration	Q2		Q2	
6 Different approaches to corporate governance	Q1	Q3	Q3	Q4
7 Corporate governance and corporate social responsibility		Q1	Q4	Q1
8 Governance: reporting and disclosure	Q1	Q3		
B – Internal control and review				
1 Management control systems in corporate governance	Q4		Q1	Q1
2 Internal control, audit and compliance in corporate governance		Q2	Q1	Q2
3 Internal control and reporting				Q4
4 Management information in audit and internal control				
C – Identifying and assessing risk				
1 Risk and the risk management process				
2 Categories of risk	Q1, Q4			
3 Identification, assessment and measurement of risk	Q1, Q4			Q1, Q4
D – Controlling risk				
1 Targeting and monitoring risk				
2 Methods of controlling and reducing risk			Q2	
3 Risk avoidance, retention and modelling			Q2	
E – Professional values and ethics				
1 Ethical theories	Q3	Q1	Q1	Q2
2 Different approaches to ethics and social responsibility		Q1	Q4	
3 Professions and the public interest	Q4			Q2
4 Professional practice and codes of ethics	Q3, Q4			Q2
5 Conflicts of interest and the consequences of unethical behaviour		Q1		
6 Ethical characteristics of professionalism				
7 Social and environmental issues in conduct of business and of ethical behaviour	Q1			Q1

* Supplementary pilot paper contained three 25 mark questions

SYLLABUS AND EXAM FORMAT

Format of the exam

		Number of marks
Section A:	1 compulsory 50-mark question, possibly in several parts	50
Section B:	2 out of 3 25-mark questions	50
		100

Total time allowed: 3 hours

This syllabus and study guide is designed to help with planning study and to provide detailed information on what could be assessed in any examination session.

The structure of the syllabus and study guide

Relational diagram of paper with other papers

This diagram shows direct and indirect links between this paper and other papers preceding or following it. Some papers are directly underpinned by other papers such as Advanced Performance Management by Performance Management. These links are shown as solid line arrows. Other papers only have indirect relationships with each other such as links existing between the accounting and auditing papers. The links between these are shown as dotted line arrows. This diagram indicates where you are expected to have underpinning knowledge and where it would be useful to review previous learning before undertaking study.

Overall aim of the syllabus

This explains briefly the overall objective of the paper and indicates in the broadest sense the capabilities to be developed within the paper.

Main capabilities

This paper's aim is broken down into several main capabilities which divide the syllabus and study guide into discrete sections.

Relational diagram of the main capabilities

This diagram illustrates the flows and links between the main capabilities (sections) of the syllabus and should be used as an aid to planning teaching and learning in a structured way.

Syllabus rationale

This is a narrative explaining how the syllabus is structured and how the main capabilities are linked. The rationale also explains in further detail what the examination intends to assess and why.

Detailed syllabus

This shows the breakdown of the main capabilities (sections) of the syllabus into subject areas. This is the blueprint for the detailed study guide.

Approach to examining the syllabus

This section briefly explains the structure of the examination and how it is assessed.

Study guide

This is the main document that students, tuition providers and publishers should use as the basis of their studies, instruction and materials.

Examinations will be based on the detail of the study guide which comprehensively identifies what could be assessed in any examination session. The study guide is a precise reflection and breakdown of the syllabus. It is divided into sections based on the main capabilities identified in the syllabus. These sections are divided into subject areas which relate to the sub-capabilities included in the detailed syllabus. Subject areas are broken down into sub-headings which describe the detailed outcomes that could be assessed in examinations. These outcomes are described using verbs indicating what exams may require students to demonstrate, and the broad intellectual level at which these may need to be demonstrated (*see intellectual levels below).

Intellectual levels

The syllabus is designed to progressively broaden and deepen the knowledge, skills and professional values demonstrated by the student on their way through the qualification.

The specific capabilities within the detailed syllabuses and study guides are assessed at one of three intellectual or cognitive levels:

Level 1: Knowledge and comprehension
Level 2: Application and analysis
Level 3: Synthesis and evaluation

Very broadly, these intellectual levels relate to the three cognitive levels at which the Knowledge module, the Skills module and the Professional level are assessed.

Each subject area in the detailed study guide included in this document is given a 1, 2, or 3 superscript, denoting intellectual level, marked at the end of each relevant line. This gives an indication of the intellectual depth at which an area could be assessed within the examination. However, while level 1 broadly equates with the Knowledge module, level 2 equates to the Skills module and level 3 to the Professional level, some lower level skills can continue to be assessed as the student progresses through each module and level. This reflects that at each stage of study there will be a requirement to broaden, as well as deepen capabilities. It is also possible that occasionally some higher level capabilities may be assessed at lower levels.

Learning hours

The ACCA qualification does not prescribe or recommend any particular number of learning hours for examinations because study and learning patterns and styles vary greatly between people and organisations. This also recognises the wide diversity of personal, professional and educational circumstances in which ACCA students find themselves.

Each syllabus contains between 23 and 35 main subject area headings depending on the nature of the subject and how these areas have been broken down.

Guide to exam structure

The structure of examination varies within and between modules and levels.

The Fundamentals level examinations contain 100% compulsory questions to encourage candidates to study across the breadth of each syllabus.

The Knowledge module is assessed by equivalent two-hour paper based and computer based examinations.

The Skills module examinations are all paper based three-hour papers. The structure of papers varies from ten questions in the *Corporate and Business Law* (F4) paper to four 25 mark questions in *Performance Management* (F5) and *Financial Management* (F9). Individual questions within all Skills module papers will attract between 10 and 30 marks.

The Professional level papers are all three-hour paper based examinations, all containing two sections. Section A is compulsory, but there will be some choice offered in Section B.

For all three hour examination papers, ACCA has introduced 15 minutes reading and planning time.

This additional time is allowed at the beginning of each three-hour examination to allow candidates to read the questions and to begin planning their answers before they start writing in their answer books. This time should be used to ensure that all the information and exam requirements are properly read and understood.

During reading and planning time candidates may only annotate their question paper. They may not write anything in their answer booklets until told to do so by the invigilator.

The Essentials module papers all have a Section A containing a major case study question with all requirements totalling 50 marks relating to this case. Section B gives students a choice of two from three 25 mark questions.

Section A of each of the Options papers contains 50-70 compulsory marks from two questions, each attracting between 25 and 40 marks. Section B will offer a choice of two from three questions totalling 30-50 marks, with each question attracting between 15 and 25 marks.

Guide to examination assessment

ACCA reserves the right to examine anything contained within the study guide at any examination session. This includes knowledge, techniques, principles, theories, and concepts as specified.

For the financial accounting, audit and assurance, law and tax papers, ACCA will publish *examinable documents* every six months to indicate exactly what regulations and legislation could potentially be assessed at the following examination session. Knowledge of new examinable regulations will not be assessed until at least six calendar months after the last day of the month in which documents are issued or legislation is passed. The relevant cut-off date for the June examinations is 30 November of the previous year, and for the December examinations, it is 31 May of the same year.

The study guide offers more detailed guidance on the depth and level at which the examinable documents will be examined. The study guide should therefore be read in conjunction with the examinable documents list.

New Professional Ethics Module

ACCA are introducing a new Professional Ethics module which all students registering from January 2007 are required to take, preferably before or at the same time as Paper P1, *Professional Accountant*. If you are an existing student transferring to the new syllabus this module is not compulsory - however you are encouraged to take it to improve your understanding of ethical issues facing accountants. This should also assist you in answering questions on the P1 paper. Further information on the Ethics Module can be found on the ACCA website.

SYLLABUS

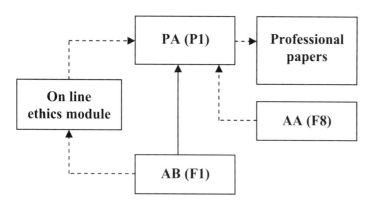

Aim

To apply relevant knowledge, skills and exercise professional judgement in carrying out the role of the accountant relating to governance, internal control, compliance and the management of risk within an organisation, in the context of an overall ethical framework.

Relational diagram of main capabilities

Main capabilities

On successful completion of this paper, candidates should be able to:

A   Define governance and explain its function in the effective management and control of organisations and of the resources for which they are accountable

B   Evaluate the professional accountant's role in internal control, review and compliance

C   Explain the role of the accountant in identifying and assessing risk

D   Explain and evaluate the role of the accountant in controlling and mitigating risk

E   Demonstrate the application of professional values and judgement through an ethical framework that is in the best interests of society and the profession, in compliance with relevant professional codes, laws and regulations.

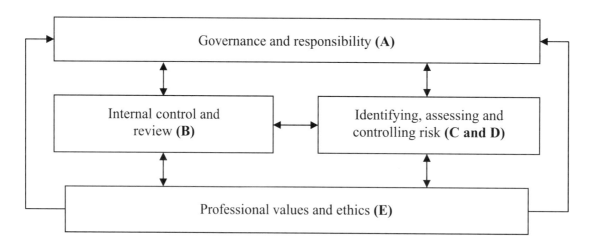

Rationale

The syllabus for Paper P1, *Professional Accountant*, acts as the gateway syllabus into the professional level. It sets the other Essentials and Options papers into a wider professional, organisational, and societal context.

The syllabus assumes essential technical skills and knowledge acquired at the Fundamentals level where the core technical capabilities will have been acquired, and where ethics, corporate governance, internal audit, control, and risk will have been introduced in a subject-specific context.

The PA syllabus begins by examining the whole area of governance within organisations in the broad context of the agency relationship. This aspect of the syllabus focuses on the respective roles and responsibilities of directors and officers to organisational stakeholders and of accounting and auditing as support and control functions.

The syllabus then explores internal review, control, and feedback to implement and support effective governance, including compliance issues related to decision-making and decision-support functions. The syllabus also examines the whole area of identifying, assessing, and controlling risk as a key aspect of responsible management.

Finally, the syllabus covers personal and professional ethics, ethical frameworks – and professional values – as applied in the context of the accountant's duties and as a guide to appropriate professional behaviour and conduct in a variety of situations.

Detailed syllabus

A   Governance and responsibility

1   The scope of governance

2   Agency relationships and theories

3   The board of directors

4   Board committees

5   Directors' remuneration

6   Different approaches to corporate governance

7   Corporate governance and corporate social responsibility

8   Governance: reporting and disclosure

B   Internal control and review

1   Management control systems in corporate governance

2   Internal control, audit and compliance in corporate governance

3   Internal control and reporting

4   Management information in audit and internal control

C   Identifying and assessing risk

1   Risk and the risk management process

2   Categories of risk

3   Identification, assessment and measurement of risk

D   Controlling risk

1   Targeting and monitoring risk

2   Methods of controlling and reducing risk

3   Risk avoidance, retention and modelling

E   Professional values and ethics

1   Ethical theories

2   Different approaches to ethics and social responsibility

3   Professions and the public interest

4   Professional practice and codes of ethics

5   Conflicts of interest and the consequences of unethical behaviour

6   Ethical characteristics of professionalism

7   Social and environmental issues in the conduct of business and of ethical behaviour

Approach to examining the syllabus

The syllabus will be assessed by a three-hour paper-based examination. The examination paper will be structured in two sections. Section A will be based on a case study style question comprising a compulsory 50 mark question, with requirements based on several parts with all parts relating to the same case information. The case study will usually assess a range of subject areas across the syllabus and will require the candidate to demonstrate high level capabilities to evaluate, relate and apply the information in the case study to several of the requirements.

Section B comprises three questions of 25 marks each, of which candidates must answer two. These questions will be more likely to assess a range of discrete subject areas from the main syllabus section headings, but may require application, evaluation and the synthesis of information contained within short scenarios in which some requirements may need to be contextualised.

Study Guide

A   GOVERNANCE AND RESPONSIBILITY

1   The scope of governance

(a)   Define and explain the meaning of corporate governance.[2]

(b)   Explain, and analyse the issues raised by the development of the joint stock company as the dominant form of business organisation and the separation of ownership and control over business activity.[3]

(c)   Analyse the purposes and objectives of corporate governance.[2]

(d)   Explain, and apply in context of corporate governance, the key underpinning concepts of: [3]

   (i)   fairness

   (ii)   openness/transparency

   (iii)   independence

   (iv)   probity/honesty

   (v)   responsibility

   (vi)   accountability

   (vii)   reputation

   (viii)   judgment

   (ix)   integrity

(e)   Explain and assess the major areas of organisational life affected by issues in corporate governance.[3]

   (i)   duties of directors and functions of the board (including performance measurement)

   (ii)   the composition and balance of the board (and board committees)

   (iii)   reliability of financial reporting and external auditing

   (iv)   directors' remuneration and rewards

   (v)   responsibility of the board for risk management systems and internal control

   (vi)   the rights and responsibilities of shareholders, including institutional investors

   (vii)   corporate social responsibility and business ethics.

(f)   Compare, and distinguish between public, private and non-governmental organisations (NGO) sectors with regard to the issues raised by, and scope of, governance.[3]

(g)   Explain and evaluate the roles, interests and claims of, the internal parties involved in corporate governance.[3]

   (i)   Directors

   (ii)   Company secretaries

   (iii)   Sub-board management

   (iv)   Employee representatives (e.g. trade unions)

(h)   Explain and evaluate the roles, interests and claims of, the external parties involved in corporate governance.[3]

   (i)   Shareholders (including shareholders' rights and responsibilities)

   (ii)   Auditors

   (iii)   Regulators

   (iv)   Government

   (v)   Stock exchanges

   (vi)   Small investors (and minority rights)

   (vii)   Institutional investors (see also next point)

(i)   Analyse and discuss the role and influence of institutional investors in corporate governance systems and structures, for example the roles and influences of pension funds, insurance companies and mutual funds.[2]

2   Agency relationships and theories

(a) Define agency theory.[2]

(b) Define and explain the key concepts in agency theory.[2]

    (i)   Agents

    (ii)   Principals

    (iii) Agency

    (iv)   Agency costs

    (v)   Accountability

    (vi)   Fiduciary responsibilities

    (vii) Stakeholders

(c) Explain and explore the nature of the principal-agent relationship in the context of corporate governance.[3]

(d) Analyse and critically evaluate the nature of agency accountability in agency relationships.[3]

(e) Explain and analyse the following other theories used to explain aspects of the agency relationship.[2]

    (i)   Transaction costs theory

    (ii)   Stakeholder theory

3   The board of directors

(a) Explain and evaluate the roles and responsibilities of boards of directors.[3]

(b) Describe, distinguish between and evaluate the cases for and against, unitary and two-tier board structures.[3]

(c) Describe the characteristics, board composition and types of, directors (including defining executive and non-executive directors (NED).[2]

(d) Describe and assess the purposes, roles and responsibilities of NEDs.[3]

(e) Describe and analyse the general principles of legal and regulatory frameworks within which directors operate on corporate boards:[2]

    (i)   legal rights and responsibilities,

    (ii)   time-limited appointments

    (iii) retirement by rotation,

    (iv)   service contracts,

    (v)   removal,

    (vi)   disqualification

    (vii) conflict and disclosure of interests

    (viii) insider dealing/trading

(f) Define, explore and compare the roles of the chief executive officer and company chairman.[3]

(g) Describe and assess the importance and execution of, induction and continuing professional development of directors on boards of directors.[3]

(h) Explain and analyse the frameworks for assessing the performance of boards and individual directors (including NEDs) on boards.[2]

4   Board committees

(a) Explain and assess the importance, roles and accountabilities of, board committees in corporate governance.[3]

(b) Explain and evaluate the role and purpose of the following committees in effective corporate governance:[3]

    (i)   Remuneration committees

    (ii)   Nominations committees

    (iii) Risk committees.

5   Directors' remuneration

(a) Describe and assess the general principles of remuneration.[3]

    (i)   purposes

    (ii)   components

    (iii) links to strategy

    (iv)   links to labour market conditions.

(b) Explain and assess the effect of various components of remuneration packages on directors' behaviour.[3]

    (i) basic salary

    (ii) performance related

    (iii) shares and share options

    (iv) loyalty bonuses

    (v) benefits in kind

(c) Explain and analyse the legal, ethical, competitive and regulatory issues associated with directors' remuneration.[3]

6 Different approaches to corporate governance

(a) Describe and compare the essentials of 'rules' and 'principles' based approaches to corporate governance. Includes discussion of 'comply or explain'.[3]

(b) Describe and analyse the different models of business ownership that influence different governance regimes (e.g. family firms versus joint stock company-based models).[2]

(c) Describe and critically evaluate the reasons behind the development and use of codes of practice in corporate governance (acknowledging national differences and convergence).[3]

(d) Explain and briefly explore the development of corporate governance codes in principles-based jurisdictions.[2]

    (i) impetus and background

    (ii) major corporate governance codes

    (iii) effects of

(e) Explain and explore the Sarbanes-Oxley Act (2002) as an example of a rules-based approach to corporate governance.[2]

    (i) impetus and background

    (ii) main provisions/contents

    (iii) effects of

(f) Describe and explore the objectives, content and limitations of, corporate governance codes intended to apply to multiple national jurisdictions.[2]

    (i) Organisation for economic cooperation and development (OECD) Report (2004)

    (ii) International corporate governance network (ICGN) Report (2005)

7 Corporate governance and corporate social responsibility

(a) Explain and explore social responsibility in the context of corporate governance.[2]

(b) Discuss and critically assess the concept of stakeholders and stakeholding in organisations and how this can affect strategy and corporate governance.[3]

(c) Analyse and evaluate issues of 'ownership,' 'property' and the responsibilities of ownership in the context of shareholding.[3]

(d) Explain the concept of the organisation as a corporate citizen of society with rights and responsibilities.[3]

8 Governance: reporting and disclosure

(a) Explain and assess the general principles of disclosure and communication with shareholders.[3]

(b) Explain and analyse 'best practice' corporate governance disclosure requirements.[2]

(c) Define and distinguish between mandatory and voluntary disclosure of corporate information in the normal reporting cycle.[2]

(d) Explain and explore the nature of, and reasons and motivations for, voluntary disclosure in a principles-based reporting environment (compared to, for example, the reporting regime in the USA).[3]

(e) Explain and analyse the purposes of the annual general meeting and extraordinary general meetings for information exchange between board and shareholders.[2]

(f) Describe and assess the role of proxy voting in corporate governance.[3]

B INTERNAL CONTROL AND REVIEW

1 Management control systems in corporate governance

(a) Define and explain internal management control.[2]

(b) Explain and explore the importance of internal control and risk management in corporate governance.[3]

(c) Describe the objectives of internal control systems.[2]

(d) Identify, explain and evaluate the corporate governance and executive management roles in risk management (in particular the separation between responsibility for ensuring that adequate risk management systems are in place and the application of risk management systems and practices in the organisation).[3]

(e) Identify and assess the importance of the elements or components of internal control systems.[3]

2 Internal control, audit and compliance in corporate governance

(a) Describe the function and importance of internal audit.[1]

(b) Explain, and discuss the importance of, auditor independence in all client-auditor situations (including internal audit).[3]

(c) Explain, and assess the nature and sources of risks to, auditor independence. Assess the hazard of auditor capture.[3]

(d) Explain and evaluate the importance of compliance and the role of the internal audit committee in internal control.[3]

(e) Explore and evaluate the effectiveness of internal control systems.[3]

(f) Describe and analyse the work of the internal audit committee in overseeing the internal audit function.[2]

(g) Explain and explore the importance and characteristics of, the audit committee's relationship with external auditors.[2]

3 Internal control and reporting

(a) Describe and assess the need to report on internal controls to shareholders.[3]

(b) Describe the content of a report on internal control and audit.[2]

4 Management information in audit and internal control

(a) Explain and assess the need for adequate information flows to management for the purposes of the management of internal control and risk.[3]

(b) Evaluate the qualities and characteristics of information required in internal control and risk management and monitoring.[3]

C   IDENTIFYING AND ASSESSING RISK

1   Risk and the risk management process

(a)   Define and explain risk in the context of corporate governance.[2]

(b)   Define and describe management responsibilities in risk management.[2]

2   Categories of risk

(a)   Define and compare (distinguish between) strategic and operational risks.[2]

(b)   Define and explain the sources and impacts of common business risks.[2]

(i)   market

(ii)   credit

(iii)   liquidity

(iv)   technological

(v)   legal

(vi)   health, safety and environmental

(vii)   reputation

(viii) business probity

(ix)   derivatives

(c)   Recognise and analyse the sector or industry specific nature of many business risks.[2]

3   Identification, assessment and measurement of risk

(a)   Identify, and assess the impact upon, the stakeholders involved in business risk.[3]

(b)   Explain and analyse the concepts of assessing the severity and probability of risk events.[2]

(c)   Describe and evaluate a framework for board level consideration of risk.[3]

(d)   Describe the process of (externally) reporting internal control and risk.[2]

D   CONTROLLING RISK

1   Targeting and monitoring of risk

(a)   Explain and assess the role of a risk manager in identifying and monitoring risk.[3]

(b)   Explain and evaluate the role of the risk committee in identifying and monitoring risk.[3]

(c)   Describe and assess the role of internal or external risk auditing in monitoring risk.[3]

2   Methods of controlling and reducing risk

(a)   Explain the importance of risk awareness at all levels in an organisation.[2]

(b)   Describe and analyse the concept of embedding risk in an organisation's systems and procedures.[3]

(c)   Describe and evaluate the concept of embedding risk in an organisation's culture and values.[3]

(d)   Explain and analyse the concepts of spreading and diversifying risk and when this would be appropriate.[2]

3   Risk avoidance, retention and modelling

(a)   Define the terms 'risk avoidance' and 'risk retention'.[2]

(b)   Explain and evaluate the different attitudes to risk and how these can affect strategy.[3]

(c)   Explain and assess the necessity of incurring risk as part of competitively managing a business organisation.[3]

(d)   Explain and assess attitudes towards risk and the ways in which risk varies in relation to the size, structure and development of an organisation.[3]

E   PROFESSIONAL VALUES AND ETHICS

1   Ethical theories

(a)   Explain and distinguish between the ethical theories of relativism and absolutism.[2]

(b)   Explain, in an accounting and governance context, Kohlberg's stages of human moral development.[3]

(c)   Describe and distinguish between deontological and teleological/consequentialist approaches to ethics.[2]

(d)   Apply commonly used ethical decision-making models in accounting and professional contexts:

    (i)   American Accounting Association model

    (ii)   Tucker's 5-question model

2   Different approaches to ethics and social responsibility

(a)   Describe and evaluate Gray, Owen & Adams (1996) seven positions on social responsibility.[2]

(b)   Describe and evaluate other constructions of corporate and personal ethical stance:[2]

    (i)   short-term shareholder interests

    (ii)   long-term shareholder interests

    (iii)   multiple stakeholder obligations

    (iv)   shaper of society

(c)   Describe and analyse the variables determining the cultural context of ethics and corporate social responsibility (CSR).[2]

3   Professions and the public interest

(a)   Explain and explore the nature of a 'profession' and 'professionalism'.[2]

(b)   Describe and assess what is meant by 'the public interest'.[2]

(c)   Describe the role of, and assess the widespread influence of, accounting as a profession in the organisational context.[3]

(d)   Analyse the role of accounting as a profession in society.[2]

(e)   Recognise accounting's role as a value-laden profession capable of influencing the distribution of power and wealth in society.[3]

(f)   Describe and critically evaluate issues surrounding accounting and acting against the public interest.[3]

4   Professional practice and codes of ethics

(a)   Describe and explore the areas of behaviour covered by *corporate* codes of ethics.[3]

(b)   Describe and assess the content of, and principles behind, *professional* codes of ethics.[3]

(c)   Describe and assess the codes of ethics relevant to accounting professionals such as the IFAC or professional body codes.[3]

5   Conflicts of interest and the consequences of unethical behaviour

(a)   Describe and evaluate issues associated with conflicts of interest and ethical conflict resolution.[3]

(b)   Explain and evaluate the nature and impacts of ethical threats and safeguards.[3]

(c)   Explain and explore how threats to independence can affect ethical behaviour.[3]

6   Ethical characteristics of professionalism

(a)   Explain and analyse the content and nature of ethical decision-making using content from Kohlberg's framework as appropriate.[2]

(b)   Explain and analyse issues related to the application of ethical behaviour in a professional context.[2]

(c) Describe and discuss 'rules based' and 'principles based' approaches to resolving ethical dilemmas encountered in professional accounting.[2]

7   Social and environmental issues in the conduct of business and ethical behaviour

(a) Describe and assess the social and environmental effects that economic activity can have (in terms of social and environmental 'footprints').[3]

(b) Explain and assess the concept of sustainability and evaluate the issues concerning accounting for sustainability (including the contribution of 'full cost' accounting).[3]

(c) Describe the main features of internal management systems for underpinning environmental accounting such as EMAS and ISO 14000.[1]

(d) Explain the nature of social and environmental audit and evaluate the contribution it can make to the development of environmental accounting.[3]

REVISION GUIDANCE

Planning your revision

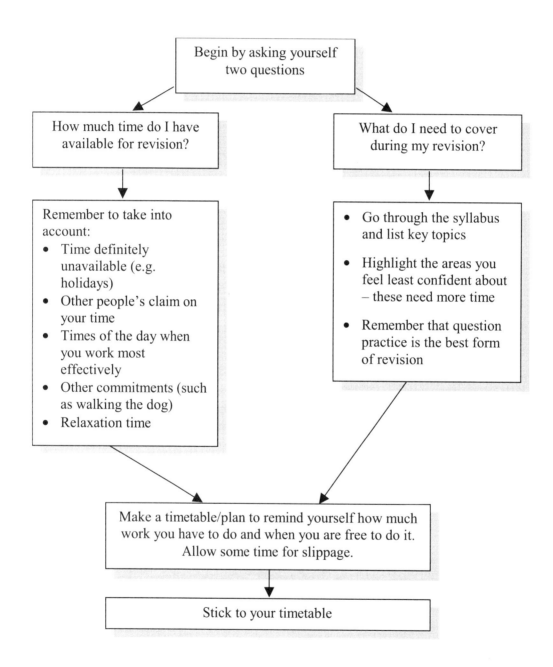

Begin by asking yourself two questions

How much time do I have available for revision?

What do I need to cover during my revision?

Remember to take into account:
- Time definitely unavailable (e.g. holidays)
- Other people's claim on your time
- Times of the day when you work most effectively
- Other commitments (such as walking the dog)
- Relaxation time

- Go through the syllabus and list key topics
- Highlight the areas you feel least confident about – these need more time
- Remember that question practice is the best form of revision

Make a timetable/plan to remind yourself how much work you have to do and when you are free to do it. Allow some time for slippage.

Stick to your timetable

Revision techniques

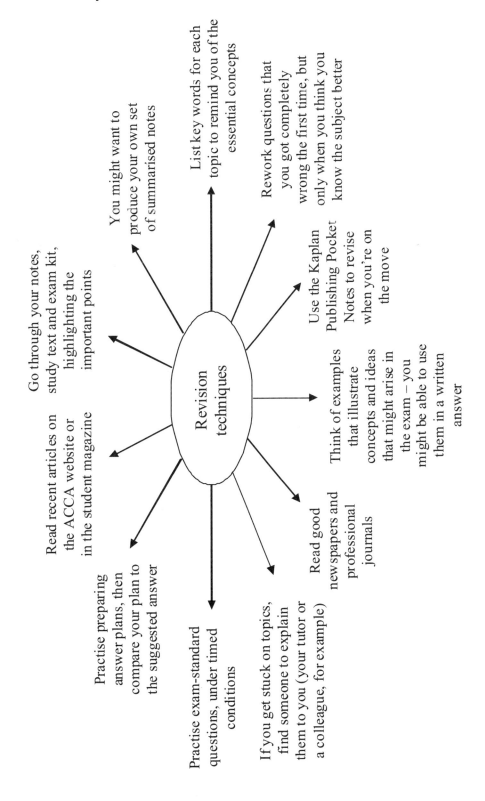

- Go through your notes, study text and exam kit, highlighting the important points
- You might want to produce your own set of summarised notes
- List key words for each topic to remind you of the essential concepts
- Rework questions that you got completely wrong the first time, but only when you think you know the subject better
- Use the Kaplan Publishing Pocket Notes to revise when you're on the move
- Think of examples that illustrate concepts and ideas that might arise in the exam – you might be able to use them in a written answer
- Read good newspapers and professional journals
- If you get stuck on topics, find someone to explain them to you (your tutor or a colleague, for example)
- Practise exam-standard questions, under timed conditions
- Practise preparing answer plans, then compare your plan to the suggested answer
- Read recent articles on the ACCA website or in the student magazine

Revision techniques

EXAM TECHNIQUES

- Use the allocated **15 minutes reading and planning time** at the beginning of the exam to read the questions and begin planning your answers.

- You might want to spend the first few minutes of the exam **reading the paper**.

- Where you have a **choice of question**, decide which questions you will do.

- Unless you know exactly how to answer the question, spend some time **planning** your answer.

- **Divide the time** you spend on questions in proportion to the marks on offer. One suggestion is to allocate 1½ minutes to each mark available, so a 10-mark question should be completed in 15 minutes.

- Spend the last **five minutes** reading through your answers and **making any additions or corrections**.

- **Essay questions**: Your essay should have a clear structure. It should contain a brief introduction, a main section and a conclusion. Be concise. It is better to write a little about a lot of different points than a great deal about one or two points.

- If you **get completely stuck** with a question, leave space in your answer book and **return to it later.**

- Stick to the question and **tailor your answer** to what you are asked. Pay particular attention to the verbs in the question.

- If you do not understand what a question is asking, **state your assumptions**. Even if you do not answer in precisely the way the examiner hoped, you should be given some credit, if your assumptions are reasonable.

- You should do everything you can to make things easy for the marker. The marker will find it easier to identify the points you have made if your **answers are legible**.

- **Computations**: It is essential to include all your workings in your answers. Many computational questions require the use of a standard format: company profit and loss account, balance sheet and cash flow statement for example. Be sure you know these formats thoroughly before the examination and use the layouts that you see in the answers given in this book and in model answers.

- **Case studies**: To write a good case study, first identify the area in which there is a problem, outline the main principles/theories you are going to use to answer the question, and then apply the principles/theories to the case.

- **Reports, memos and other documents**: Some questions ask you to present your answer in the form of a report or a memo or other document. So use the correct format – there could be easy marks to gain here.

Section 1

PRACTICE QUESTIONS – SECTION A

1 MANAGE LTD

Background information

Manage Ltd is a large family-owned private company operating in the UK in the contract services sector. The principle business that Manage undertakes is project management on large, long-term building projects in the UK. Manage Ltd has no overseas customers. The company provides a complete project management service, enabling the customers to deal just with Manage Ltd. Manage deal with all sub-contractors. The business has been very successful in recent years and as a result has become a potential acquisition target for a major international company, Utopia Inc, based in the US. Utopia Inc is listed on the New York Stock Exchange and is interested in furthering its businesses in Europe.

Some of the members of the family that own Manage Ltd (the Inglesons) are keen to dispose of their shares and it is therefore expected they will sell to Utopia if a suitable price can be agreed. The managing director of Manage, Jean Smith (not in the Ingleson family), is currently negotiating with the directors of Utopia over a price for the shares. Following the negotiation Jean will make a proposal to the Ingleson family. Jean and other selected staff have already been offered positions in Utopia if the acquisition proceeds. } *inducement.*

Financing the acquisition

Utopia Inc have a corporate policy of financing their acquisitions through loans. In previous foreign acquisitions, they have used either US or foreign loans depending on their views on economic and political factors in the US and in the foreign markets. They have no strong views on where to raise finance. They expect to need to borrow in 4 months' time to finance the acquisition.

One factor that the directors of Utopia Inc do feel needs to be considered however is that they are considering selling an existing UK division within a year and the proceeds are expected to be in the region of the acquisition price for Manage Ltd. The disposal will definitely occur after the acquisition of Manage Ltd, probably six months later.

Corporate governance

In anticipation of Manage Ltd becoming part of the Utopia Group the group CFO, Bert Bailey, has forwarded to Jean Smith a memo he sent last year to all divisional CEOs on corporate governance. He told Jean that the same process would operate for Manage Ltd, but with the dates about a year on.

MEMO

To: Divisional CFOs and CEOs
From: Bert Bailey
Subject: SOX compliance
Date: 15 January 20X4

As you are all no doubt aware, we are implementing Sarbanes-Oxley (SOX) this year. This memo summarises the timetable; more detail on the processes and procedures required will follow later.

Feb – May   Document key financial reporting systems and controls. Decide key controls and report any material design weaknesses in systems;

Jun – July   Divisional management to test key controls to confirm compliance and the effectiveness of the systems;

Aug – Sept   Group internal audit to review documentation and testing, and report on each division to the audit committee;

Oct – Nov   External audit to conduct the majority of their attestation work;

Dec   Management certification and assertions as required by sections 302 and 404.

The control framework the US companies will be using is the COSO framework. Overseas companies can use a local framework, if desired, provided it is approved in advance by the group SOX project team. Documentation must be standard across the group.

Required:

acquisition

(a)   Explain the difference between strategic and operational risks.   **(10 marks)**

(b)   Explain the risks that could exist for Utopia in making the investment in Manage Ltd and discuss how Utopia could assess their likely impact on the company.   **(15 marks)**

Jean Smith does not understand the memo she has been sent. She knows that Sarbanes-Oxley is the American corporate governance requirements but has not heard of any 'control frameworks'.

(c)   (i)   List some of the typical requirements for corporate governance in the areas of:

   • directors and the board

   • accountability and audit.   **(10 marks)**

   (ii)   Explain the elements of an effective internal control system (such as in the COSO framework or Turnbull report) giving practical examples of how Manage Ltd could demonstrate they have met all elements.   **(15 marks)**

↳ C – Control Environment
R – Risk assessment
I – Information technology
C – Control activities
M – Monitoring control.

   (Total: 50 marks)

2   WORLDWIDE MINERALS
(DEC 07)

The board of Worldwide Minerals (WM) was meeting for the last monthly meeting before the publication of the yearend results. There were two points of discussion on the agenda. First was the discussion of the year-end results; second was the crucial latest minerals reserves report.

WM is a large listed multinational company that deals with natural minerals that are extracted from the ground, processed and sold to a wide range of industrial and construction companies. In order to maintain a consistent supply of minerals into its principal markets, an essential part of WM's business strategy is the seeking out of new sources and the measurement of known reserves. Investment analysts have often pointed out that WM's value rests principally upon the accuracy of its reserve reports as these are the best indicators of future cash flows and earnings. In order to support this key part of its strategy, WM has a large and well-funded geological survey department which, according to the company website, contains 'some of the world's best geologists and minerals scientists'. In its investor relations literature, the company claims that:

'our experts search the earth for mineral reserves and once located, they are carefully measured so that the company can always report on known reserves. This knowledge underpins market confidence and keeps our customers supplied with the inventory they need. You can trust our reserve reports – our reputation depends on it!'

At the board meeting, the head of the geological survey department, Ranjana Tyler, reported that there was a problem with the latest report because one of the major reserve figures had recently been found to be wrong. The mineral in question, mallerite, was WM's largest mineral in volume terms and Ranjana explained that the mallerite reserves in a deep mine in a certain part of the world had been significantly overestimated. She explained that, based on the interim minerals report, the stock market analysts were expecting WM to announce known mallerite reserves of 4.8 billion tonnes. The actual figure was closer to 2.4 billion tonnes. It was agreed that this difference was sufficient to affect WM's market value, despite the otherwise good results for the past year. Vanda Monroe, the finance director, said that the share price reflects market confidence in future earnings. She said that an announcement of an incorrect estimation like that for mallerite would cause a reduction in share value. More importantly for WM itself, however, it could undermine confidence in the geological survey department. All agreed that as this was strategically important for the company, it was a top priority to deal with this problem.

Ranjana explained how the situation had arisen. The major mallerite mine was in a country new to WM's operations. The WM engineer at the mine said it was difficult to deal with some local people because, according to the engineer, 'they didn't like to give us bad news'. The engineer explained that when the mine was found to be smaller than originally thought, he was not told until it was too late to reduce the price paid for the mine. This was embarrassing and it was agreed that it would affect market confidence in WM if it was made public.

The board discussed the options open to it. The chairman, who was also a qualified accountant, was Tim Blake. He began by expressing serious concern about the overestimation and then invited the board to express views freely. Gary Howells, the operations director, said that because disclosing the error to the market would be so damaging, it might be best to keep it a secret and hope that new reserves can be found in the near future that will make up for the shortfall. He said that it was unlikely that this concealment would be found out as shareholders trusted WM and they had many years of good investor relations to draw on. Vanda Monroe, the finance director, reminded the board that the company was bound to certain standards of truthfulness and transparency by its stock market listing. She pointed out that they were constrained by codes of governance and ethics by the stock market and that colleagues should be aware that WM would be in technical breach of these if the incorrect estimation was concealed from investors. Finally, Martin Chan, the human resources director, said that the error should be disclosed to the investors because he would not want to be deceived if he were an outside investor in the company. He argued that whatever the governance codes said and whatever the cost in terms of reputation and market value, WM should admit its error and cope with whatever consequences arose. The WM board contains three non-executive directors and their views were also invited.

At the preliminary results presentation some time later, one analyst, Christina Gonzales, who had become aware of the mallerite problem, asked about internal audit and control systems, and whether they were adequate in such a reserve-sensitive industry. WM's chairman, Tim Blake, said that he intended to write a letter to all investors and analysts in the light of the mallerite problem which he hoped would address some of the issues that Miss Gonzales had raised.

Required:

(a) Define 'transparency' and evaluate its importance as an underlying principle in corporate governance and in relevant and reliable financial reporting. Your answer should refer to the case as appropriate. **(10 marks)**

(b) Explain Kohlberg's three levels of moral development and identify the levels of moral development demonstrated by the contributions of Gary Howells, Vanda Monroe and Martin Chan. **(12 marks)**

(c) Critically discuss FOUR principal roles of non-executive directors and explain the potential tensions between these roles that WM's non-executive directors may experience in advising on the disclosure of the overestimation of the mallerite reserve.

(12 marks)

(d) Draft a letter for Tim Blake to send to WM's investors to include the following:

(i) why you believe robust internal controls to be important; and

(ii) proposals on how internal systems might be improved in the light of the overestimation of mallerite at WM.

Note: four professional marks are available within the marks allocated to requirement (d) for the structure, content, style and layout of the letter. **(16 marks)**

(Total: 50 marks)

3 VCF

VCF is a small listed company that designs and installs high technology computer numerical control capital equipment used by multinational manufacturing companies. VCF is located in one Pacific country, but almost 90% of its sales are exported. VCF has sales offices in Europe, Asia, the Pacific, Africa, and North and South America and employs about 300 staff around the world.

VCF has annual sales of $200 million but the sales value of each piece of equipment sold is about $2 million so the sales volume is relatively low. Sales are always invoiced in the currency of the country where the equipment is being installed. The time between the order being taken and the final installation is usually several months. However, a deposit is taken when the order is placed and progress payments are made by the customer before shipment and upon delivery, with the final payment being made after installation of the equipment.

The company has international patents covering its technology and invests heavily in research and development (R&D, about 15% of sales) and marketing costs to develop export markets (about 25% of sales). VCF's manufacturing operations are completely outsourced in its home country and the cost of sales is about 20%. The balance of costs is for installation, servicing and administration, amounting to about 15% of sales. Within each of these cost classifications the major expenses (other than direct costs) are salaries for staff, all of whom are paid well above the industry average, rental of premises in each location and travel costs. Area managers are located in each sales office and have responsibility for achieving sales, installing equipment and maintaining high levels of after-sales service and customer satisfaction.

Although the head office is very small, most of the R&D staff are located in the home country, along with purchasing and logistics staff responsible for liaising with the outsource suppliers and a small accounting team that is primarily concerned with monthly management accounts and end of year financial statements.

VCF has a majority shareholding held by Jack Viktor, an entrepreneur who admits to taking high risks, both personally and in business. The board of four is effectively controlled by Viktor who is both chairman and chief executive. The three other directors were appointed by Viktor. They are his wife, who has a marketing role in the business, and two non-executive directors, one an occasional consultant to VCF and the other a long-time family friend. Board meetings are held quarterly and are informal affairs, largely led by Viktor's verbal review of sales activity.

Viktor is a dominating individual who exercises a high degree of personal control, often bypassing his area managers. Because the company is controlled by him, Viktor is not especially concerned with short-term profits but with the long-term. He emphasises two objectives: sales growth to generate increased market share and cash flow; and investment in R&D to ensure the long-term survival of VCF by maintaining patent protection and a technological lead over its competitors.

Viktor is in daily contact with all his offices by telephone. He travels extensively around the world and has an excellent knowledge of VCF's competitors and customers. He uses a limited number of non-financial performance measures, primarily concerned with sales, market share, quality and customer satisfaction. Through his personal contact and his twin objectives, Viktor encourages a culture committed to growth, continual innovation, and high levels of customer satisfaction. This is reinforced by high salary levels, but Viktor readily dismisses those staff not committed to his objectives.

The company has experienced rapid growth over the last 10 years and is very profitable although cash flow is often tight. A high margin is achieved because VCF is able to charge its customers premium prices. The equipment sold by VCF enables faster production and better quality than its competitors can offer.

Viktor has little time for traditional accounting. Product costing is not seen as valuable because the cost of sales is relatively low and most costs incurred by VCF, particularly R&D and export marketing costs, are incurred a long time in advance of sales being made. R&D costs are not capitalised in VCF's balance sheet.

Although budgets are used for expense control and monthly management accounts are produced, they have little relevance to Viktor who recognises the fluctuations in profit caused by the timing of sales of low volume but high value capital equipment. Viktor sees little value in comparing monthly profit figures against budgets because sales are erratic. However, Viktor depends heavily on a spreadsheet to manage VCF's cash flow by using sensitivity analysis against his sales and cash flow projections. Cash flow is a major business driver and is controlled tightly using the spreadsheet model.

The major risks facing VCF have been identified by Viktor as:

- competitor infringement of patents, which VCF always meets by instituting legal actions;

- adverse movements in the exchange rate between the home country and VCF's export markets, which VCF treats as an acceptable risk given that historically gains and losses have balanced each other out;

- the reduction in demand for his equipment due to economic recession;

- a failure of continued R&D investment to maintain technological leadership; and

- a failure to control costs.

Viktor considers that the last three of these risks are addressed by his policy of outsourcing manufacture and continuous personal contact with staff, customers and competitors.

Required:

(a)   With the aid of a diagram, explain the role of the board of a company in relation to risk management.   **(10 marks)**

(b)   Identify and evaluate the existing controls within VCF (including those applied by Viktor). Where appropriate, recommend actions to mitigate any risks identified.
                                                                                          (20 marks)

(c)   Write a report to the board of VCF recommending improvements to the company's corporate governance, risk management strategy and internal controls.

Note: You should use examples from the case to illustrate your answer.   **(20 marks)**

(Total: 50 marks)

4   EMEA

East Midlands Estate Agents (EMEA) is one of the largest estate agents and property valuers in the country. It has over 30 agency branches and 12 auction rooms, employing over 200 mainly full-time staff.

EMEA has expanded massively over the last five years on the back of a property boom. Typically they charge 1.75% of the sales value as their fee. The sale of property has slowed recently, however, due to a restructuring of stamp duty levels by the government. This has meant that houses being bought for over $500,000 are now charged 4% of the purchase price in stamp duty (over $20,000) and houses worth $250,000 are charged 3% (over $7,500).

EMEA has a board of seven executive directors, four of whom are from the same, founding family. The company is quoted on the stock market but family members still own 40% of the shares in the business. The three other directors, who are not shareholders, were brought in for their expertise in fields such as accountancy and law. The directors do not work together at the same location very often, but tend to have an office at the nearest big city to which they live. These tend to have the largest branches of EMEA. Regional managers help manage the larger offices and oversee any other smaller offices in the surrounding area, although they are based at the larger city branches, spending some time travelling to the smaller offices. Each smaller office has a manager who oversees the staff and reports back to the regional manager regarding any issues operationally, but they do not take part in making any major business decisions. The number of staff they are responsible for can vary between two and 10.

EMEA have taken the slow down as a chance to look at the direction of their business and any improvements that could be made. One improvement identified by the directors has been information technology used in the agency branches and auction rooms. It is very slow to bring up house or property details due to the images it has to download, and is based on three databases – one for house, one for property and one holding potential client details. The staff find the system very frustrating due to the number of times they have to change between the databases whilst on the telephone to a potential client. The client has often made the call and is not happy about having to hold on for the system to do its job.

Required:

Tactical

(a) Contrast controls at a strategic, management and operational level, and illustrate your answer with examples of these present in EMEA. **(10 marks)**

(b) Discuss the controls that will influence the employees' behaviour at EMEA so that it is legally correct, consistent, efficient and fair. **(10 marks)**

(c) Discuss the responsibility of the directors of the business towards the shareholders of EMEA. **(12 marks)**

(d) Identify governance issues which could arise from having four family members on the board. Discuss how the situation may be improved by appointing non-executive directors.

(18 marks)

(Total: 50 marks)

5 IDAN

Company overview

IDAN is a large banking and financial services group that is listed on both the London Stock Exchange and the New York Stock Exchange. The group has over 20 million customers throughout the world and operates in 35 countries on four continents. The IDAN Group is composed of a mix of retail and commercial businesses that include corporate and investment banking, private banking and commercial banking.

Trends within the Financial Services Sector

The board of directors of IDAN is aware that a number of trends within the sector will require the bank to substantially re-design a number of its operating and information systems and review the nature of the interface between the internal audit and risk management functions. Current issues that are having an impact on the financial services sector include:

• A new European Union law requiring banks to provide details of interest paid on personal savings accounts held by non-residents. A withholding tax of 15% is to be imposed on such income and details must be sent by the bank to the tax authorities in the EU country where the recipient resides.

• Forecast rises in interest rates over the next two years.

• The elimination within the UK of the use of personal signatures as the authorisation method for credit and debit card transactions and their replacement with personal identification (PIN) numbers.

• The increasing use, by personal customers, of both telephone and internet banking services. Over 40% of bill payments, standing order amendments and balance transfers by such customers were processed in this way during the last 12 months compared with 28% the previous year.

- A growth in the number of cases being sent to the financial ombudsman or the financial industry regulator relating to claims of mis-selling or incorrect advice on the part of financial services companies in the supply of a range of savings and investment products.

- As a result of threats of terrorist activity, money laundering legislation has been introduced or tightened in all of the countries in which IDAN has banking operations.

Required:

(a) Discuss the main categories of risk that are faced by a bank such as IDAN and the advantages of risk categorisation in the design of a risk management system.

(10 marks)

(b) For each of the six issues identified in the question, recommend the controls that might be introduced to minimise IDAN's exposure to such risks. **(15 marks)**

(c) Compare and contrast the roles played by internal audit and risk management in organisations. Discuss the likely nature of the interaction between these two activities.

(10 marks)

(d) Identify the key attributes of internal audit and suggest criteria which a company such as IDAN could use to evaluate internal audit services. **(15 marks)**

(Total: 50 marks)

6   KEVIN'S KITCHENS

Kevin's Kitchens (KK) has been trading for the last 50 years. The company was floated three years ago and has recently undergone a significant restructuring. The company's main activity is the design and manufacture of kitchen cabinets and worktops, which it sells to do-it-yourself stores. Demand has been buoyant for the last five years and operating profits have steadily increased. Turnover has increased 20% this financial year (based on draft figures) and budgeted to increase 25% next year (based on forecast prepared by CEO).

The board is chaired by Kevin Jones, whose father founded the company. His brother Jack acts as managing director. Kevin and Jack have both worked at KK since they left school 40 years ago and still own 20% of the company between them. The directors meet every six weeks and due to the company restructuring during the last year their recent board meetings have concentrated on strategic issues and marketing plans.

All of the directors are members of the executive share option plan which vests in two years' time.

Currently there are six executive directors and two non-executive directors. The board is trying to recruit two more non-executive directors but are finding it difficult to find people with experience in the industry or financial reporting familiarity. This is largely because Kevin and Jack will only pay a nominal fee to non executive directors, as they don't see the point of having them at all. There is currently no formal audit committee, a fact which is disclosed in the annual report.

The finance director, William Micawber, was recruited from a large accountancy practice six months ago. The previous FD left following a disagreement with the other directors over the profit related bonus scheme which is in place for the directors. William produces a set of management accounts each month which is emailed to the directors in advance of the board meeting. He is responsible for performing analytical review on the management accounts and for explaining variances between actual and budgeted figures to the board. No formal analysis is produced by the FD, but he answers any questions raised about the management accounts at board meetings.

At the beginning of this year the directors decided to restructure the business. This involved two main issues:

- The closure of a design studio and factory close to the head office. This factory produced a specific range of fancy kitchen cabinets for which demand had been steadily decreasing over the last 10 years. The business unit became loss making two years ago and contributed only 10% to total company turnover. The factory ceased production seven months ago and staff have either been made redundant, or reallocated to more successful factories in the region. There are some Grecian-style cabinets in inventory remaining at the factory, considered unlikely to be sold. There was considerable bad press surrounding the factory closure as it resulted in 300 job losses in an area of high unemployment.

- The 100% acquisition last month of Camel Kitchens, a small design and manufacturing company based about 100 km from the head office. This business was started five years ago by two design school graduates who specialise in bespoke kitchen designs for exclusive architect-designed houses. The team comprises the two designers, a part time accountant and a small production team. It is hoped that this side of the business will grow over the next 10 years, with a budgeted annual turnover increase of 35%. This is the first acquisition ever made by BB, and due diligence was provided by the external audit firm Copperfield and Sons.

In the run up to the flotation the directors were told by the external auditors about the importance of improving the controls operating within the business. The directors felt that they lacked the skills and knowledge to do this without outside help, so Copperfields were heavily involved in creating a control system for the accounting function. Copperfields also provided accounting manuals at the time of the flotation which have since been followed by the finance department. The finance team which is separately located from most of the manufacturing operations is quite small and suffers from high staff turnover.

As KK does not have a dedicated internal audit department, this function is outsourced. The internal auditors visit the accounting department for two days every six months and send a report to the board outlining weaknesses identified in the system and suggesting recommendations. Kevin and Jack leave this report to be dealt with by William Micawber.

The IT system is a bespoke system introduced two years ago and was developed by a small local company IT4U. Any operational problems with the system are resolved by IT4U. All of the finance staff had training in the new system when it was introduced. There was some resistance to the new software and documentation as many of the finance team thought it over complicated and difficult to understand compared to the previous system. There is still some reliance on manual records that were used in the old system. Additionally the financial controller often issues verbal amendments to the practices outlined in the manual.

It is now nearly the end of the financial year. The audit is due to commence in four weeks' time, and the AGM is planned for three months' time. Due to the restructuring during the year there is considerable media attention expected on this year's results and AGM. It is planned that William Micawber will present the operating and financial results at the AGM, as Kevin and Jack are worried about being asked about compliance with the corporate governance requirements for listed companies, which they don't fully understand. A tax planning meeting is to be held tomorrow with the tax partner from Copperfields.

Required:

(a)   List the factors mentioned in the case study which could threaten compliance with general corporate governance principles. **(12 marks)**

(b)   Identify and discuss the factors that indicate weaknesses are likely to exist in the internal control function. Use a recognised method of assessing controls such as COSO to structure your answer. **(25 marks)**

(c)   Explain the benefits of appointing additional non-executive directors to Kevin and Jack.   **(13 marks)**

(Total: 50 marks)

7   WATER AGENCY

The Water Agency (WA) is a government department responsible for dealing with rivers, canals, reservoirs, lakes, flooding and sea defences.

The WA, like many government organisations, has struggled to keep up with information technology because of constraints on government funding, and has many legacy systems in place. Investment has recently started in a time-recording system for its staff. Until recently, the staff did not have to justify their time and projects frequently went over budget or were late.

The new system involves each member of staff recording each 10 minutes to a cost code on their computerised timesheet, each month. It has been communicated to staff that at least 75% of their time should be charged to productive tasks, i.e. projects, while the other 25% might be for undertaking general administrative tasks or for going on courses.

The system arrived two months ago in the offices of the WA, almost two years' late and at a cost so far of $5 million. It has not been fully debugged and keeps crashing, mainly as a result of the number of staff trying to access the system at the same time, i.e. the first Monday morning of the month when their timesheets must be entered for the previous month. There has been no training on how to use the system. The more IT-literate staff have had to show others how to use it. Mistakes are frequently made during input and any errors must be reported to the line manager responsible for that staff member, who may be at a different office elsewhere in the region. The line manager has to 'unsubmit' the data and then inform the staff member to resubmit. This has led to staff leaving the errors on the system because of the effort required to change them.

Owing to early teething problems with the system, no-one has been specifically allocated to check its output. The reason for the lateness of the system was that it was to feed into the costing system for materials used, so that budget managers could keep an eye on total costs. This proved reasonably problematic because of the age of the costing system and the language in which it was written. This information is now being produced in part, and the managers are horrified by the amount of money being spent on consultants. Information as to the labour cost of the full-time staff is still not available since the finance department have yet to calculate a charge-out rate for each staff member. At present the system simply shows a number of hours next to a name.

The Flood Defence Department in one small regional office comprises only 11 people – a manager, an assistant manager, three seniors, three juniors, two consultants and one administrator. One of the seniors with a project budget of $100,000 has reported to the manager his concerns about the amount of consultant time being charged to this project. The manager has not dealt with this issue yet because he has been out of the office recently. The senior has tried to contact him but he never answers the company mobile phone with which he is provided.

The consultants are usually qualified engineers charging around $300 per day for their input into projects with specialised areas in which full-time members of staff may not have experience. Consultants were contracted originally on a daily basis. Over the years, however, many consultants have worked full-time at the WA. This has caused resentment by some of the full-time staff who feel they make work for themselves at times. Also, one junior member of staff has seen a consultant playing solitaire on his computer for an afternoon.

The full-time staff have a flexi-time system. There are core hours of work when a staff member must be at work (10 am to 12 noon and 2 pm until 4 pm). Non-core hours are at the discretion of the staff member, although the standard working week is 37 hours.

A representative salary of a full-time, newly-qualified engineer is around $22,000, whereas a manager's salary is around $27,000. Increases in the salary of all staff depend on many things, but include 'coming in under budget and within the deadlines set'.

In the past, the administrator, aged 56, was given the responsibility of 'keeping an eye' on staff hours by the manager. However, recently she has been on long-term sick leave. Staff presume that she will be back soon because they received a postcard from the Sierra Nevada mountains in Spain from her last week. It is common knowledge that she hopes to retire early on the grounds of ill-health (a bad back).

While the administrator has been off sick, it has been noted by a junior that a senior has been arriving for work at 10 am, leaving at 4 pm, having 2 hours at the gym at lunchtime most days, and still accumulates a flexi-day off each month by recording more than a 37-hour week.

An internal auditor (ACCA-qualified and newly employed by the WA) has recently been assigned with the task of reviewing the Flood Defence Department's work. One of the projects he has selected for review is the $100,000 project mentioned earlier. When comparing the budget with the actual costs so far, he noticed an amount not budgeted for of $5,000 paid to the local council where the project was to take place. When he spoke to the senior in charge of the project, it came to light that this payment was a 'sweetener' so that an electricity cable could be run through a council run children's play area, the $5,000 being used to improve the play area. (The cable was required to supply a pump to combat flooding in the area.) Following review of other projects, it appears that the flood defence manager has authorised many 'sweeteners' (some as large as $20,000) so that the project is finished on time. The internal auditor has approached the manager about this issue but has been told it is normal business practice and to leave him alone to get on with his job. The manager then drove off in his Porsche to another meeting off-site.

The Water Agency is currently implementing a new directive on the internal control systems of the organisation. The requirement is that the Water Agency must employy 'best practice' in terms of corporate governance, risk management and ethical principles.

Required:

(a) Explain the implications of the directive to the internal control systems of the WA with specific reference to a principles-based corporate governance code of your choice.

Your answer should include discussions of the key elements of governance codes, the roles of directors and internal control systems. **(15 marks)**

(b) Identify the lack of controls over the full-time employees at the WA, and make recommendations to overcome these issues. **(12 marks)**

(c) Recommend how the controls over outsourcing (using consultant engineers) can be improved in the WA. **(8 marks)**

(d) Evaluate the findings of the internal auditor and incorporate ACCA's ethical principles in your recommendation for the auditors' subsequent actions. **(15 marks)**

(Total: 50 marks)

8 FUEL SURCHARGES

TY and JK are two airline companies providing scheduled flights between a number of major cities on two continents. Both companies are respected and have policies of providing full and detailed information in their financial statements as well as providing excellent customer service. TY and JK maintain some element of rivalry, and frequently produce adverts explaining how, for example, their seats have the most distance between them or their in-flight menus and entertainment are 'better' than the other company's.

As part of their pricing policy, both companies charge a basic price for each seat purchased. The basic price is then supplemented by an excess to travel at weekends, airport taxes and a fuel surcharge. The latter varies during the year depending on the price of oil and is designed to allow the airline companies to pass on increases in fuel price to their customers. Over the past 20 months, the fuel surcharges of TY and JK have changed on six occasions, with both airlines' surcharges changing at the same time and by the same amount.

One week ago, the legal department of the JK airline discovered that both airlines had colluded to set identical surcharges and that this collusion was illegal under the Anti-Competition laws of most jurisdictions. The matter was brought to the attention of the board of JK and a full disclosure statement was made to the airline industry regulator and the relevant governmental departments. JK stated that this action was being taken 'in the public interest'. As a result of the disclosure JK escaped any liability for damages, but TY was fined €250 million for entering into a price fixing agreement.

The chairman of JK promised to provide additional disclosure on this and other matters in the company's new Corporate and Social Responsibility (CSR) report. The board of TY were obviously annoyed with the decision by JK to disclose, and even more annoyed when it was discovered that the surcharges had been agreed by senior managers below board level without board approval. Those managers were immediately suspended.

The remuneration policy for directors in each company is slightly different.

- In TY, remuneration is determined 40% as a fixed salary, 40% based on a proportion of profit for the year and 20% on long-term incentives by granting share options.

- In JK, remuneration is determined 30% as a fixed salary, 30% based on the movement in share price over the last 12 months and 40% on share options.

Board remuneration in TY fell as a result of the fine and the board are now considering amending their remuneration to include a higher fixed element to overcome this shortfall.

Required:

(a) (i) Explain Kohlberg's levels of moral development.

 (ii) Discuss the price fixing agreement for fuel surcharges in terms of Kohlberg's theory and evaluate whether the action of JK to disclose the agreement was morally correct. **(20 marks)**

(b) (i) Define and explain the term 'public interest'.

 (ii) Evaluate whether the decision to disclose the fuel surcharge by JK was in the 'public interest' as the directors maintain. **(8 marks)**

(c) With respect to the elements of remuneration in TY and JK, discuss whether the elements are correctly implemented according to codes of corporate governance and evaluate the effectiveness of each element. **(15 marks)**

(d) Explain the reasons for JK providing a CSR report. **(7 marks)**

(Total: 50 marks)

9 AEI

You are the audit manager in charge of the field work of the AEI Co; it is the first year you have been involved with this client, although your audit firm has carried out the audit for the last eight years. AEI is a general manufacturing company which is listed on the stock exchange of the country it is based in. The company manufactures and distributes household products including kitchen equipment, chairs, tables, and bedroom furniture.

The audit work for the year to 30 June has been in progress for the last three weeks, and there is one week to go before it is completed. The audit team of five staff comprises two juniors, two seniors and yourself.

Ethical issues

P, one of the audit juniors, has been working exclusively on checking the existence and valuation of the inventory in the kitchen equipment division of AEI. The work is not particularly difficult, but it is quite time-consuming and means checking many items of inventory in a large warehouse. A lot of the inventory is old and dirty and P normally brings old clothes each day to wear around the warehouse. The warehouse manager recently approached P and offered a free re-fitting of P's kitchen as a 'thank you' for carrying out the inventory work. The warehouse manager stated this was a normal activity each year, in recognition of P's difficult working conditions. During the audit P has identified that the inventory is over-valued, particularly in respect of many old kitchen units being maintained at full cost price, even though those units have had no sales in the last 18 months. The extent of the over-valuation appears to be material to the financial statements.

Q, an audit senior, has been working on the disclosure elements of directors' remuneration for the financial statements and the directors' remuneration regulations disclosure for that jurisdiction. Q has discovered that disclosure in the financial statements and remuneration regulations is different from the information provided by and checked by the audit committee. When queried, the newly appointed chair of the audit committee stated that share options were not considered part of disclosable remuneration as the value was uncertain, being based on future share price, which could not be determined. This element of remuneration was therefore omitted from the financial statements and remuneration regulations disclosure. The chair informed Q that due to the confidential nature of directors' remuneration, no further disclosure of this situation was to be made. The chair also noted *[– ethical threat]* that recent review of shareholdings indicated that Q had a 2.5% share of the company and again this would not be disclosed due to the confidential nature of the information. Finally, the chair noted that the facts that the chair of the remuneration committee was also a director *[cross directorship]* of IEA and that the chair of the remuneration committee of IEA was also a director of AEI should not be disclosed in the financial statements; again citing confidentiality issues.

R, the second audit junior, has been auditing the bank reconciliations on AEI's 26 different bank accounts. The work is considered suitable for a junior member as it mainly entails checking that cheques issued prior to the year end were presented to the bank for payment after the end of the year. R has completed work on the reconciliations, and stated correctly that all cheques were presented to AEI's bank for payment after the end of the year. However, R failed to state that a number of cheques, material in amount, were only presented two months after the year end. In other words the financial statements were 'window dressed' to show a lower creditors' amount than was actually the case at the year end. When queried about this omission during final review of the audit files, R correctly stated that he was never informed that timing of presentation of cheques was part of the audit procedures.

Governance issues

Recently, under pressure from the governing body of the stock exchange where AEI is listed, all four NEDs were urged to resign. Four new NEDs have recently been appointed; the NEDs have the knowledge and experience to be able to assist the board in their strategic and scrutinising roles, the NEDs have backgrounds in production, operations and HR roles. The term of the NED contracts of employment is the same as executive directors; that is three years between renewals. One minor concern is that the NEDs were appointed in a hurry and they have not worked with the executive directors on the board of AEI before.

Required:

(a) Discuss the extent to which provision of an ethical code assists in resolving ethical dilemmas. **(11 marks)**

(b) (i) Explain the terms 'ethical threat' and 'ethical safeguard'. **(2 marks)**

(ii) From the information above, identify any ethical threats and recommend appropriate ethical safeguards explaining why that safeguard is appropriate. **(20 marks)**

(c) Explain the advantages and disadvantages of having NEDs on the board of a listed company. **(7 marks)**

(d) Explain the key functions of NEDs and evaluate whether those functions are being carried out effectively on the board of AEI. **(10 marks)**

(Total: 50 marks)

10 BMB

The BMB company provides rail passenger services between 152 different towns in one country. BMB is relatively successful in providing this service and has just had its lease to operate rail services renewed by the government. The terms of the lease state that BMB must provide payments of €100 million (or about 15% of turnover) to the government each year for the benefit of having a protected market in the area it provides rail services. However, the €100 million lease is a fixed sum not dependent on the number of passengers carried. So far, BMB has always been able to meet payment dates on the lease. Provision of rail services below the standard set out in the lease is also a breach of the lease terms, which is punishable as a fine.

Payment for rail transport is straightforward; customers purchase tickets prior to travel using cash, debit or credit cards. Creditors include loans and payment for the new trains as well as lease payments to the government.

As part of the bid to renew the lease, BMB stated that it was investing in a new type of train which will use bio-diesel as a fuel. Provision of the new train helps to maintain and enhance the culture of BMB being an innovative and forward-looking company. Design and initial testing of the trains has been completed, and results are promising, although final speed and safety trials are currently outstanding.

BMB is committed to purchasing 15 train units from their supplier N&D. Failure of the trains to pass the safety tests and be available to carry passengers will mean that BMB cannot meet its performance targets with the government, leaving the company open to fines for not meeting conditions in its lease. N&D is based in a different country with a volatile exchange rate; however, the contract with BMB is denominated in the currency of N&D's country. For the purchase to be completed, is it likely that BMB will need to take out additional loans.

The use of bio-diesel fuel represents an attempt by BMB to obtain good publicity from reduction in carbon emissions as well as showing that train services can be provided using renewable fuel sources. Bio-diesel is also in relatively short supply while new crops are cultivated to provide the fuel.

The ability of BMB to meet performance targets for provision of train services is further limited by government policy on updating of the rail network. While demand for rail transport has grown for each of the last five years, investment in the rail network has fallen to an all-time low and government funding has been directed instead to building more roads. This means that BMB is locked into a lease to provide more rail services where the rail network infrastructure may not be able to cope with the number of trains that BMB wants to run.

Directors' remuneration in BMB is heavily weighted towards a percentage of net profits. The board recognise this is a reason for arguing the profit element is not equitable, and open to manipulation by the directors.

Required:

(a)   Explain the concepts of *risk* and *risk management* and a process for managing risks in an organisation.   **(10 marks)**

(b)   Identify and explain the sources of business risk that could affect BMB. For each of those risks evaluate the impact of the risk on BMB and where necessary, discuss how that risk can be mitigated by BMB.   **(26 marks)**

(c)   Explain the concept of risk mapping and produce a risk map for BMB. Justify your categorisation of events in the risk map.   **(14 marks)**

(Total: 50 marks)

11   ROWLANDS & MEDELEEV
(JUN 08)

Rowlands & Medeleev (R&M), a major listed European civil engineering company, was successful in its bid to become principal (lead) contractor to build the Giant Dam Project in an East Asian country. The board of R&M prided itself in observing the highest standards of corporate governance. R&M's client, the government of the East Asian country, had taken into account several factors in appointing the principal contractor including each bidder's track record in large civil engineering projects, the value of the bid and a statement, required from each bidder, on how it would deal with the 'sensitive issues' and publicity that might arise as a result of the project.

The Giant Dam Project was seen as vital to the East Asian country's economic development as it would provide a large amount of hydroelectric power. This was seen as a 'clean energy' driver of future economic growth. The government was keen to point out that because hydroelectric power did not involve the burning of fossil fuels, the power would be environmentally clean and would contribute to the East Asian country's ability to meet its internationally agreed carbon emission targets. This, in turn, would contribute to the reduction of greenhouse gases in the environment. Critics, such as the environmental pressure group 'Stop-the-dam', however, argued that the project was far too large and the cost to the local environment would be unacceptable. Stop-the-dam was highly organised and, according to press reports in Europe, was capable of disrupting progress on the dam by measures such as creating 'human barriers' to the site and hiding people in tunnels who would have to be physically removed before proceeding. A spokesman for Stop-the-dam said it would definitely be attempting to resist the Giant Dam Project when construction started.

The project was intended to dam one of the region's largest rivers, thus creating a massive lake behind it. The lake would, the critics claimed, not only displace an estimated 100,000 people from their homes, but would also flood productive farmland and destroy several rare plant and animal habitats. A number of important archaeological sites would also be lost. The largest community to be relocated was the indigenous First Nation people who had lived on and farmed the land for an estimated thousand years. A spokesman for the First Nation community said that the 'true price' of hydroelectric power was 'misery and cruelty'. A press report said that whilst the First Nation would be unlikely to disrupt the building of the dam, it was highly likely that they would protest and also attempt to mobilise opinion in other parts of the world against the Giant Dam Project.

The board of R&M was fully aware of the controversy when it submitted its tender to build the dam. The finance director, Sally Grignard, had insisted on putting an amount into the tender for the management of 'local risks'. Sally was also responsible for the financing of the project for R&M. Although the client was expected to release money in several 'interim payments' as the various parts of the project were completed to strict time deadlines, she anticipated a number of working capital challenges for R&M, especially near the beginning where a number of early stage costs would need to be incurred. There would, she explained, also be financing issues in managing the cash flows to R&M's many subcontractors. Although the major banks financed the client through a lending syndicate, R&M's usual bank said it was wary of lending directly to R&M for the Giant Dam Project because of the potential negative publicity that might result. Another bank said it would provide R&M with its early stage working capital needs on the understanding that its involvement in financing R&M to undertake the Giant Dam Project was not disclosed. A press statement from Stop-the-dam said that it would do all it could to discover R&M's financial lenders and publicly expose them. Sally told the R&M board that some debt financing would be essential until the first interim payments from the client became available.

When it was announced that R&M had won the contract to build the Giant Dam Project, some of its institutional shareholders contacted Richard Markovnikoff, the chairman. They wanted reassurance that the company had fully taken the environmental issues and other risks into account. One fund manager asked if Mr Markovnikoff could explain the sustainability implications of the project to assess whether R&M shares were still suitable for his environmentally sensitive clients. Mr Markovnikoff said, through the company's investor relations department, that he intended to give a statement at the next annual general meeting (AGM) that he hoped would address these environmental concerns. He would also, he said, make a statement on the importance of confidentiality in the financing of the early stage working capital needs.

(a) Any large project such as the Giant Dam Project has a number of stakeholders.

Required:

(i) Define the terms 'stakeholder' and 'stakeholder claim', and identify from the case FOUR of R&M's external stakeholders as it carries out the Giant Dam Project;   **(6 marks)**

(ii) Describe the claim of each of the four identified stakeholders.   **(4 marks)**

(b) Describe a framework to assess the risks to the progress of the Giant Dam Project. Your answer should include a diagram to represent the framework.   **(6 marks)**

(c) Using information from the case, assess THREE risks to the Giant Dam Project.
                                                                          (9 marks)

Risk to R&M

(d)   Prepare the statement for Mr Markovnikoff to read out at the AGM. The statement you construct should contain the following.

    (i)   A definition and brief explanation of 'sustainable development';   **(3 marks)**

    (ii)   An evaluation of the environmental and sustainability implications of the Giant Dam Project;   **(8 marks)**

    (iii)   A statement on the importance of confidentiality in the financing of the early stage working capital needs and an explanation of how this conflicts with the duty of transparency in matters of corporate governance.   **(6 marks)**

Professional marks for layout, logical flow and persuasiveness of the statement.
(4 marks)

(e)   Internal controls are very important in a complex civil engineering project such as the Giant Dam Project.

Required:

Describe the difficulties of maintaining sound internal controls in the Giant Dam Project created by working through sub-contractors.   **(4 marks)**

(Total: 50 marks)

12   POOL PUBLISHING

(a)   POOL Publishing is a publisher of books with a listing on the national stock exchange of the country in which it is based. The company has been profitable in recent years. However, although total annual profits have been growing at a good rate, the directors are searching for a strategy that will enable the company to achieve even better growth.

One proposal is to grow through acquisition. The directors believe that growth opportunities in book publishing in their country are limited. They also take the view that the company should be diversifying to reduce risk and should therefore be developing into a conglomerate organisation operating a range of different businesses in different industries. They have therefore been looking at four potential takeover targets:

    (1)   a foreign book publisher in a country where the same language is spoken;

    (2)   a magazine publisher;

    (3)   a company operating a chain of internet cafes;

    (4)   a company operating a chain of restaurants.

The last three companies in the list all operate in the same country as POOL.

The chairman has reported, however, that several of the major shareholders in the company have expressed strong misgivings about the strategy of the board. They believe that a diversification strategy of the kind proposed would be inadvisable and unnecessary.

Required:

    (i)   Explain how diversification reduces risk.

    (ii)   Explain why the diversification strategy of the POOL board might be inappropriate.   **(20 marks)**

(b) POOL has a large number of customers. Almost five years ago, it outsourced its accounting to an external service provider, ITW. The accounting system is fully computerised, and is a bespoke system developed several years ago for POOL, and updated occasionally since that time.

The service from ITW has operated fairly well until recently, but ITW now appears to have difficulty in dealing with the rapidly-growing accounting requirements of POOL, as its business has expanded.

A decision has therefore been taken that the contract with ITW will not be renewed when it expires in six months' time. The accounting work will be given to a different outsourcing firm.

As a finance manager and internal auditor for POOL, you have been asked to plan the changeover from ITW to the new outsourcing firm. In addition, in accordance with the contractual agreement with ITW, you will be required to carry out an audit of the accounts system before the changeover occurs.

Required:

Describe the potential risks that need to be considered in the changeover from ITW to the new outsourcing firm, and recommend measures to limit those risks. **(15 marks)**

(c) Discuss the role and characteristics of internal audit in a company such as POOL and its effectiveness should be assessed. **(15 marks)**

(Total: 50 marks)

13 COMPLETE COMPUTER CARE

Complete Computer Care (also known as 3C) provides computer services and repairs on a regional basis to home computer users. Over recent years there has been an explosion in the numbers of householders owning computers which are running more sophisticated systems. Many homes now contain several computers linked together over their own network. However most PC owners have very little IT experience and encounter problems related to new software installations, software and hardware incompatibility, viruses and internet connections.

The majority of customers have bought their computers in superstores or over the internet, and although a large proportion come with 12 month warranties, these do not usually cover problems related to the installation by computer owners of additional software or peripherals. Where the computer retailer does provide such support it is often only provided over the telephone at very high rates.

Four years ago, 3C was set up by three individuals who met when working together as computer engineers in an IT company. Janet and John, a married couple, and Henry owned equal shares in the business. John is the Chairman of the company. They were recently joined by James, who purchased 10% of the business in return for an investment of capital. The other three shareholders currently each own 30% of the shares. The four all work as directors of the company, which now employs a large team of PC support and repair engineers, with the use of contract staff to cover occasional peaks in demand.

The services offered by include a helpline to resolve straightforward problems, supported by a repair service provided through home visits. Customers also have the option of paying for an annual contract which covers telephone support and one home visit per year. Any subsequent visits are charged at a discounted rate to these customers. 3C prides itself on providing a very friendly service and building up a relationship with customers who, as far as possible, speak to the same service engineer each time they contact the company.

Following the success of the company on a regional basis, Henry and James have been encouraging the other shareholders to consider expansion on a national basis. Although Janet and John are not so sure that this is a good idea, the four have been in discussions with a venture capital company which is interested in providing an injection of capital in return for a 40% share of the business.

In addition to the 40% share in the company, the venture capital company have also said that they would want to appoint a non-executive director of their choice, and have suggested Katy, who is the former finance director of a white goods repair company. They would also like the company to recruit two more non-executive director. They have also expressed concern that the directors do not all seem to be committed to expansion. In addition they have identified as a problem a lack of risk awareness and risk management within the business, which they believe will be essential for 3C if the company embarks on an expansion plan in a very fast-changing environment. The four directors are unsure of the implications of these requirements for the management of the business.

Required:

(a)   Identify issues which could arise from the current board structure of 3C.

(13 marks)

(b)   Explain why the venture capital company wants to appoint non-executive directors to the board and identify any benefits would Katy and the other directors could bring. Are there any potential problems resulting from their appointment?   **(12 marks)**

(c)   Suggest reasons why the venture capital company would be concerned about the lack of risk awareness and risk management. What actions would they expect 3C to take to address this?   **(25 marks)**

(Total: 50 marks)

PAPER P1 : PROFESSIONAL ACCOUNTANT

Section 2

PRACTICE QUESTIONS – SECTION B

GOVERNANCE AND RESPONSIBILITY

14   STAKEHOLDERS

Private sector companies have multiple stakeholders who are likely to have divergent interests.

Required:

(a)   Identify five stakeholder groups and discuss their financial and other objectives.

(12 marks)

(b)   Discuss the extent to which good corporate governance procedures can help manage the problems arising from the divergent interests of multiple stakeholder groups in private sector companies. You should answer with reference to a principles-based system of corporate governance with which you are familiar.   **(13 marks)**

(Total: 25 marks)

15   CORPORATE GOVERNANCE GUIDELINES

The following are extracts from the corporate governance guidelines issued by a large, publicly-quoted company:

(i)   All auditors' fees, including fees for services other than audit, should be fully disclosed in the annual report. In order to ensure continuity of standards the same audit partner, wherever possible, should be responsible for a period of at least three years.

(ii)   The board shall establish a remuneration committee comprising 50% executive directors, and 50% non-executive directors. A non-executive director shall chair the committee.

(iii)   The Chairman of the company may also hold the position of Chief Executive, although this shall not normally be for a period of more than three years.

(iv)   The annual report shall fully disclose whether principles of good corporate governance have been applied.

(v)   No director shall hold directorships in more than 20 companies.

(vi)   Directors should report regularly on the effectiveness of the company's system of internal control.

Required:

(a) Discuss the extent to which each of points (i) – (vi) is likely to comply with a principles-based corporate governance system. Use examples from a system with which you are familiar to illustrate your answer. **(12 marks)**

(b) Prepare a brief report advising senior managers of your company who are going to work in subsidiaries in:

  (i) A country with a rules-based corporate governance system which is similar to that in the USA and which applies to subsidiaries of overseas companies.

  (8 marks)

  (ii) A country where companies have two-tier boards. **(5 marks)**

  (Total: 25 marks)

16 INFLUENCE ON OBJECTIVES

Required:

(a) Discuss, and provide examples of, the types of non-financial, ethical and environmental issues that might influence the objectives of companies.

Consider the impact of these non-financial, ethical and environmental issues on the achievement of primary financial objectives such as the maximisation of shareholder wealth. **(15 marks)**

(b) Explain what is meant by corporate citizenship and discuss its implications for the objectives of businesses. **(10 marks)**

  (Total: 25 marks)

17 MULTI-JURISDICTIONAL GOVERNANCE
(DEC 07)

At a recent international meeting of business leaders, Seamus O'Brien said that multi-jurisdictional attempts to regulate corporate governance were futile because of differences in national culture. He drew particular attention to the Organisation for Economic Co-operation and Development (OECD) and International Corporate Governance Network (ICGN) codes, saying that they were, 'silly attempts to harmonise practice'. He said that in some countries, for example, there were 'family reasons' for making the chairman and chief executive the same person. In other countries, he said, the separation of these roles seemed to work. Another delegate, Alliya Yongvanich, said that the roles of chief executive and chairman should always be separated because of what she called 'accountability to shareholders'.

One delegate, Vincent Viola, said that the right approach was to allow each country to set up its own corporate governance provisions. He said that it was suitable for some countries to produce and abide by their own 'very structured' corporate governance provisions, but in some other parts of the world, the local culture was to allow what he called, 'local interpretation of the rules'. He said that some cultures valued highly structured governance systems while others do not care as much.

Required:

(a) Explain the roles of the chairman in corporate governance. **(5 marks)**

(b) Assess the benefits of the separation of the roles of chief executive and chairman that Alliya Yongvanich argued for and explain her belief that 'accountability to shareholders' is increased by the separation of these roles. **(12 marks)**

(c) Critically evaluate Vincent Viola's view that corporate governance provisions should vary by country. **(8 marks)**

(Total: 25 marks)

18 FOOTBALL CLUB
(DEC 07)

When a prominent football club, whose shares were listed, announced that it was to build a new stadium on land near to its old stadium, opinion was divided. Many of the club's fans thought it a good idea because it would be more comfortable for them when watching games. A number of problems arose, however, when it was pointed out that the construction of the new stadium and its car parking would have a number of local implications. The local government authority said that building the stadium would involve diverting roads and changing local traffic flow, but that it would grant permission to build the stadium if those issues could be successfully addressed. A number of nearby residents complained that the new stadium would be too near their homes and that it would destroy the view from their gardens. Helen Yusri, who spoke on behalf of the local residents, said that the residents would fight the planning application through legal means if necessary. A nearby local inner-city wildlife reservation centre said that the stadium's construction might impact on local water levels and therefore upset the delicate balance of animals and plants in the wildlife centre. A local school, whose pupils often visited the wildlife centre, joined in the opposition, saying that whilst the school supported the building of a new stadium in principle, it had concerns about disruption to the wildlife centre.

Helen

Local School

Local inner city wildlife reservation centre.

The football club's board was alarmed by the opposition to its planned new stadium as it had assumed that it would be welcomed because the club had always considered itself a part of the local community. The club chairman said that he wanted to maintain good relations with all local people if possible, but at the same time he owed it to the fans and the club's investors to proceed with the building of the new stadium despite local concerns.

fiduciary Relationship

Required:

(a) Define 'stakeholder' and explain the importance of identifying all the stakeholders in the stadium project. **(10 marks)**

② ⑧ — 4 points

(b) Compare and contrast Gray, Owen and Adams's 'pristine capitalist' position with the 'social contractarian' position. Explain how these positions would affect responses to stakeholder concerns in the new stadium project. **(8 marks)**

(c) Explain what 'fiduciary responsibility' means and construct the case for broadening the football club board's fiduciary responsibility in this case. **(7 marks)**

(Total: 25 marks)

19 DELCOM

Jason Kumas is the CEO and majority shareholder of Delcom, a large conglomerate listed on a European stock exchange. Mr Kumas created the company less than ten years ago and during this time has successfully acquired a portfolio of manufacturing businesses across the region. The company was listed three years ago in order to gain access to the large amounts of capital needed to continue growth through acquisition. Since his decision to float the company institutional investors have begun to take an increasingly active role in the governance of Delcom.

Investors are concerned about the risk profile of the organisation. In particular, they point to two recent takeovers of production companies where, in his haste to close the deal, Mr Kumas failed to adequately carry out due diligence, relying instead on his own intuitive feelings as to the value of the going concerns. This insight was subsequently found to be impaired as it is generally agreed that much of the companies' technologies are poor and the price paid was therefore far too high. Acquisitive transactions such as this are common and although Delcom has a board of directors it is evident that such decision making authority rests solely with the CEO.

Disclosure through the annual report is also considered to be inadequate. Mr Kumas has repeatedly failed to address this issue, privately viewing disclosure as little more than a paper exercise since he is the majority shareholder and has an insider's perspective on the success of the business.

Concerns have been voiced at the AGM calling for Mr Kumas to recognise the need to adhere to global governance standards such as those published by the OECD and ICGN. In response, Mr Kumas insists that local stock exchange regulation, although far below these global standards, provides an adequate basis upon which to operate, and that if change is necessary, it is for regulators to enforce such measures.

Required:

(a)   Define 'insider governance' structure and evaluate the worth of such structures.

(8 marks)

(b)   Describe the application of transaction cost theory to corporate governance. **(6 marks)**

(c)   Recommend improvements to disclosure that would be applicable in the situation of Delcom. **(6 marks)**

(d)   Discuss the focus for action within global governance standards. **(5 marks)**

(Total: 25 marks)

20   VESTEL

Vestel is a drinks manufacturer that specialises in producing wine and spirit products for consumption in its home markets and abroad. The company has been very successful in recent years culminating in its ability to gain listing on the local stock exchange.

Acceptance as a member of the stock exchange has placed pressure on the board of directors to ensure the company is fully compliant with the principles-based governance regime currently in operation. This compliance includes the need for appropriate committee structures and support for all board members in ensuring appropriate skills and expertise are developed over time.

As a relatively small public company Vestel has needed to be innovative and adaptive in order to compete against global competitors that operate in its markets. In addition, it has recently been faced with a number of market challenges that threaten shareholder prospects over the next period. These include the rising price of grapes, molasses and grain due to a series of harsh winters and poor harvests as well as rising costs in energy and transport. At the retail end, government taxation on alcoholic drinks has dramatically increased following public outcry over levels of alcohol abuse amongst the country's citizens.

Ethics, environmentalism, skills in government lobbying and operational infrastructure are all seen as key areas for improvement following a recent review of board performance. In response a nomination committee is being created for the first time in the company's history in order to recruit a number of non-executive directors onto the board. Finding suitable candidates may be difficult in a country where the size of the economy and number of large companies is relatively small.

The need to ensure such individuals' take an active role as soon as possible has highlighted the importance of induction as part of the recruitment process.

Required:

(a) Explain why a nomination committee is suggested to be essential for effective board operations. **(6 marks)**

(b) Describe how the committee might tackle the recruitment process. **(7 marks)**

(c) Briefly discuss the business case for induction and consider the content of such a process.

(12 marks)

(Total: 25 marks)

21 CORPORATE GOVERNANCE

Required:

(a) Identify the key reasons for the emergence of corporate governance regulations around the world. **(5 marks)**

(b) Explain the key areas and principles of corporate governance regulations. **(10 marks)**

(c) Discuss the role and responsibilities of audit committees as laid down in a major principles-based corporate governance code of your choice. **(10 marks)**

(Total: 25 marks)

22 MANAGERS AND SHAREHOLDERS

Required:

(a) Explain what is meant by agency theory and discuss how this can be used to explain the relationship between directors and shareholders. **(12 marks)**

(b) A function of non-executive directors is to reduce potential conflicts of interest between management and shareholders.

Required:

Discuss the major potential conflicts of interest that affect non-executive directors. **(13 marks)**

(Total: 25 marks)

23 ANDROM

Androm is a large manufacturing company. The board are currently considering obtaining additional finance via a listing on a recognised stock exchange.

Mr Hunt, the chairman and CEO of Androm, is convinced this course of action is appropriate for the company, although a minority of directors on the board disagree with the move. If necessary, Mr Hunt is prepared to appoint other directors who support his views to ensure that listing proceeds.

Mr Tyr, the non-executive director, recommends an external review to provide unbiased guidance to the board. He recognises that this advice may not be accepted because he only just resigned as chairman of Androm two years ago, and maintains his share options in the company.

Unfortunately, information about the possible listing was only provided to the board at the most recent board meeting to try to maintain secrecy, as Mr Hunt stated to the board. While this is correct, given a lack of appropriate skills on preparing for listing, board members suggested that they should have been made aware of the information prior to the board meeting so appropriate research could be undertaken.

Required:

Write a formal report to the board of Androm that:

(i)   Explains the principles of good corporate governance for boards of directors.

(ii)   Recommends amendments to the board structure of Androm to meet those principles.

(25 marks)

(Total: 25 marks)

24   GISTC

The Great International Stores Trading Company (GISTC) supplies a wide range of products via a catalogue distributed to two million customers, and a website. Products sold range from clothes through to kitchen appliances, furniture, electronic games, and household electronic goods. Customers make their selections from the catalogue or Internet site and then send orders via mail, telephone ordering, or direct from the Internet site.

Profits in GISTC have been rising steadily over the last five years following successful promotional activities, and a good reputation for fast delivery of goods and customer service.

To continue its expansion, GISTC will be investing in a new distribution centre located near two important motorways. The centre will take one year to build, and the financial accountant estimates that the company will need to borrow $500 million over two years to fund the expansion. TMC, GISTC's auditors for the last 14 years, have been asked to provide advice on alternative methods of raising finance for this operation, as well as performing a detailed review of the internal controls currently in operation within GISTC.

GISTC continues to be controlled by the board of directors, with Mr Wallace being the CEO and board chairman – an arrangement which works in the interest of GISTC regarding timely decision making. The company has the required number of non-executive directors, all with previous experience from within the financial services sector. The audit committee meets on a regular basis, and includes the chairman and senior executive directors as its membership. The chairman aims to continue dialogue with shareholders at the next AGM; important resolutions such as extending directors' service contracts to five years, and providing additional meetings for major shareholders will be proposed.

Required:

(a)   Discuss how the independence of external auditors can be maintained in a large entity, making reference to GISTC where possible.   **(12 marks)**

(b)   Discuss how good corporate governance principles affect the board of a company and its sub-committees, identifying any areas where GISTC breaches those principles.

(13 marks)

(Total: 25 marks)

25 SYKES ENGINEERING GROUP

Jerome Sykes is the grandson of the founder of Sykes Engineering Group. This company is now a publicly quoted company with 2,000 employees, and although Jerome, the chairman and managing director, only owns less than 2% of the equity of the Group he behaves as if it is his personal possession. His behaviour is becoming increasingly autocratic, involving himself in all levels of decision-making. This personalised decision-making has not brought consistency, clarity or rationality to the strategy process. Instead the company has suffered from confused improvisation, uncertainty and wild swings in corporate direction. Unfortunately this culture appears to have influenced many managers below board level.

The board of directors has now been forced into action after extensive media coverage has criticised the company for a number of accounting irregularities over several years, the bribing of key foreign customers and sexual and racial harassment. This has inevitably adversely affected the share price. The key financial institutions who have invested in the Group are now demanding the removal of Jerome Sykes from office.

Required:

(a) Discuss actions which might have been taken to prevent the problems within the Sykes Engineering Group. **(12 marks)**

(b) Describe the legal framework for the duties of directors of a company and the actions which the company can take following a breach of these duties. **(10 marks)**

(c) Explain the circumstances in which an individual could be disqualified from acting as a director. **(3 marks)**

(Total: 25 marks)

26 ROSH AND COMPANY
(JUN 08)

Mary Hobbes joined the board of Rosh and Company, a large retailer, as finance director earlier this year. Whilst she was glad to have finally been given the chance to become finance director after several years as a financial accountant, she also quickly realised that the new appointment would offer her a lot of challenges. In the first board meeting, she realised that not only was she the only woman but she was also the youngest by many years.

Rosh was established almost 100 years ago. Members of the Rosh family have occupied senior board positions since the outset and even after the company's flotation 20 years ago a member of the Rosh family has either been executive chairman or chief executive. The current longstanding chairman, Timothy Rosh, has already prepared his slightly younger brother, Geoffrey (also a longstanding member of the board) to succeed him in two years' time when he plans to retire. The Rosh family, who still own 40% of the shares, consider it their right to occupy the most senior positions in the company so have never been very active in external recruitment. They only appointed Mary because they felt they needed a qualified accountant on the board to deal with changes in international financial reporting standards.

Several former executive members have been recruited as non-executives immediately after they retired from full-time service. A recent death, however, has reduced the number of non-executive directors to two. These sit alongside an executive board of seven that, apart from Mary, have all been in post for over ten years.

Mary noted that board meetings very rarely contain any significant discussion of strategy and never involve any debate or disagreement. When she asked why this was, she was told that the directors had all known each other for so long that they knew how each other thought. All of the other directors came from similar backgrounds, she was told, and had worked for the company for so long that they all knew what was 'best' for the company in any given situation. Mary observed that notes on strategy were not presented at board meetings and she asked Timothy Rosh whether the existing board was fully equipped to formulate strategy in the changing world of retailing. She did not receive a reply.

Required:

(a)   Explain 'agency' in the context of corporate governance and criticise the governance arrangements of Rosh and Company.   **(12 marks)**

Good & bad.

(b)   Explain the roles of a nominations committee and assess the potential usefulness of a nominations committee to the board of Rosh and Company.   **(8 marks)**

(c)   Define 'retirement by rotation' and explain its importance in the context of Rosh and Company.   **(5 marks)**

(Total: 25 marks)

27   CORPORATE GOVERNANCE DEBATE
(JUN 08)

At an academic conference, a debate took place on the implementation of corporate governance practices in developing countries. Professor James West from North America argued that one of the key needs for developing countries was to implement rigorous systems of corporate governance to underpin investor confidence in businesses in those countries. If they did not, he warned, there would be no lasting economic growth as potential foreign inward investors would be discouraged from investing.

In reply, Professor Amy Leroi, herself from a developing country, reported that many developing countries are discussing these issues at governmental level. One issue, she said, was about whether to adopt a rules-based or a principles-based approach. She pointed to evidence highlighting a reduced number of small and medium sized initial public offerings in New York compared to significant growth in London. She suggested that this change could be attributed to the costs of complying with Sarbanes-Oxley in the United States and that over-regulation would be the last thing that a developing country would need. She concluded that a principles-based approach, such as in the United Kingdom, was preferable for developing countries.

Professor Leroi drew attention to an important section of the Sarbanes-Oxley Act to illustrate her point. The key requirement of that section was to externally report on – and have attested (verified) – internal controls. This was, she argued, far too ambitious for small and medium companies that tended to dominate the economies of developing countries.

Professor West countered by saying that whilst Sarbanes-Oxley may have had some problems, it remained the case that it regulated corporate governance in the 'largest and most successful economy in the world'. He said that rules will sometimes be hard to follow but that is no reason to abandon them in favour of what he referred to as 'softer' approaches.

(a)   There are arguments for both rules and principles-based approaches to corporate governance.

   Required:

   (i)   Describe the essential features of a rules-based approach to corporate governance;   **(3 marks)**

   (ii)   Construct the argument against Professor West's (and in favour of Professor Leroi's) opinion that a principles-based approach would be preferable in developing countries. Your answer should consider the particular situations of developing countries.   **(10 marks)**

(b)   The Sarbanes-Oxley Act contains provisions for the attestation (verification) and reporting to shareholders of internal controls over financial reporting.

Required:

Describe the typical contents of an external report on internal controls.   **(8 marks)**

(c)   Construct the arguments in favour of Professor Leroi's remark that external reporting requirements on internal controls were 'too ambitious' for small and medium companies.   **(4 marks)**

(Total: 25 marks)

28   BERT BROWN

Bert Brown, an ACCA member, works as the finance director of a small, private company which manages large, long-term construction projects on behalf of clients. The company has four shareholders, all of whom are members of the same family. Two shareholder own 30% of the business each and the other two own 20% each. One of the 20% shareholders does not play a large part in the business and has been discussing the possibility of selling his share of the business to the other shareholders.

The company has recently been in discussions with a large potential client. If successful this would bring the company significant business over the next five years and would have a considerable impact on the value of the business. The directors have estimated the likelihood of gaining this contract at 80%. As part of the company's strategic planning process Bert has been producing some forecasts of the company's activities and cash flow over the next three years to be presented at the next board meeting. However, the three active shareholders have asked him to exclude the potential contract from all the forecasts and not to discuss it with the fourth shareholder. Bert is concerned that this may be because they want to buy his shareholding and do not want him to be aware of the potential increase in business when assessing the value of his share of the business and is unhappy about not including this business in his forecasts.

Required:

(a)   Discuss Bert's concerns about not including information about the potential contract in the forecast information of the company.   **(7 marks)**

(b)   Discuss other ways in which the structure of a small family-run company like this one can affect the governance of the business.   **(10 marks)**

(c)   One of the active shareholders has said that as the company is small, private and a family business, they do not need to worry about corporate governance.

Discuss the points Bert could make in response to this statement.   **(8 marks)**

(Total: 25 marks)

29   CODES OF GOVERNANCE

(a)   Discuss the advantages and disadvantages of a rules-based system of corporate governance, and identify the key requirements of such codes. You should illustrate your answer with reference to the Sarbanes-Oxley Act.   **(15 marks)**

(b)   Explain the reasons behind the development of international convergence codes. Outline the areas covered by an international convergence code of your choice.

(10 marks)

(Total: 25 marks)

30   ROLES AND RELEVANCE

Many countries have developed best practice guidelines for corporate governance, although the details of what constitutes best practice vary from one country to another. There are also differences between statutory and regulatory corporate governance, as in the US, and voluntary codes of practice, as in Europe.

In all countries with a corporate governance regime, the composition of the board of directors is a key issue. In some countries, the remuneration of directors is another important aspect of corporate governance.

Required:

(a)   Explain why it is considered appropriate for the positions of chairman and chief executive officer of a company to be held by different individuals.   **(5 marks)**

 (b)   Describe the roles of non-executive directors, and suggest why there might be tension in these roles between contributing to strategy development and monitoring executive activity.   **(8 marks)**

(c)   Explain the reasons why directors' remuneration might be regarded as an important issue in corporate governance, and explain the principles that should be applied by a remuneration committee when negotiating a remuneration package with an executive director.   **(12 marks)**

(Total: 25 marks)

31   METTO MINING

There have been articles in the media recently regarding Metto Mining's operations around the world. In one 'whistleblower' documentary carried out by an investigative journalist, a hidden camera revealed a scandalous disregard for safety at three mines, with employees working in conditions far below legal standards set by the host country.

Local activist groups and citizens have been demonstrating outside one of the facilities for the past two months, ever since an underground explosion killed a number of employees. The company's response has been to pay local police to keep the crowds away from the gates of the mine. It has also issued a statement referring to the incident as 'regrettable but unavoidable'. Most impartial observers believe improved safety standards could have prevented the disaster.

At its European head quarters, Professor Lee, Metto's ethics manager has been handling questions from reporters all week. Due to the gravity of the situation he is now blaming local explosives suppliers for providing faulty products to the mines whilst also pointing out that the company contributes financially to the health and schooling of the local population through payments for mining rights paid to the local government. This government refuses to comment on any issues involving the mines.

Professor Lee's words have done little to appease institutional investors such as Julie Walker, head of Walker investments. She believes that share ownership is coupled with an obligation to act responsibly and is now threatening to divest unless Metto takes positive action to improve its ethical positioning. This includes making large charitable donations direct to families and communities affected by its operations. Professor Lee and the board of directors have so far failed to respond to her written request.

Required:

(a)   Describe how Carrol's model of Corporate Social Responsibility (CSR) can be applied to Metto and identify possible responses to ethical conflict.   **(12 marks)**

(b)   Discuss Metto's rights and responsibilities with regard to its position of corporate citizenship.   **(6 marks)**

(c) Briefly explain FOUR classifications of stakeholders that may assist in determining a response to the ethical conflict at Metto. **(4 marks)**

(d) Assess the responsibilities of ownership and property as identified by Julie Walker.

(3 marks)

(Total: 25 marks)

INTERNAL CONTROL AND REVIEW

32 REVIEW OF INTERNAL CONTROL

You are the internal auditor of Gash, a listed company. The company has recently appointed a new non-executive director, who is being given induction to the company and some training for carrying out his role on the board of directors. You have been asked to give him some information and guidance about the annual review of internal control, which is a requirement of best practice in corporate governance. (As a listed company, Gash applies best practice.)

He presents you with a list of questions about the review, which he would like you to answer. The questions are as follows:

objectives of internal control

(1) What aspects of the company's operations and activities will be covered by the review?

(2) What is the responsibility for the review and evaluation of internal control of (i) senior management, (ii) the audit committee and (iii) the board of directors?

Required:

(a) Provide an answer to the questions of the non-executive director. **(5 marks)**

(b) Describe a method for carrying out a review of the internal control system that you believe would be consistent with the guidelines for best practice. **(12 marks)**

(c) The non-executive director is aware that it is company policy for the internal auditors to carry out regular checks on internal controls, outside the annual review. He is rather surprised that the internal auditors, who report to the Finance Director, should be asked to do this work, due to ethical issues that could arise. He is not certain that the internal auditors could conduct an impartial and effective review of controls.

Explain the ethical issues that could arise for the internal auditor, and the relevance of the fundamental principles in ACCA's Code of Ethics and Conduct to the conduct of an impartial and effective review of internal controls. **(8 marks)**

(Total: 25 marks)

33 SPQ

As an ACCA member, you have recently been appointed as the head of internal audit for SPQ, a multinational listed company that carries out a large volume of Internet sales to customers who place their orders using their home or work computers. You report to the chief executive, although you work closely with the finance director. You have direct access to the chair of the audit committee whenever you consider it necessary.

One of your internal audit teams has been conducting a review of IT security for a system which has been in operation for 18 months and which is integral to Internet sales. The audit was included in the internal audit plan following a request by the chief accountant. Sample testing by the internal audit team has revealed several transactions over the last three months which have raised concerns about possible hacking or fraudulent access to the customer/order database. Each of these transactions has disappeared from the database after deliveries have been made, but without sales being recorded or funds collected from the customer. Each of the identified transactions was for a different customer and there seems to be no relationship between any of the transactions.

You have received the draft report from the internal audit manager responsible for this audit which suggests serious weaknesses in the design of the system. You have discussed this informally with senior managers who have told you that such a report will be politically very unpopular with the chief executive as he was significantly involved in the design and approval of the new system and insisted it be implemented earlier than the IT department considered was advisable. No post-implementation review of the system has taken place.

You have been informally advised by several senior managers to lessen the criticism and work with the IT department to correct any deficiencies within the system and to produce a report to the audit committee that is less critical and merely identifies the need for some improvement. They suggest that these actions would avoid criticism of the Chief Executive by the board of SPQ.

Required:

(a)   Explain the role of internal audit in internal control and risk management.   **(5 marks)**

(b)   Analyse the potential risks faced by SPQ that have been exposed by the review of IT security and recommend controls that should be implemented to reduce them.

(8 marks)

(c)   Discuss the issues that need to be considered when planning an audit of activities and systems such as the one undertaken at SPQ.   **(5 marks)**

(d)   Explain the ethical principles you should apply as the head of internal audit for SPQ when reporting the results of this internal review and how any ethical conflicts should be resolved.   **(7 marks)**

(Total: 25 marks)

34   INTERNAL CONTROL ASSESSMENT

Your finance director has been asked to prepare a paper for the next board meeting on the assessment of internal control and risk management within the company. Many board members think that the internal control system consists of accounting procedures and checks, and that internal audit is about testing whether these checks work properly. The finance director wants to explain to his colleagues that internal control is much wider in scope than procedures and checks.

Required:

(a)   Explain the objectives of a system of internal control.   **(8 marks)**

(b)   Explain the principles for the assessment of the internal control system within the company, under the following broad headings:

   •   the control environment

   •   risk recognition and assessment

   •   control activities and segregation of duties

   •   information and communication

   •   monitoring control activities and correcting deficiencies.   **(17 marks)**

(Total: 25 marks)

35   YAHTY

The YAHTY organisation provides investment services to individuals living away from their country of residence. For example, a person may be required to work in a foreign country for two or three years, but will retain an investment portfolio of shares, bank account deposits, pension contributions, etc in their home country. The YAHTY organisation manages this portfolio for the individual until they return to their country.

YAHTY employs 35 investment accountants to provide the investment services. Each accountant controls the portfolio of up to 200 clients, with an average fund value of €500,000. Decisions regarding the companies to invest in, the pension scheme funds to use, etc are made by the individual financial accountant. The accountant retains a computer record for each client which shows the funds invested in, the values and recent transfers. As long as the individual requirements of the client are met, then the YAHTY organisation is deemed to have been successful in managing that client. A senior accountant provides additional investment advice should the need arise.

For each client, the investment accountant is the authorised signatory on the client accounts, enabling funds transfers to be made by that individual. Any payment over €100,000 has to be authorised by the senior accountant. Most transfers are between €10,000 and €50,000 – the senior accountant only checking material transactions. At any time, the list of investments on the computer must agree to share certificates, etc retained by the accountant. The list of investments is not, however, linked to the payments systems in YAHTY.

Documentation for each transfer has to be retained by each investment accountant. Documents regarding fund transfers are retained in date order within a central filing system. This procedure provides YAHTY with significant savings in storage costs while ensuring that documentation can be obtained when necessary.

When a client returns to their home country, the investment manager transfers all funds back into the client's name. A list of the investments is printed off from the accountant's computer system and this is given to the client along with share certificates, pension scheme reports, etc. Full transaction histories are not available due to the time required for obtaining detailed historical documentation from the filing system already mentioned above. To ensure completeness and accuracy of transfer, the senior accountant reviews all funds with a value of more than €750,000 by checking the list of investments to the supporting documentation.

Required:

Prepare a report for the directors of YAHTY which:

(a)   Explains the principles of a sound system of internal control within the context of corporate governance. You should include examples based on guidance with which you are familiar.   **(6 marks)**

(b)   Identifies and describes the directors' responsibilities in relation to internal controls.   **(6 marks)**

(c)   Evaluates the YAHTY organisation's internal control systems, identifying any weaknesses; assesses the effectiveness of any controls over those weaknesses; and recommends improvements to the system of internal controls.   **(13 marks)**

(Total: 25 marks)

36 GERANIUM

Geranium grows and sells indoor and outdoor plants to a wide range of retailers and through its own garden centres. It has seen enormous growth in recent years, now operating from 10 sites and almost doubling turnover and profits each year. In the last year, the company invested significantly in new poly tunnel technology, which allows plants shelter from weather extremes and hence significantly increases productivity.

This financial year, Geranium has, for the first time, achieved the sales revenue level at which an external audit is required. The directors of Geranium have decided to set up a small internal audit department and an audit committee to help assist in the audit.

Required:

(a)   Advise Geranium's board of directors and the audit committee as to their separate responsibilities for internal control, and explain their relationship with both the internal and external auditors.   **(13 marks)**

(b)   Using relevant examples, recommend the financial and non-financial controls that should be present in Geranium Ltd.   **(12 marks)**

(Total: 25 marks)

37 AUDITOR INDEPENDENCE

'Much has been written recently about the need for internal auditors to be independent. However auditor independence is an ideal which can never be achieved.'

Required:

In the light of the statement above discuss:

(a)   why auditor independence is important   **(5 marks)**

(b)   the threats to independence of internal and external auditors   **(12 marks)**

(c)   whether it is possible for auditors to be completely independent.   **(8 marks)**

(Total: 25 marks)

38 FIS

FIS Ltd is located in the capital of a large country. Its main business is investing money from a variety of clients in stocks, shares, government bonds and other similar products. The investment portfolio managed by FIS runs into hundreds of millions of dollars across several hundred different investments.

Three fund managers are responsible for investing client money, and transferring funds between different investments, depending on their view of the risk of each investment and expected return from that investment. Funds can be moved between investments in a matter of minutes, if required.

To help the managers assess the risk of each investment, FIS maintains a management information system, linked to the Internet, which provide the managers with an hourly update on the value of the investments and current news stories which may affect the value of those investments. Detailed information on the value of each fund, the investment history, number of stocks and shares held, location of the appropriate certificates etc. is also provided automatically by the MIS. However, the system is relatively old (being installed four years ago) and has to be supplemented with information from other sources including:

- newspapers, and

- Internet news services (available on a separate computer system).

Information may also be available from an in-house information system maintained in the new business department. The new business department is responsible for contacting potential clients and offering investment services to those clients. This MIS provides information to assist with the initial investment decision for client funds. However, fund managers do not have access to this system.

The board of FIS has proposed a new system for the fund managers, because the old system is old and fund mangers have made some poor investment decisions in the last few months. However, the cost appears to outweigh the tangible benefits of installing the system.

Required:

Identify and explain the inefficiencies in the knowledge management information system for the fund managers in FIS Ltd. Recommend processes for removing these inefficiencies.

(25 marks)

39 RG

RG manufactures industrial glues and solvents in a single large factory. Approximately 400 different inputs are used to produce the 35 specialist outputs, which range from ultra-strong glues used in aircraft manufacture to high-impact adhesives that are required on construction sites.

Two years ago, with the company only just breaking even, the directors recognised the need for more information to control the business. To assist them with their strategic control of the business, they decided to establish a MIS. This is now operational but provides only the following limited range of information to the directors via their networked computer system:

- A summary business plan for this and the next two years. The plan includes details of the expected future incomes and expenditure on existing product lines. It was produced by a new member of the accounting department without reference to past production data.

- Stock balances on individual items of raw materials, finished goods etc. This report is at a very detailed level and comprises 80% of the output from the MIS itself.

- A summary of changes in total demand for glues and solvents in the market place for the last five years. This information is presented as a numerical summary in six different sections. Each section takes up one computer screen so only one section can be viewed at a time.

Required:

(a) (i)   Comment on the weaknesses in the information currently being provided to the directors of the company. **(11 marks)**

(ii)   Suggest how the information may be improved, with particular reference to other outputs which the MIS might usefully provide to the directors. **(8 marks)**

(b)   Explain what strategic information any MIS is unlikely to be able to provide.

(6 marks)

(Total: 25 marks)

40   SUPERMARKET

In pursuit of ever greater profits to satisfy the shareholders, the supermarket chain had searched overseas for cheaper suppliers. Unfortunately this strategy failed when the following headline appeared in the newspapers:

'Supermarket poisons customers'

Government inspections of farming facilities in the chosen countries were almost non-existent so the supermarket had employed a local inspector to work closely with factory managers and to carry out food hygiene audits. When the news of the disaster was first reported to the board six months after problems begun the inspector simply disappeared and still cannot be traced.

In their defence, the suppliers say they were forced to cut veterinary attention to their herds because of the low rate paid by the supermarket for their meat. The result was that large amounts of infected foodstuffs were exported to the supermarket's home country.

When interviewed as part of a review of the failure in control supermarket store managers said that they had known for some time that there was something wrong with the meat. As part of their routine goods inward inspection they examined the cellophane wrapped cuts and threw out any that seemed discoloured. Most say that they had not received any complaints from customers regarding ill effects following consumption of the product.

The Chief Executive (CEO) of the supermarket chain, Jon Cooper, fears that the repercussions of this event will have a serious effect on this year's profit. Some customers have defected to competitors whilst an environmental group is protesting at some of the larger stores. There are rumours of a government audit of the company's supplier systems and they have, of course, needed to commence a search for a new and hopefully cheaper supplier in another country.

Required:

(a)   Examine failures in internal control and recommend improvements.   **(16 marks)**

(b)   Describe a process through which the board of directors can carry out a formal review of internal control in this company.   **(9 marks)**

(Total: 25 marks)

41   CC & J

Audit firm CC & J had worked extensively with the global banking organisation Banco for many years. Senior audit partner, Andrezej Puczynski, had built up a close working and personal relationship with the Chief Finance Officer (CFO), often attending private family barbeques. In return for his diligent support and low fee audit work he had been rewarded with hugely lucrative management consultancy contracts that made his local office profits the envy of senior CC&J partners around the world.

The closeness of the relationship could be seen in the automatic selection of CC & J by the CFO, operating as chair of the audit committee of Banco, despite the existence of cut price tenders from audit firm competitors. Andrezej had only met the other two members of the committee once on a shooting trip organised by the CFO. The other members of the committee had no financial expertise and little, if any, involvement in Banco outside of an annual meeting with the committee chairman.

Last week significant financial impropriety was uncovered at Banco leading to the collapse of the firm and its suspension on the stock exchange. Andrezej knew that many of the accounting treatments he had personally signed off were, at the least, stretching the interpretation of accounting standards to their breaking point.

Required:

(a) Discuss the nature of threats to auditor independence and identify a measure to reduce each threat. **(10 marks)**

(b) Assess an appropriate composition of an audit committee using evidence within the scenario. **(5 marks)**

(c) Describe how an audit committee operates as an interface within an organisation.

(5 marks)

(d) Identify the characteristics of good quality information required by an audit committee.

(5 marks)

(Total: 25 marks)

IDENTIFYING AND ASSESSING RISK

42 LANDMASS

Landmass is a property company that is planning to obtain a listing for its shares on the stock market of the country in which it is based. The directors are aware, however, that the company will be required to comply with the corporate governance requirements including an annual review by the directors of the adequacy of its risk management systems. This country has a principles-based system of corporate governance which covers all companies with a listing on the stock market.

At the moment, the company does not have any formal risk management system, and the directors need advice on how such a system might be established. They have been informed that the risks of the business should be categorised, but they do not know how this might be done.

The company operates in three different areas:

1   It manages business property which it rents to business customers under short-term and medium-term lease arrangements.

2   It buys and re-sells office property and property used by retail businesses (such as shopping arcades).

3   It has a subsidiary that specialises in building high-quality residential property.

Required:

(a) Explain how risks might be categorised by companies, and suggest the risk categories that might be used by Landmass. **(9 marks)**

(b) Recommend how Landmass might establish a risk management system prior to its listing and the introduction of its shares to trading on the stock exchange. **(16 marks)**

(Total: 25 marks)

43 STREAK

Streak is a listed company operating in the entertainment industry. You are an internal auditor for the company, carrying out a range of tasks including reviews of management controls and audits of different parts of the company's accounting, operational and compliance systems.

Within the internal audit department, you are a member of a small management team responsible for planning the annual programme for control review, and for agreeing the annual programme of internal audits.

An item on the agenda for the next departmental meeting is the system of authorising capital expenditure in each division, particularly the film production division. Each division within the company is treated as an investment centre. Divisional management is responsible for authorising capital expenditures within their division, within the annual budget for the division and below a specified level. Larger capital expenditures are reserved to the board of directors for a decision.

There is a concern within the management team that capital expenditure within the film-making division is not properly controlled. For example, it has been alleged that $2 million approved for the purchase of new cameras was actually spent on completion of a new film that has exceeded its expenditure budget.

Required:

(a)   Suggest who has the responsibility for reviewing internal controls, and the importance of such a review. **(10 marks)**

(b)   Identify the risks that might be significant within the capital expenditure system within the film-making division, that a planned internal audit of the system should consider.
(15 marks)

(Total: 25 marks)

44   CALL CENTRE

A credit card company has a call centre. Cardholders with queries or complaints call the centre by telephone, where they are dealt with by the first junior operator to respond to the call. The junior operators are required to deal with the customer's query or complaint if they can, and to refer more complicated problems to a senior operator.

When customers have a valid complaint about items incorrectly included in their monthly statement, the account details must be corrected, and inappropriate interest charges must be cancelled.

The costs of the centre are high, but the board of directors and senior management believe that providing a high quality service is essential to maintain the reputation of the company's brand name and the continued support of its customers.

Required:

As a person newly-appointed to the role of manager of the call centre:

(a)   list the components of an internal control system, **(5 marks)**

(b)   identify the main risks within the call centre and explain the main controls that you would expect to see in operation with respect of those risks. **(20 marks)**

(Total: 25 marks)

45   REGIONAL POLICE FORCE

A regional police force has the following corporate objectives:

*   to reduce crime and disorder;

*   to promote community safety;

*   to contribute to delivering justice and maintaining public confidence in the law.

The force aims to achieve these objectives by continuously improving its resources management to meet the needs of its stakeholders. It has no stated financial objective other than to stay within its funding limits.

The force is mainly public-funded but, like other regional forces, it has some commercial operations, for example policing football matches when the football clubs pay a fee to the police force for its officers working overtime. The police force uses this money to supplement the funding it receives from the government.

Required:

(a) Discuss the risks to the achievement of the corporate objectives of the regional police force. **(12 marks)**

(b) Discuss the risks associated with a regional structure for the national police force. **(7 marks)**

(c) Describe the types of internal controls that might be applied by the police force in order to assist with the achievement of its objectives. **(6 marks)**

(Total: 25 marks)

46 GHI GROUP

The GHI Group is a major listed travel company based in northern Europe, with a market capitalisation of €200 million. GHI specialises in the provision of budget-priced short and long haul package holidays targeted at the family market. The term 'package holiday' means that all flights, accommodation and overseas transfers are organised and booked by the tour operator on behalf of the customer.

The GHI Group encompasses a number of separate companies that include a charter airline, a chain of retail travel outlets, and several specialist tour operators who provide package holidays. Each subsidiary is expected to be profit generating, and each company's performance is measured by its residual income. The capital charges for each company are risk adjusted, and new investments are required to achieve a base hurdle rate of 10% before adjustment for risk.

The package holiday market is highly competitive, with fewer than five main players all trying to gain market share in an environment in which margins are continually threatened. The key threats include rising fuel prices, last minute discounting and the growth of the 'self managed' holiday, where individuals by-pass the travel retailers and use the Internet to book low cost flights and hotel rooms directly with the service providers. Also, customer requirements regarding product design and quality are continuously changing, thereby increasing the pressure on travel companies to devise appropriate strategies to maintain profitability.

Sales of long haul packages to North America are relatively static, but the number of people travelling to South East Asian destinations has fallen substantially following the 2004 tsunami disaster. Africa, New Zealand, Australia and certain parts of the Caribbean are the only long haul growth areas, but such growth is from a small base. Sales within the European region are shifting in favour of Eastern Mediterranean destinations such as Cyprus and Turkey as the traditional resorts of Spain and the Balearic Islands fall out of favour. Short 'city breaks' are also growing rapidly in popularity, reflecting higher spending power particularly amongst the over 50s.

The shift in patterns of demand has created some problems for GHI in a number of Eastern Mediterranean resorts over the last two summer seasons. There are not many hotels that meet the specified quality standards, and consequently there is fierce competition amongst travel operators to reserve rooms in them. In addition GHI customers have experienced very poor service from hotels, which has resulted in adverse publicity and high compensation payments.

GHI has recently invested €8 million in purchasing two new hotels in the affected resorts. Sales forecasts indicate demand will grow at approximately 15% per year in the relevant resorts over the next five years. It is anticipated that the hotels will supply 70% of the group's accommodation requirements for the next season. The package holidays to the GHI owned hotels will be sold as premium all-inclusive deals that include all food, soft drinks and local beers, wines and spirits. Such all-inclusive deals are not currently offered by other hotels in the target resorts.

GHI's local currency is the Euro.

Required:

(a) Identify and briefly discuss two risks that are likely to be faced by the GHI Group under each of the following categories:

- Financial

- Political

- Environmental

- Economic. **(12 marks)**

(b) Identify and comment upon the changes in risks to GHI Group that might arise from the decision to sell premium all-inclusive deals, and suggest methods by which these risks might be monitored and controlled. **(8 marks)**

(c) List the tasks that the internal audit department of GHI should have performed to ensure that the risks associated with the new hotel purchases are managed effectively. You should assume that its involvement commenced immediately the strategic decision was made to purchase overseas property – in other words, prior to identification of target sites. **(5 marks)**

(Total: 25 marks)

CONTROLLING RISK

47 BTS COMPANY

Required:

(a) Explain the importance of monitoring risks at the strategic, tactical and operational levels in an organisation, discussing any problems that may occur from not doing this effectively. **(13 marks)**

(b) The BTS company manufactures and sells chairs and sofas for use in the 'sitting' or 'living' rooms of houses. The company's products are displayed on an internet site and orders received via this site only. Order processing takes place on the company's in-house computer systems along with inventory control and payment to suppliers. The computer systems are managed in-house with no external links other than the Internet for selling.

Production is carried out in BTS's factory. There is little automation and production is dependent on the knowledge of Mr Smith and Mr Jones, the production controllers. Similarly, BTS rely on the Woody company for the supply of 80% of the wood used in the manufacture of BTS products. BTS's supplier policy is to pay as late as possible, providing little information on future production requirements.

Other raw materials purchased include fabrics for chair and sofa covers. However, a minority of sales orders are lost because the correct fabric is not available for the customer. The main reason for these stock-outs appears to be that the procurement manager forgets to order the fabric when inventory levels are low.

BTS's products are distributed by FastCour – a nationwide courier firm. However, due to the size of the chairs and sofas it is essential that the customer is available to take delivery of the goods when the courier arrives at their house. FastCour offer a 2-hour 'window' for delivery although only 55% of deliveries are actually meeting this criteria providing poor publicity for BTS and an increasing number of customer complaints. The board of BTS do not believe a strategic review of courier services is required at this time.

Required:

Identify and explain any strategic, tactical and operational risks affecting the BTS company. For each risk, discuss method(s) of alleviating this risk.   **(12 marks)**

(Total: 25 marks)

48   SOUTHERN CONTINENTS COMPANY
(DEC 07)

The risk committee at Southern Continents Company (SCC) met to discuss a report by its risk manager, Stephanie Field. The report focused on a number of risks that applied to a chemicals factory recently acquired by SCC in another country, Southland. She explained that the new risks related to the security of the factory in Southland in respect of burglary, to the supply of one of the key raw materials that experienced fluctuations in world supply and also an environmental risk. The environmental risk, Stephanie explained, was to do with the possibility of poisonous emissions from the Southland factory.

The SCC chief executive, Choo Wang, who chaired the risk committee, said that the Southland factory was important to him for two reasons. First, he said it was strategically important to the company. Second, it was important because his own bonuses depended upon it. He said that because he had personally negotiated the purchase of the Southland factory, the remunerations committee had included a performance bonus on his salary based on the success of the Southland investment. He told Stephanie that a performance-related bonus was payable when and if the factory achieved a certain level of output that Choo considered to be ambitious. 'I don't get any bonus at all until we reach a high level of output from the factory,' he said. 'So I don't care what the risks are, we will have to manage them.'

Stephanie explained that one of her main concerns arose because the employees at the factory in Southland were not aware of the importance of risk management to SCC. She said that the former owner of the factory paid less attention to risk issues and so the staff were not as aware of risk as Stephanie would like them to be. 'I would like to get risk awareness embedded in the culture at the Southland factory,' she said.

Choo Wang said that he knew from Stephanie's report what the risks were, but that he wanted somebody to explain to him what strategies SCC could use to manage the risks.

Required: *TARA*

(a)   Describe four strategies that can be used to manage risk and identify, with reasons, an appropriate strategy for each of the three risks mentioned in the case.   **(12 marks)**

(b)   Explain the meaning of Stephanie's comment: 'I would like to get risk awareness embedded in the culture at the Southland factory.' — *control environment* **(5 marks)**

(c)   Explain the benefits of performance-related pay in rewarding directors and critically evaluate the implications of the package offered to Choo Wang.   **(8 marks)**

e.g share option

(Total: 25 marks)

49   TASS

The grocery business is heavily dominated by four major players, between them accounting for approximately 80% of householder purchases. The cost of competing for the dwindling additional market share in the home country makes the substantial returns available from opening stores in new countries seem very attractive.

The Chief Executive of TASS, one of the major players, knows that this strategy is not without its risks. Capital from existing operations is available to finance the investment, but each targeted country has a distinct culture and appetites that might not match the supermarket's high volume, limited choice offering. TASS knows that one of its competitors has already tried to breach this cultural divide but is finding it hard to attract customers, whilst dealing with local trading difficulties and a highly bureaucratic government.

TASS's risk auditor has raised a number of concerns. She stated that existing supply chain challenges were creating problems in ensuring continued supply of fresh vegetable and fruit products to its stores and these issues are likely to be exacerbated by the poor road infrastructure in some of the target countries and the need to import many more exotic products from abroad. Those sourced from local markets would need to be rigorously quality controlled, and competition from a network of well known local brands was likely to be fierce.

The Chief Executive, with thirty years experience in the industry, has absolute faith in the retail model that has created the stores' success over the last decades. He knows that the company's buying power, possibly assisted by the existence of some of its main competitors in the new markets, will, over time, drive out local competition and create trading conditions similar to those in its home markets.

His is acutely aware of the need for sustained profits in order to meet the expectations of the market. Talk of recession in the company's home market makes him even more determined to spread the risk of fluctuating profits through a number of different markets rather than remain reliant on one.

Required:

(a)   Describe a risk management process that could assist the company in determining strategy.   **(14 marks)**

(b)   Explain the role of a risk auditor.   **(6 marks)**

(c)   Discuss how risk can be embedded into the systems of an organisation.   **(5 marks)**

(Total: 25 marks)

50 RISK STRATEGY

Required:

(a) Explain how the risk appetite of an organisation can affect its risk strategy and discuss how risk management approaches such as TARA (Transference, Avoidance, Reduction and Acceptance) can also affect the overall risk strategy. **(10 marks)**

(b) Explain Ansoff's product/market matrix and discuss how this can be used in assisting an organisation in determining its risk strategy. **(10 marks)**

(c) Discuss the extent to which the size of an organisation affects its risk strategy.

(5 marks)

(Total: 25 marks)

51 DOCTORS' PRACTICE

A large doctors' practice, with six partners and two practice nurses, has decided to increase its income by providing day surgery facilities. The existing building would be extended to provide room for the surgical unit and storage facilities for equipment and drugs. The aim is to offer patients the opportunity to have minor surgical procedures conducted by a doctor at their local practice, thus avoiding any unfamiliarity and possible delays to treatment that might result from referral to a hospital. Blood and samples taken during the surgery will be sent away to the local hospital for testing but the patient will get the results from their doctor at the practice. It is anticipated that the introduction of the day surgery facility will increase practice income by approximately 20%.

Required:

(a) Identify the additional risks that the doctors' practice may expect to face as a consequence of the introduction of the new facility. **(12 marks)**

(b) A partner in another practice has suggested that in order to improve the way in which the practice manages its risks, risk management should be embedded in the organisation. Explain what is meant by 'embedding' risk and what steps need to be taken to ensure that this happens. **(13 marks)**

(Total: 25 marks)

PROFESSIONAL VALUES AND ETHICS

52 VAN BUREN
(JUN 08)

It was the final day of a two-week-long audit of Van Buren Company, a longstanding client of Fillmore Pierce Auditors. In the afternoon, Anne Hayes, a recently qualified accountant and member of the audit team, was following an audit trail on some cash payments when she discovered what she described to the audit partner, Zachary Lincoln, as an 'irregularity'. A large and material cash payment had been recorded with no recipient named. The corresponding invoice was handwritten on a scrap of paper and the signature was illegible.

Zachary, the audit partner, was under pressure to finish the audit that afternoon. He advised Anne to seek an explanation from Frank Monroe, the client's finance director. Zachary told her that Van Buren was a longstanding client of Fillmore Pierce and he would be surprised if there was anything unethical or illegal about the payment. He said that he had personally been involved in the Van Buren audit for the last eight years and that it had always been without incident. He also said that Frank Monroe was an old friend of his from university days and that he was certain that he wouldn't approve anything unethical or illegal. Zachary said that Fillmore Pierce had also done some consultancy for Van Buren so it was a very important client that he didn't want Anne to upset with unwelcome and uncomfortable questioning.

When Anne sought an explanation from Mr Monroe, she was told that nobody could remember what the payment was for but that she had to recognise that 'real' audits were sometimes a bit messy and that not all audit trails would end as she might like them to. He also reminded her that it was the final day and both he and the audit firm were under time pressure to conclude business and get the audit signed off.

When Anne told Zachary what Frank had said, Zachary agreed not to get the audit signed off without Anne's support, but warned her that she should be very certain that the irregularity was worth delaying the signoff for. It was therefore now Anne's decision whether to extend the audit or have it signed off by the end of Friday afternoon.

Required:

(a)   Explain why 'auditor independence' is necessary in auditor-client relationships and describe THREE threats to auditor independence in the case.   **(9 marks)**

(b)   Anne is experiencing some tension due to the conflict between her duties and responsibilities as an employee of Fillmore Pierce and as a qualified professional accountant.

   Required:

   (i)   Compare and contrast her duties and responsibilities in the two roles of employee and professional accountant.   **(6 marks)**

   (ii)   Explain the ethical tensions between these roles that Anne is now experiencing.   **(4 marks)**

(c)   Explain how absolutist (dogmatic) and relativist (pragmatic) ethical assumptions would affect the outcome of Anne's decision.   **(6 marks)**

                                                                     (Total: 25 marks)

53   PHARMA

Pharma is a global pharmaceutical company producing many of the world's leading over-the-counter and prescription drugs. Many of these brands are household names sold through major retail chains in over 100 countries or direct to governments for use through public sector health services. Recently, the company has funded a research project into the effectiveness of one of its new products designed to combat a particular childhood disease. The project is designed to evaluate effectiveness in comparison with a competitor brand as a foundation for a future marketing campaign. The drug was released into markets around the world two years ago.

All trials of the new drug have been carried out by Professor Zac Jones at the Massachusetts State University who receive a multi-million dollar support grant for their assistance in projects of this nature. The contract with Pharma insists on no publicity being given to projects and that all findings are kept strictly confidential.

Professor Jones has just returned from a meeting with Chief Executive and Chief Finance Officer (CFO) of Pharma. He has told them that, in his view, although the new product is effective, its side effects can be damaging to children in some cases and possibly even fatal. Although the probability of loss of life is small he is recommending removing the product from the shelves immediately. Professor Jones also states that he is ethically bound to publish his findings so that governments and health services around the world may take appropriate action.

The CFO has reminded him of the considerable revenue loss involved in such a move and of the size of the grant given to the University. He insists the findings remain confidential, pointing out a clause in the contract between Pharma and the University that forbids the disclosure of 'trade secrets' to third parties. Professor Jones is appalled and has openly questioned the CFO's integrity as a member of an esteemed profession.

Required:

(a) Define 'profession' and evaluate the role of the accountant in support of the public interest. **(10 marks)**

(b) Discuss how an accountant might support a wider, value laden role in society. **(6 marks)**

(c) Define 'confidentiality' and assess its importance as an underlying ethical principle. **(5 marks)**

(d) Advise Professor Jones as to possible courses of action given the ethical dispute with Pharma. **(4 marks)**

(Total: 25 marks)

54 DEONTOLOGICAL ETHICS

Required:

(a) Explain the deontological approach to ethics and the application of this approach by Kant in his three maxims. **(12 marks)**

(b) A recent newspaper report explained that a toy re-seller was recalling over 500,000 toys because they were unsafe. Following use of the toys, it was discovered that small magnets attached to each toy could become dislodged and accidentally swallowed by children. Swallowing a number of magnets could produce digestion problems and in extreme cases death. Subsequent investigation by the Trading Standards Authority (TSA) identified that these toys were produced in a country where the use of child labour is common – this was not the case in the country of sale. Also the manufacturer did not always provide safe conditions for the workers. Workers were also paid on a piece-rate which meant they hurried to complete each toy, and the magnets were not always properly attached to the toy. The reason for the lack of safety and poor working conditions was ascribed to pressure from the toy re-seller to provide toys at a low price. The toy re-seller indicated that low prices were expected by its customers, and that the use of child labour had not been publicised.

Required:

Apply Kant's deontological maxims to the above situation evaluating whether the use of child labour is acceptable. **(13 marks)**

(Total: 25 marks)

55 EEF AND TUCKER

Required:

(a) Explain the four stage Ethics Education Framework model and discuss how an ACCA member can show each stage of the model has been completed. **(16 marks)**

(b) An accountancy firm normally provides CPD training for its staff using an external training provider. This means that staff members have to travel to the training venue but then receive quality training in a classroom environment.

In an attempt to decrease costs, the training manager has decided to provide training in-house using computer-based training. Training can be undertaken at a time to suit each member of staff, although some unpaid late afternoon and evening use of the CBT will be expected.

Required:

Explain Tucker's five-question model and assess the change in training method against this model. **(9 marks)**

(Total: 25 marks)

56 PUBLIC INTEREST

Required:

(a) Explain the term 'public interest' and discuss when an accountant could be deemed to be acting for or against 'the public interest'. **(11 marks)**

(b) The accountant of QPT is nearing the completion of the audit of this company. Various issues have been raised with the directors of the company including:

1 One of the company's factories accidentally disposed of some toxic waste into a river. Information on this accident has been kept confidential within the company although there is risk to stakeholders and the general public.

2 One of the company's subsidiaries has been used for money-laundering activities (payment of 'fake' invoices to suppliers in another jurisdiction). The directors do not want this information to be made public.

3 The un-published results for QPT for the year show that the company has made a large loss (as compared to market expectations of a small profit). Official publication of the financial statements takes place in seven days.

Required:

Taking each of these issues one at a time, discuss whether information regarding each issue should be disclosed in the public interest. **(14 marks)**

(Total: 25 marks)

57 INO COMPANY

Required:

(a) Explain the term 'corporate ethics', discussing the extent to which organisations must have corporate ethics and how those ethics are reported. **(6 marks)**

(b) The INO Company produces a range of motor vehicles in a central European country. INO currently produces nine different models, and it has a good reputation for safety and has build up customer trust in its products in this respect.

One model produced by INO, the N920, has been identified as having a potential failure. There is a remote chance that the engine will overheat during use, causing the vehicle to stop. The INO R&D department estimates that this error will affect one car in 125,000 (or five cars overall). The board considers that the costs of rectification are excessive and far outweigh the potential costs of rectifying faults as and when they occur.

INO obtains tyres for its vehicles from the UIN Company. UIN is part of INO's preferred supplier scheme and enjoy close working relations with INO as well as prompt payment of invoices for goods supplied. However, INO has recently learnt that UIN are employing children as young as nine in an overseas production facility, although this is not against the law in that particular country.

As part of its perceived duty to society, the board of INO does promote charitable giving and support of community projects such as sponsorship of local schools and colleges. Employees are also providing with 'fair' wages and additional facilities such as a sports hall providing fitness training. However, INO does not produce any CSR report and the board prefers to invest in ethical activities as and when it chooses to rather than having any formal structure or systems in place.

INO has a range of shareholders from large corporate investors to smaller personal investments. Shareholders are generally pleased with the way in which directors run their business; growth in turnover and profits has been steady in recent years while dividends have consistently exceeded competitors by 25% or more.

The board of INO also recognises that motor vehicles are potentially damaging to the environment. An R&D budget of €25 million has therefore been targeted at reducing emissions from INO's vehicles.

Required:

Identify and explain any issues relevant to the ethical stance of INO and discuss the potential impact of those issues on the company and its stakeholders. Where appropriate, recommend amendments to the corporate ethics of INO. **(19 marks)**

(Total: 25 marks)

58 CODES OF ETHICS

Required:

(a) Explain the elements of a code of ethics including the introduction, fundamental principles, conceptual framework and detailed application. **(5 marks)**

(b) You are a recently qualified management accountant and have just accepted a new post as management accountant in MilesForDosh Co, a company specialising in provision of credit and loans to wealthy individuals. You report to Mr. M, the senior management accountant and your duties involve performing credit checks on new customers through to the preparation of monthly management accounts and cash and profit forecasts for the company.

An initial review of the receivables ledger shows one debt from Mr. MoneyPenny is quite old; there have been no loan repayments for the last six months, and the outstanding balance has risen to nearly €150,000 with accrued interest. When queried, Mr. M suggests not making a provision for this amount because to make a provision would decrease profit and cash flow by an unacceptable amount.

After leaving work for the day, you stop at the local wine bar for a drink with the junior management accountant, Lex. After a few drinks, Lex informs you that Mr MoneyPenny is a personal friend of Mr M, which may be a reason Mr M does not want to make a provision at this time.

Required:

Explain whether Lex or Mr. M have broken the ACCA professional code of ethics stating which principles, if any, have been broken, analysing reasons for any potential breach and suggesting actions that you should take. **(20 marks)**

(Total: 25 marks)

59 FIVE ETHICAL SITUATIONS

In all of the ethical situations below, the people involved are qualified members of ACCA.

1. A applies for a job and enhances his CV by indicating he obtained first time passes in all his examinations, although he actually failed three exams at the first attempt.

2. B is the management accountant in C Ltd. B is paid a bonus based on the profits of C Ltd. During accounts preparation B notices an error in the inventory calculation which has the effect of overstating profits. B decides to take no action as this would decrease the bonus payable.

3   D is responsible for the purchase of computer equipment in E Ltd. Quotes from three suppliers have been received for installation of new hardware; one supplier, F Co, has promised a 10% discount payable to D if their quote is accepted.

4. G is preparing the management accounts in H Ltd. Part of the information presented to him indicates that H Ltd entered into an illegal agreement with I Ltd to fix price increases in the goods H and I supply. H and I together supply 90% of the total market. The price setting enabled H and I to obtain higher than expected profits for their sales.

5. J is preparing the management accounts for K Ltd. L, the senior management accountant, has instructed J to omit the negative overhead variance from the accounts on the grounds that they show an 'unacceptable loss' with the inclusion of the variance.

Required:

(a) Explain how professional codes of ethics address possible conflicts of interest facing accountants. **(5 marks)**

(b) For each of the situations above:

(i)   Identify and explain the ethical threat to the accountant. **(10 marks)**

(ii) Discuss the ethical safeguards available to overcome that threat. **(10 marks)**

NB: Each situation is worth four marks – two for part (i) and two for part (ii).

(Total: 25 marks)

60 CARPETS AND FLOOR COVERINGS

BK is a company specialising in the sale of carpets and floor coverings to sports clubs, sports halls and social centres around the country. It obtains its carpeting and other materials directly from suppliers in Eastern Asia.

When it provides new carpeting to a customer, BK also undertakes to remove and dispose of the old carpeting or floor covering, but charges a fee for the service. The old carpets are taken to waste disposal sites or occasionally burned.

You have recently been appointed as an internal auditor to the company, and you are discussing your plan of work for the next 12 months with the finance director. The following points arise in your discussion.

The work of the internal audit section has so far been largely restricted to audits of elements of the financial accounting system, although there have been occasional management audits. You suggest that it might be appropriate to carry out some value for money audits.

The board of directors has come under pressure from its major shareholders to publish an annual Social and Environmental Report for inclusion in the annual report and accounts. You suggest that it might be appropriate to check and verify the contents of this report before publication.

There has been considerable publicity in the national press recently about the use of child labour and slave labour in certain parts of the country from which BK purchases its carpets. The finance director expresses the view that BK benefited from low purchase costs for carpets and floor coverings, but he would be disappointed if BK's suppliers were associated with these labour practices.

The finance director informs you that your predecessor as internal auditor resigned from the company after a dispute with the executive director concerning a department where the auditor had carried out a management audit. Apparently, the internal auditor had criticised the director and his department severely for lax controls and inefficiency. The director had argued that the internal auditor had not discussed any of the criticisms before preparing the report, had been deceitful in asking questions and was probably not qualified to do the audit work. On being told that the auditor was a ACCA member, you express the view that this seemed to be a matter where the Institute's Ethical Guidelines should have been followed.

Required:

(a)   Explain the difference between a value for money audit of the accounts department and an audit of the accounting system.   **(7 marks)**

(b)   Suggest how you might plan a social and environmental audit of the company and what you would consider to be the main social and environmental risks facing BK.
                                                                                    (8 marks)

(c)   From the information available about the dispute between the previous internal auditor and the executive director, suggest how ACCA's Code of Ethics and Conduct might have been relevant to the way in which the auditor acted, or ought to have acted.
                                                                                    (10 marks)

(Total: 25 marks)

61   COMPANY A AND COMPANY B

Required:

(a)   Explain how the environmental and social effects of a company's activities can be considered and what is meant by a company's social and environmental footprints.
                                                                                    (10 marks)

(b)   Two multinational companies have recently published their objectives:

Company A:

'Our company's objective is to focus on the maximisation of global shareholder wealth. We will use sophisticated measures to maximise cash flow in each country in which we operate. We will also extensively outsource internationally in order to increase profitability.'

Company B:

'Our company's primary objectives are to enhance our customers' satisfaction and to grow our business. We aim to supply our customers with the highest quality products and provide outstanding levels of sales and delivery service, incapable of being matched by our competitors, and thereby increasing our market share.'

Required:

Discuss and contrast these objectives. Comment upon any possible ethical implications of the objectives.   **(15 marks)**

(Total: 25 marks)

62   MATTI

(a)   As a newly-qualified certified accountant, you are assisting in the preparation of the accounts of MATTI. Part of your duties involves calculating the provision for inventory. Part way through this calculation, the senior accountant notices that you are providing against inventory lines which have not sold any units for the last six months. 'That provision will adversely affect profit by €520,000' he notes. 'The company cannot afford that additional fall in profit and anyway, provision for those items has not been made in this way before; we normally wait and see what the scrap value will be in 12 months time.' The senior accountant states that the provision must not be entered into the accounting system.

Required:

Explain each of Kohlberg's levels of Cognitive Mental Development (6 levels in total) and using the above example, provide an example of a decision and the rationale behind it for each level of development.   **(18 marks)**

(b)   Z's son needs a drug costing €40,000 to improve the quality of his son's life, and potentially stop him from dying. Z lives in a state where healthcare requirements are provided almost exclusively by the state.

Z has a discussion with M, a doctor. M informs Z that the hospital budget (which is set by the state) cannot afford this amount of expenditure on one individual. M advises Z to try and obtain the money privately – Z informs M this is not possible.

Z takes a job as a hospital cleaner and one night breaks into the hospital storeroom and steals the drug. Z's son recovers from his illness.

Required:

Using Kohlberg's model of CMD, explain the actions of Z and M.   **(7 marks)**

(Total: 25 marks)

63   SOCIAL ACCOUNTABILITY

Required:

(a)   Explain Gray, Owen and Adams' seven positions on social responsibility.   **(14 marks)**

(b)   Outline what is meant by social auditing and identify its limitations.   **(11 marks)**

(Total: 25 marks)

Section 3

ANSWERS TO PRACTICE QUESTIONS – SECTION A

1   MANAGE LTD

Key answer tips

This question is typical of the scenario questions for this exam in that it covers many syllabus areas. You must use the marks to guide you as to the depth of your answer. Part (a) requires plenty of detail to earn five marks about each risk categorisation – you will need to be very explicit as to what is meant by strategic and operational.

In part (b) only make reference to risks resulting from the investment in Manage Ltd. Make sure that you explain your risks precisely and clearly, don't just stop at things like 'interest rate risk'. Note the careful wording of the second part of the requirement: you are asked to discuss **how** they could assess impact on the company. As such you are **not** required to formulate a view on the impact or likelihood, but discuss how Utopia could assess these. Be careful that you answer this precise question.

Part (c) is a much more theoretical part on corporate governance.

(a)   **Strategic risks**

Strategic risks are those which have a direct impact on the overall mission of the company. The first group of strategic risks is those which arise from the possible consequences of strategic decisions taken by the company. For example, one company might pursue a strategy of growth by acquisitions, whilst another might seek slower, organic growth. Growth by acquisition is likely to be much more high-risk than organic growth, although the potential returns might also be much higher.

A second group of strategic risks arises from the way in which an organisation is strategically positioned within its environment. A company may decide to expand into higher or lower risk areas, for example by manufacturing new products or simply enhancing older products

Adverse consequences can also result from failings in the strategic management of an organisation. A company may have the right strategy but fail to monitor or implement it effectively, or identify and follow the wrong strategy.

Strategic risks should be identified and assessed at senior management and board or director level.

Operational risks

Operational risks affect the day-to-day activities of the company. These risks are potential losses which may arise from the people or processes or the structure of the organisation. Operational risks can be defined as 'the risk of losses resulting from inadequate or failed internal processes, people and systems, or external events' (Basel Committee on Banking Supervision). Operational risks include risks of fraud or employee malfeasance as well as risks from production (such as poor quality) or lack of production (not having inputs available at the correct time).

Other examples include:

- business interruption

- product design failures

- loss of key people

- termination of contracts by suppliers.

Operational risks can be most effectively identified, assessed and managed at the level in the organisation at which they arise. Most can be managed by internal control systems.

(b) A number of risks exist for Utopia Inc in making the acquisition of Manage Ltd. The following explains some of the main risks.

Strategic risks – understanding market

The investment in Manage Ltd is a strategic investment and there is the chance that the investment will not generate the returns expected. The reason for this could be that Utopia has not understood the market in which Manage Ltd operates and therefore predicts growth that may not actually arise. There is perhaps a danger of this in the scenario as Manage Ltd has been very successful in recent years and Utopia could be paying a price based on the growth continuing, which it may not.

Carrying out market research will enable Utopia to assess the likelihood of the sales revenue failing to grow as expected. The use of scenario planning to assess the outcome of different levels of sales would enable the company to quantify the impact on the business.

Loss of staff

There is a danger that key staff in Manage Ltd will leave after the acquisition and as a result there will be a loss of goodwill and customer support. If the staff leave they may join competitors or set up in competition with Manage. It appears that Utopia Inc is attempting to reduce this risk by offering positions to Jean Smith and other selected staff.

Utopia may be able to assess the probability of staff leaving based on the experience from previous acquisitions. Feedback from discussions with selected staff could also give an indication of the likelihood that staff will leave. The company will also be able to estimate the cost of replacing staff who leave.

Culture

There is a serious risk of a cultural issue in Utopia investing in Manage. It is possible that Utopia's management style will not fit with the style of Manage. This could result in the existing Manage staff being demotivated and therefore either leaving or not putting their full effort into making Utopia a successful business.

There is also a risk that Utopia will not understand the UK culture and therefore as a result they might operate in a way which is unacceptable to UK customers.

It may be possible for Utopia to gain an understanding of the culture of Manage and assess how different it is and the likely problems from the conversations it is having with staff. Utopia should also be able to draw on the company's experience of previous acquisitions of UK companies to make an assessment of the risk of losing customers due to differences between the cultures in the US and the UK.

Financial risk

There are distinct financial risks for Utopia in different areas. One area is interest rate risk. As Utopia is planning to finance the acquisition of Manage through loans, there is the chance that interest rates will increase meaning that the loans become more expensive.

In addition there is currency risk. Even though Manage does not have any foreign suppliers or customers and therefore is not exposed to currency risk in the Manage business, Utopia will be exposed to translation risk as they will have a foreign asset and economic risk as they are now exposed to the UK economy affecting exchange rates. The final area to consider with currency risk is the issue of remitting funds to the US. If sterling weakens in the future against the dollar, the value of the dollar profits made by Manage Ltd will fall, as will the level of dividends Manage Ltd could remit to the US.

If Utopia is planning to use the proceeds from the sale of an existing UK division to finance this acquisition or repay any loan, then there is a risk that if the sale does not achieve the price expected or takes place later than anticipated. This will affect the amount of finance required and the level of interest paid.

To assess the risks arising from the disposal of the division, Utopia needs to ensure that sufficient research has been carried out to give as much information as possible about the likely timing and proceeds. The company should then evaluate the different financial options, varying the level of factors such as interest and exchange rates.

Political and regulatory risks

There is an increased political and regulatory risk if operations are conducted in overseas countries as it is unlikely Utopia will understand the political and regulatory environment in the UK as well as the environment in the US. This may not be a significant extra risk because Utopia is continuing to employ key staff of Manage and it already has operations in the UK.

(c)   (i)   **Directors and the board**

- There should be a significant number of independent non-executive directors on the board.

- The board should take responsibility for controlling the activities of a business and devising long-term strategy.

- There should be separate people in the positions of chairman and chief executive.

- There should be full transparency of directors' pay with disclosure of the levels of directors' pay and policies for setting pay in the annual report.

- Directors should be allowed to seek independent advice if they feel it necessary at the expense of the company.

- There should be biographical details of all proposed directors sent to the shareholders prior to the directors' appointment.

- Directors should have service contracts of relatively short duration (e.g. one or two years) and they should have to be re-elected by shareholders regularly (for example every three years).

Accountability and audit

- Directors should be responsible for maintaining an adequate system of internal control and have to report on its effectiveness annually.

- All listed companies should have an audit committee of independent non-executive directors (including financial experts) that appoints external auditors and receives internal audit reports.

- There should be restrictions on the non-audit work performed by the company's external auditors.

- Directors should review the need for internal audit and ensure an internal audit function is maintained if necessary.

(ii) The five main elements of an effective internal control framework are as follows:

Control environment

A company must have a strong control environment which means that the senior management must have a good attitude towards internal controls, awareness of the need for controls and take action to improve and monitor controls.

For Manage Ltd, senior management could demonstrate this by, for example:

- Employing people who have the appropriate experience and qualification for a position and having a good training regime.

- Acting on recommendations for control improvements that are sent to them.

- Establishing internal audit as an important function with independence from operational departments.

- Establishing good segregation of duties between different parts of systems and also establishing good supervisory and authorisation controls.

Risk assessment

An integral part of good control is an assessment of risk. It should only be acceptable for management to accept low risks in significant and material areas of the business and therefore risks must be assessed. Greater internal control will be needed over areas with high risks.

Manage Ltd could do the following to improve risk assessment:

- Establish risk management committees that set up processes for the review of risk and suggest policies to reduce it.

- Management of operational departments could be asked to prepare risk assessments in their areas of operation.

- If it was felt serious enough, or there were inadequate skills within Manage Ltd, risk consultants could be employed.

Control activities

These are the detailed internal controls that operate over business processes to ensure that those processes remain low risk. Every business will have many controls, some of which will be key (i.e. they will have to work if overall risk is to be low) and some of which will be non-key.

To understand and improve its control activities Manage Ltd could:

- Document fully the key business processes and controls that should operate over them. This may well lead to the identification of areas where there are deficiencies in the controls and improvements are necessary.

- Identify key controls as these will require more management time and effort to ensure they are operating effectively.

- Ensure that any material weaknesses in the design or operation of the controls are reported to the audit committee.

Information and communication

Manage Ltd must have good information systems that supply high quality control information to the people that need it at the time that they need it. In addition there must be communication lines established within the organisation that communicate control actions and recommendations swiftly both vertically and horizontally.

Actions that Manage Ltd could take are:

- A review of control information that is used by managers (such as budgets and variance analysis) to ensure that it is presented in an efficient and user-friendly way.

- Asking Jean Smith and the other directors to set procedures for communication of control issues so that all staff are clear about the reporting lines.

- Appointing or nominating a person to be responsible for communication of control suggestions around the organisation.

Monitoring

The final element of an effective internal control system is good monitoring. The internal controls need to be reviewed regularly to ensure they are working properly and also to ensure that they develop as the business develops. Internal audit is often a key function in effective monitoring.

To demonstrate effective monitoring, Manage Ltd could:

- Establish an effective, relatively independent internal audit department (if they currently do not have one) that has the right to investigate and report on all aspects of internal control.

- Set up, possibly through internal audit, a regular control testing regime that would identify if controls are being followed and what improvements in the control system are necessary.

Overall

If all of these elements work together then Manage Ltd should have an effective system of internal control.

2 WORLDWIDE MINERALS *Walk in the footsteps of a top tutor*

Key answer tips

It is critical to break down all parts of the requirements in this question. Sections (a) to (c) all have two or more parts to them, and these should be tackled separately in your answer to score full marks.

Part (a) starts with a definition, which is a common question style for your exam. To help you to evaluate the importance of transparency it is sometimes easier to consider it in reverse, i.e. what would happen if there wasn't any transparency? The things that would go wrong will provide ideas for your answer as to the importance.

Part (b) is a straightforward application of Kohlberg's Cognitive Moral Development model. It is essential that you explain why, citing examples from the scenario, you have selected the level for each of the directors mentioned.

Part (c) starts with a theoretical element about roles of non-executive directors. The second part of the requirement is very precise in referring to tensions in advising on the disclosure point. Ensure that your answer only focuses on this matter, general tensions between the roles would not earn marks.

There is no specific theory that is required to answer part (d). In fact, your answer to part (ii) needs to be very specific to the situation in WM. To gain the full professional marks ensure that you correctly focus your letter, addressing the investors at all stages. References to 'your company' and 'we, on the board' will keep this targeted as is necessary.

The highlighted words are key phrases that markers are looking for.

(a) **Transparency and its importance at WM**

Define transparency

Transparency is one of the underlying principles of corporate governance. As such, it is one of the 'building blocks' that underpin a sound system of governance. In particular, transparency is required in the agency relationship. In terms of definition, transparency means openness (say, of discussions), clarity, lack of withholding of relevant information unless necessary and a default position of information provision rather than concealment. This is particularly important in financial reporting, as this is the primary source of information that investors have for making effective investment decisions.

Evaluation of importance of transparency

There are a number of benefits of transparency. For instance, it is part of gaining trust with investors and state authorities (e.g. tax people). Transparency provides access for investors and other stakeholders to company information thereby dispelling suspicion and underpinning market confidence in the company through truthful and fair reporting. It also helps to manage stakeholder claims and reduces the stresses caused by stakeholders (e.g. trade unions) for whom information provision is important. Reasons for secrecy/confidentiality include the fact that it may be necessary to keep strategy discussions secret from competitors. Internal issues may be private to individuals, thus justifying confidentiality. Finally, free (secret or confidential) discussion often has to take place before an agreed position is announced (cabinet government approach).

Reference to case

At Worldwide Minerals, transparency as a principle is needed to deal with the discussion of concealment. Should a discussion of possible concealment even be taking place? Truthful, accurate and timely reporting underpins investor confidence in all capital-funded companies including WM. The issue of the overestimation of the mallerite reserve is clearly a matter of concern to shareholders and so is an example of where a default assumption of transparency would be appropriate.

(b)   **Kohlberg's levels of moral development**

Description of levels

Kohlberg described human moral development in terms of three consecutive levels.

Preconventional moral responses view morality in terms of rewards, punishments and whether or not the act will be penalised, found out or rewarded.

Conventional moral responses view morality in terms of compliance with the agreed legal and regulatory frameworks relevant at the time and place in which the decision is taking place.

Postconventional responses go beyond the other two and frame morality in terms of the effects of the action on oneself and others, on how it will affect one's own moral approach and how it will accord with wider systems of ethics and social norms.

Three people in the case

The three people mentioned in the case exhibit different levels of moral development.

Gary Howells is demonstrating the *preconventional* in that he sees the decision to disclose or not in terms of whether WM can get away with it. He was inclined to conceal the information because of the potential impact on the company's share price on the stock market. His suggestion was underpinned by his belief that the concealment of the incorrect valuation would not be 'found out'.

Vanda Monroe demonstrates *conventional* behaviour, reminding the WM board of its legal and regulatory obligations under the rules of its stock market listing. In particular, she reminded the board about the importance of the company's compliance with corporate governance and ethics codes by the stock market. To fail to disclose would, in Vanda's view, be a breach of those stock market expectations. Rather than rewards and punishments, Vanda was more concerned with compliance with rules and regulations.

Martin Chan is demonstrating *postconventional* morality by referring to consistency of treatment and the notion of 'do as you would be done by'. He said that he wouldn't want to be deceived if he were an outside investor in the company. His response was underpinned neither by rewards or punishments, nor by compliance with regulations, but rather than a persuasion that moral behaviour is about doing what one believes to be right, regardless of any other factors.

(c)   **Non-executive directors**

Roles of NEDs

Non-executive directors have four principal roles.

The *strategy* role recognises that NEDs are full members of the board and thus have the right and responsibility to contribute to the strategic success of the organisation for the benefit of shareholders. The enterprise must have a clear strategic direction and NEDs should be able to bring considerable experience from their lives and business experience to bear on ensuring that chosen strategies are sound. In this role they may challenge any aspect of strategy they see fit and offer advice or input to help to develop successful strategy.

In the *scrutinising* or performance role, NEDs are required to hold executive colleagues to account for decisions taken and company performance. In this respect they are required to represent the shareholders' interests against the possibility that agency issues arise to reduce shareholder value.

The *risk* role involves NEDs ensuring the company has an adequate system of internal controls and systems of risk management in place. This is often informed by prescribed codes (such as Turnbull in the UK) but some industries, such as chemicals, have other systems in place, some of which fall under ISO standards. In this role, NEDs should satisfy themselves on the integrity of financial information and that financial controls and systems of risk management are robust and defensible.

Finally, the '*people*' role involves NEDs overseeing a range of responsibilities with regard to the management of the executive members of the board. This typically involves issues on appointments and remuneration, but might also involve contractual or disciplinary issues and succession planning.

Tensions in NED roles in the case

This refers to a potential tension in the loyalties of the NEDs. Although the NED is accountable, through the chairman to the shareholders and thus must always act in the economic best interests of the shareholders, he or she is also a part of the board of the company and they may, in some situations, advise discretion. Withholding information might be judged correct because of strategic considerations or longer-term shareholder interests. In most situations, NEDs will argue for greater transparency, less concealment and more clarity of how and why a given action will be in the interests of shareholders.

The case of mallerite overestimation places the WM NEDs in a position of some tension. Any instinct to conceal the full extent of the overestimate of the reserve for the possible protection of the company's short-term value must be balanced against the duty to serve longer-term strategic interests and the public interest. Whilst concealment would protect the company's reputation and share price in the short term, it would be a duty of the NEDs to point out that WM should observe transparency as far as possible in its dealing with the shareholders and other capital market participants.

*(**Tutorial note:** these four roles are as described in the UK Higgs Report and are also contained in the Combined Code 2003)*

(d) **Letter for Tim Blake to send to WM's investors**

Worldwide Minerals plc

Address line 1

Address line 2

Address line 3

Date

Dear Shareholders,

Estimation of mallerite reserves

You will be aware of the importance of accurate resource valuation to Worldwide Minerals (WM). Unfortunately, I have to inform you that the reserve of mallerite, one of our key minerals in a new area of exploration, was found to have been overestimated after the purchase of a mine. It has been suggested that this information may have an effect on shareholder value and so I thought it appropriate to write to inform you of how the board intends to respond to the situation.

In particular, I would like to address two issues. It has been suggested that the overestimation arose because of issues with the internal control systems at WM. I would firstly like to reassure you of the importance that your board places on sound internal control systems and then I would like to highlight improvements to internal controls that we shall be implementing to ensure that the problem should not recur.

(i) **Importance of internal control**

Internal control systems are essential in all public companies and Worldwide Minerals (WM) is no exception. If anything, WM's strategic position makes internal control even more important, operating as it does in many international situations and dealing with minerals that must be guaranteed in terms of volume, grade and quality. Accordingly, your board recognises that internal control *underpins investor confidence*. Investors have traditionally trusted WM's management because they have assumed it capable of managing its internal operations. This has, specifically, meant *becoming aware of and controlling known risks*. Risks would not be known about and managed without adequate internal control systems. Internal control, furthermore, *helps to manage quality throughout the organisa*tion and it provides management with *information on internal operations and compliance*. These features are important in ensuring quality at all stages in the WM value chain from the extraction of minerals to the delivery of product to our customers. Linked to this is the importance of internal control in helping to *expose and improve underperforming internal operations*. Finally, internal control systems are essential in providing *information for internal and external reporting* upon which, in turn, investor confidence rests.

(ii) **Proposals to improve internal systems at WM**

As you may be aware, mineral estimation and measurement can be problematic, particularly in some regions. Indeed, there are several factors that can lead to under or overestimation of reserves valuations as a result of geological survey techniques and regional cultural/social factors. In the case of mallerite, however, the issues that have been brought to the board's attention are matters of internal control and it is to these that I would now like to turn.

In first instance, it is clear from the fact that the overestimate was made that we will need to audit geological reports at an appropriate (and probably lower) level in the organisation in future.

Once a claim has been made about a given mineral resource level, especially one upon which investor returns might depend, appropriate systems will be instituted to ask for and obtain evidence that such reserves have been correctly and accurately quantified.

We will recognise that single and verbal source reports of reserve quantities may not necessarily be accurate. This was one of the apparent causes of the overestimation of mallerite. A system of auditing actual reserves rather than relying on verbal evidence will rectify this.

The purchase of any going concern business, such as the mallerite mine, is subject to due diligence. WM will be examining its procedures in this area to ensure that they are fit for purpose in the way that they may not have been in respect of the purchase of the mallerite mine. I will be taking all appropriate steps to ensure that all of these internal control issues can be addressed in future.

Thank you for your continued support of Worldwide Minerals and I hope the foregoing goes some way to reassure you that the company places the highest value on its investors and their loyalty.

Yours faithfully,

Tim Blake

Chairman

Examiner's Report

Introduction

The case scenario for Question 1 was based around a company (Worldwide Minerals) faced with a difficult situation arising from an inaccurate estimate of a crucial mineral inventory in a recently purchased mine. The length and complexity of the scenario is typical of what candidates can expect in future P1 section A cases.

In the December 2007 paper, Question 1 consisted of four parts. **Part (a)** asked about one of the key underlying concepts in corporate governance and 10 marks were available for a definition of the term 'transparency' followed by an evaluation. Candidates were asked to evaluate the importance of transparency in financial reporting with reference to the case. The case was about the board of Worldwide Minerals (WM) considering how it should behave having discovered a value-material overestimate of a key mineral inventory in a mine. Most candidates were able to define the term and explain its relevance to the case of WM but fewer were able to perform the evaluation, which, in this case, involved a consideration of the issues surrounding fully reporting the error to shareholders. Many candidates made the case as to why WM should disclose the error but very few candidates went as far as explaining the opposite argument. There are times when full disclosure is not appropriate and a full evaluation would have brought that out. It is very important that the verb used in the question is used as the basis for the answer.

Part (b) was answered well overall. The first part was of part (b) was an explanation of Kohlberg's three levels of moral development and this was done well by most well-prepared candidates. The second part about identifying the levels of the three people in the case was answered less well with some candidates failing to interpret the evidence in the case scenario correctly.

Part (c) was a near-repeat of a question in the pilot paper on the principal roles of non-executive directors (NEDs) and candidates should therefore have been familiar with how to address the question. Most of the marks were awarded for a description of the roles with some also being available for the more challenging task of an explanation of the tensions that WM's NEDs might experience in the case scenario. This second part was not answered well overall with many answers containing descriptive content rather than serious efforts to consider the difficult situation that the NEDs were in at WM.

Part (d) was the most ambitious component of question 1. A question requiring the demonstration of professional presentation skills will be a part of future P1 papers and in the case of this first paper, the question required writing a letter from Tim Blake, the chairman of WM, to its shareholders. Most candidates made some attempt to present the answer in the form of a letter but many didn't pick up as many professional marks as they might have because:

The answer did not read like a letter (perhaps more like a memo)

It was not in the form of a formal letter to shareholders which would typically have a beginning and an end with a logical flow of content in the 'middle'.

It was addressed to the wrong audience ('Dear Mr Blake')

It used bullet points and short, unconnected paragraphs with no sense of 'flow' between them.

There were four professional marks available. In terms of marks allocation, one professional mark was available for the basic form of a letter meaning it was correctly headed, finished, addressed and physically laid out. The other three were awarded for the composition, flow and persuasiveness of the narrative itself. The letter was from a company chairman to the company's shareholders and those gaining all four professional marks were those that read most like a letter of its type would read in 'real life'. A good answer contained an explanatory introduction, a discussion in the form of narrative (rather than bullet points) of the content of parts (i) and (ii) of the question finished off with a brief paragraph drawing the threads together. Future P1 papers will ask candidates to 'draft' or 'write' content in the form of various types of written communication. Candidates are advised to pay attention to the professional marks as the four marks available could make the difference between a pass and a fail. Four marks are worth approximately seven minutes in time (4% of 180 minutes), which should give candidates some idea of how much investment to make in the professional marks.

In terms of the content of Q1 (d), part (i) asked candidates to explain why they believed internal controls to be important. This was intended to convey Mr Blake's competence to WM's shareholders and to reassure them that despite the recent problem with the mallerite measurement, they should continue having full confidence in him as chairman. Part (ii) invited candidates to put themselves in Mr Blake's position and suggest the types of measures that WM might introduce to improve things. Part (i) was not done well overall despite it being, in cognitive level terms, 'lower' than the task in part (ii). Some candidates introduced the letter and then misinterpreted the 'importance of' internal controls to mean 'components of' and such answers obviously were not well rewarded. The marking team allowed for a range of reasonable interpretations of part (ii) and answers making a serious attempt to address the types of changes that WM might make were rewarded to some extent.

	ACCA marking scheme	
		Marks
(a)	Up to 2 marks for definition of transparency. 1 mark per relevant point on advantages of transparency up to a max of 3 marks 1 mark per relevant point on reasons for confidentiality or concealment up to a max of 3 marks. Up to 2 marks for relevance to case.	$\underline{10}$
(b)	Up to 2 marks for each Kohlberg level identified and described up to a maximum of 6 marks. Up to 2 marks for each person's position identified with reasons/evidence from the case. 1 mark for identification only.	$\underline{12}$
(c)	2 marks for each NED role identified and briefly explained up to a maximum of 8 marks 4 marks for discussion of tension in advising on reserve overestimate.	$\underline{12}$
(d)	(i) 1 mark for each relevant point made on importance of internal control up to a maximum of 6 marks. (ii) Up to 2 marks for each relevant point identified and examined up to a maximum of 6 marks. Up to 4 professional marks for structure, content, style and layout of letter.	$\underline{16}$
Total		$\underline{50}$

3 VCF

Key answer tips

There appear to be significant control weaknesses in all areas of VCF. Remember to focus your answer on the control issues, noting any good control areas, but also stating the weaknesses identified. You may not have identified all the controls (or lack of controls) in your answer. However, given the imprecise wording of the question, control can be taken to apply to any area of VCF. Ensure therefore that you include a good range of points to show you have considered as many areas as possible.

(a)

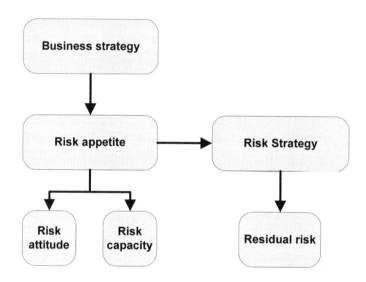

The board and risk management

The board of an organisation plays an important role in risk management.

Initially, the board considers risk at the strategic level and from this defines the organisation's attitude and approach to risk. The risk appetite relates to board (and therefore the company) attitude to risk. A higher risk appetite indicates that more risk is acceptable while a low risk appetite indicates that the company is risk averse.

The two elements of risk appetite are the risk attitude and risk capacity. The risk attitude is the overall approach to risk in terms of the board being risk adverse or risk seeking while the risk capacity is the total amount of risk that a company can bear. For some business strategies, there will be a higher risk appetite (e.g. entry into a new market) and for others a lower appetite (e.g. ensuring ongoing product quality).

The approach to risk is then summarised in the risk strategy. The strategy shows how risk will be managed within the business by reducing the likelihood of occurrence or minimising the impact, e.g. by taking out insurance or by diversification.

Finally, residual risk is risk that can not be managed, or which it is not cost-effective to manage.

Other functions of the board in relation to risk management include:

- driving the risk management process and ensuring that managers responsible for implementing risk management have adequate resources.

- ensuring that risk management supports the strategic objectives of the organisation.

- ensuring that the risk management strategy is communicated to the rest of the organisation and integrated with all the other activities.

- reviewing risks and identifying and monitoring progress of the risk management plans.

(b)   Evaluation of existing controls

Viktor – chairman and CEO

Control of the board is maintained by splitting the roles of chairman and CEO. Viktor is currently the chairman and CEO of the VCF Company. Being in charge of the board and the company indicates that Viktor may have too much power and that there is a lack of control over his actions. Splitting the functions of chairman and CEO would provide appropriate control over Viktor.

Composition of the board

Control of the board is also maintained by having an appropriate mix of board members. The other board directors are appointed by Viktor and consist of Viktor's wife, a consultant and family friend. Given that two out of these three people are likely to follow Viktor's judgments without question, there is a further lack of control at the board level. Employing some non-executive directors will enable Viktor's decisions to be challenged effectively.

Board meetings – content

Overall control of VCF is also limited by lack of any formal board agenda. The agenda provides the framework for board meetings enabling directors to review the entire operations of a company, not simply focus on sales, as happens in VCF. Effective control involves setting and reviewing budgets, authorising R&D expenditure etc which does not appear to take place in VCF.

Board meetings – frequency

The board of VCF meets every three months. This is inadequate for control purposes as the situation in the company can change significantly over this period of time. Board meetings are normally expected every month.

Chain of command

Effective control is normally carried out within a company by directors delegating work to junior managers. However, in VCF, Viktor breaks the chain of command by by-passing area managers on a regular basis. This action queries how effective the area managers can be in implementing control when Viktor creates the impression that he does not trust those managers.

Performance measures

Control of a company is maintained by monitoring financial and non-financial performance measures. Viktor correctly uses some non-financial performance measures to try to maintain control of activities of VCF. However, the implication is that he does not make use of financial measures such as gross profit or comparison of expenditure under different budget headings. Precise monetary control can only be exercised using some financial indicators.

Control of staff

Control over staff appears to be exercised by the threat of dismissal if staff do not show sufficient commitment to VCF's objectives. Viktor's approach may well result in budget reports being 'massaged' to reflect what he would like to see, weakening any control system.

Also, dismissing employees because Viktor does not think they are sufficiently committed to company objectives indicates a lack of control in the human resources area. Viktor is likely to be breaching employment legislation, leaving VCF open to claims of unfair dismissal by staff.

Cost control

VCF does not use product costing. This control system would appear to be an appropriate control given the high value and low number of individual products produced. Production is also outsourced to a third party and the only control appears to be that cost of sales is 20%. There does not appear to be any check on the actual costs incurred by the outsourcing company, leaving VCF open to being charged high prices without its knowledge.

Research and development expenditure

Development expenditure is not capitalised. This means that there is therefore a lack of financial control because development expenditure specifically is not matched with the income generated by that expenditure. VCF's financial statements may have material errors due to lack of application of appropriate International Accounting Standards.

Budget monitoring

Comparison of budget to actual expenditure is a normal method of controlling the activities of a company. Viktor's main method of budget monitoring appears to be using his own spreadsheet. While it is good to see that Viktor is monitoring the company in some way, the use of his spreadsheet indicates various control weaknesses including:

- Lack of focus on sales and expenditure; the spreadsheet only monitors cash flow.

- Lack of accuracy and completeness of input to the spreadsheet as Viktor maintains this personally outside of the normal budget monitoring systems of VCF.

- Potential lack of accuracy of output from the spreadsheet as inputs may not be complete and the integrity of the spreadsheet itself may not have been rigorously tested.

Exchange control risk

Exchange control risk is normally controlled by some form of hedging. In VCF, customers are invoiced in their own currency and VCF does not appear to hedge exchange risk. There is a lack of control in that exchange risk could be significant, but there is no information within VCF to determine this.

(c)

Key answer tips

It is unlikely that Viktor wants to amend his method of running the company and given his management style of dismissing employees you appear to run the risk of losing your job having written the report! However, the question does give areas to focus the report on. It is easier to make a mention of the control weaknesses as a method of justifying any improvements.

There is some overlap with part (b), given that controls in that question also have an impact on the same areas identified for this question.

As with part (b), our answer may be longer than you could write in an examination. However you should ensure that all three areas mentioned in the question are included in your answer, even if the number of points made is less.

Report

To:	Board of VCF
From:	Management accountant
Subject:	Improvements to control systems
Date:	24 November 20X5

Introduction

This report has been written at the request of the board to recommend improvements to systems in VCF in three specific areas. Specific examples are used from my knowledge of the company to show reasons why improvements are needed.

CORPORATE GOVERNANCE

Corporate governance relates to the way in which a company is organised and controlled, with specific emphasis on the board. It is not clear in which specific country VCF is located, or which rules of corporate governance are most applicable. However, the UK framework is used as a basis for the following comments.

Board

Chairman and CEO

The roles of chairman and CEO should be split to ensure that no one person can exercise too much power over the company and the board. Viktor is currently chairman and CEO.

Recommendation: On the assumption that Viktor were to continue running VCF (that is, being the CEO), then another individual (probably not from the current board) should be appointed as soon as possible to the position of chairman.

Composition of board

A board should comprise a mix of executive and non-executive directors, with the role of non-executives being to monitor the executive directors ensuring that they focus their attention on the best interests of the company. At present, VCF does not appear to have any non-executive directors.

Recommendation: Appoint three non-executive directors as soon as possible.

Board appointments

Board members are normally appointed by a nominations committee comprising mainly non-executive directors. The committee must take into account the skills required on the board in making its appointments. In VCF, directors are appointed by Viktor. Although the consultant may provide some appropriate skills to the board, it is unclear why Viktor's wife and friend were appointed.

Recommendation: Establish a nominations committee. Review appointment of existing board members to ensure that their skills are appropriate to the company.

Board meetings

Board meetings should be held regularly and follow a formal agenda. This ensures that the activity of the company is monitored on a regular basis and that board members can adequately prepare for meetings. In VCF, board meetings appear to be informal and focused on sales, indicating that VCF is not adequately controlled.

Recommendation: Have regular monthly board meetings which follow an agenda circulated prior to the meeting. The agenda should cover the entire operations of VCF.

RISK MANAGEMENT STRATEGY

Patents

VCF has an aggressive strategy in always instituting legal action against infringement of patents. While this protects VCF's patents, it may be an expensive strategy where infringements are limited or in fact do not occur.

Recommendation: Attempt to ensure that the extent of the infringement is identified prior to instituting legal action. Contacting the other company first to discuss the situation may be a more cost effective option.

Exchange rate movements

VCF accepts exchange rate risk as historically exchange gains and losses have been roughly the same. However, this does not mean that the situation will continue. There is also the possibility that appropriate hedging controls would have minimised losses while maintaining the gains, resulting in an overall profit for VCF.

Recommendation: Appoint a financial accountant. Part of the accountant's job description will be to review exchange risk on a contract-by-contract basis and take appropriate hedging actions.

Recession

Viktor's focus on controlling costs does not appear to allow for any significant forward budgeting activities. This means that VCF may be unprepared for any changes in world demand for its products.

Recommendation: The accountant should produce a five-year budget, taking into account changes in worldwide demand, both in general terms and in the computer numeric control area, to ensure that VCF focuses production strategy on expected demand.

R&D investment

Within VCF, there appears to be a lack of control of the R&D function (e.g. lack of reporting to the board) which may explain part of the concern that technological leadership is not maintained. Simply allocating 15% of sales to R&D may be an inappropriate method of control if results are not actually monitored.

Recommendation: Provide a monthly report to the board on the progress of R&D projects and actual expenditure during the year compared to budget.

Control of costs

Although budgets appear to be produced within VCF, cost control is focused on an independent spreadsheet maintained by Viktor. This appears to be inappropriate as no monitoring is carried out against budget and it is not certain that the spreadsheet includes details of all costs incurred, as it is separate from the main accounting systems in VCF.

Recommendation: The accountant should produce a report for the board each month showing budget and actual expenditure, clearly identifying reasons for significant variances from budget.

INTERNAL CONTROLS

Little information is provided concerning the actual internal control system in VCF. Key high-level internal controls recommended in a company such as VCF are outlined below.

Expenditure

- Board to produce and authorise an annual expenditure budget.

- Monthly reports produced for the board explaining significant variances from budget expenditure.

- Budget amounts delegated to area managers with authority to spend and accountability for over-expenditure. Recommendation that Viktor does not override the decisions of area managers.

- For individual contracts, budget amount agreed with outsourcing company prior to manufacture commencing. Actual invoice compared to budget confirming amounts agree.

- R&D expenditure. All amounts over a given limit e.g. $1,000, to be authorised by R&D controller. Invoices received reviewed by R&D controller to ensure properly incurred on R&D projects within VCF.

Income

- Contracts reviewed monthly for progress payments due – invoices raised for each customer in accordance with contract conditions.

- Sales ledger maintained with list of outstanding balances being reviewed regularly. Slow paying customers identified and monitored to ensure payments are received in a timely fashion.

- At the end of each contract, review total amounts invoiced ensuring that they agree to the total contract amount.

4   EMEA

(a)   Anthony categorised three levels of control – strategic, management and operational, which he saw as linked.

- **Strategic control** – This exists at board level and is linked to the external environment of EMEA. It includes strategic planning, governance procedures, determining the organisational structure, corporate policies and the monitoring of financial and non-financial performance measures. Strategic control involves environmental information such as competitor analysis, market information, economic forecasting (so that the government's announcement on stamp duty comes as no shock to the directors) and calculations of profitability. Information is high level, summarised, long term, external and internal, and often expensive to collate since some of it may need to be purchased.

- **Management control** – This exists at middle management level, or in the case of EMEA, it comprises the regional managers. They are concerned with implementing the strategy and procedures set by the strategic managers, and monitoring performance so that it is consistent with strategy and achieves any performance targets. It is concerned with the effective use of resources and the efficiency with which objectives are achieved. For example, with the slowing of the property market, some staff may be under-utilised and therefore redundancies might be necessary. Control is often exercised via management accounting control systems (typically budgets).

- **Operational control** – This takes place at the day-to-day level of activities, where structured and repetitive tasks occur. Control is via short-term targets such as making sure that all data inputting and filing is completed by the end of the day. Information produced will be detailed and capable of comparison with other similar branches. It might include the number of sales completed by month, the number of properties under offer, and the amount of fees received each month.

(b) Common controls found in businesses to ensure that employees' behaviour is legally correct, consistent, efficient and fair include:

- **An organisation chart** – this reflects the reporting relationships within a company: who is responsible for what and who reports to whom. The top level of management on the chart will plan and make decisions that will flow down to the lower levels of the chart.

- **Informal structures** – often there are informal management structures as well as the organisation chart in a company. This will be due to differing management styles and culture where people with informal power (natural as opposed to appointed leaders) are able to influence and change behaviour. Unfortunately this may compete with as well as complement the formal organisation structure.

- **Rules, policies and procedures** – these can include manuals, standard operating procedures, job descriptions, codes of conduct, authority levels for spending, or standing orders.

- **Physical controls** – control can be exercised over physical access to buildings via locks or security guards, computer passwords, CCTV or bag checks (although some of these controls might not be necessary in an estate agency).

- **Strategic plans** – strategy sets the long-term vision of a company. It identifies objectives, assigns resources, implements plans, sets a budget and establishes performance targets. In this way, employee efforts are directed towards a common goal for the good of the company as a whole.

- **Incentives and rewards** – companies are increasingly rewarding their staff, both management and employees, through profit-related pay, bonuses, share options and deferred compensation schemes designed to lock that member of staff into the company for the long term.

- **Personnel controls** – these cover recruitment, contracts of employment, induction processes, training, job design, promotion, performance appraisal and remuneration. They can also cover disciplinary action including dismissal procedures.

(c)   Shareholders are the legal owners of a business. In businesses such as EMEA which are quoted on a stock exchange the majority of shareholders play a passive role in the management of the business. The shareholders delegate control to professional managers, the board of directors, to run the company on their behalf.

The relationship between shareholders and directors is an example of a principal-agent relationship. Such agency relationships occur when one party, the principal, employs another party, the agent, to perform a task on their behalf. In this case the principal is the shareholders and the agent is the board of directors. Shareholders appoint the chairman and directors of the business and if they are not happy, in theory have the power to replace them (although this is not always possible in practice). As the agent directors have a 'fiduciary responsibility' to the shareholders and have a duty to act in good faith and to use reasonable skill and care in carrying out their tasks

The separation of ownership and control in a business leads to a potential conflict of interests between directors and shareholders. The principals need to find ways of ensuring that their agents act in their (the principals') interests. As a result of several high profile corporate collapses, caused by over-dominant or 'fat cat' directors, there has been a very active debate about the power of boards of directors, and how stakeholders (not just shareholders) can seek to ensure that directors do not abuse their powers. This has been a major focus of corporate governance guidelines and legislation.

Directors are accountable to the shareholders and must provide evidence that they are acting in shareholders' interests. This evidence should show that they are discharging their responsibilities in line with shareholder expectations in the form of financial results, a clean audit report and reported compliance with codes of corporate governance.

As the legal owners of the company, shareholders are entitled to sufficient information to enable them to make investment decisions. It is the board's responsibility to provide this information. The AGM is an important opportunity for the directors to communicate with the shareholders of the company. As the only legally-required disclosure to shareholders, the annual report and accounts are often the only information shareholders receive from the company.

(d)   There are a number of characteristics of companies dominated by a small number of large shareholders as is the case with EMEA which have implications for the governance of the business.

- Where members of a founding-family have substantial shareholdings in the business, they often have control rights which are disproportionate to their financial share in the business due to preferential share voting rights. This may mean that the influence of other shareholders is more limited. When controlling families participate in the management of their firms as with EMEA other large shareholders are usually not there to monitor the controlling shareholders who may be tempted to act in their own personal interest rather than that of the other shareholders.

- Although there is nothing to indicate that this is a problem with EMEA, there is a possibility that owner-managers or family members could hold the position of director due to their membership of the family, rather than because of their ability to manage the business. This may create a board which is unable to manage the business in the best interests of the shareholders.

- The closeness of relationships between the four family members may mean that they communicate well with one another, frequently on an informal basis, but not with non-family members and other shareholders.

- There is potential for problems in the future if the relationship between the family members deteriorates. Families have greater emotional ties to one another and to the business and this adds complexity to the culture of the business. In addition if the situation becomes so bad that the family members can no longer work together this could be costly in terms of buying out their shareholdings and restructuring.

- There may also be aspects of the family involvement which improve the governance of the company – there may be less risk of unethical behaviour if threats to the reputation of the business are seen as threats to family honour. There is also likely to be less short-termism as long-term growth is usually particularly important to the family.

Non-executive directors (NEDs) would provide an independent, impartial voice on the board to counteract any problems resulting from the powerful position of the family members. NEDs have four main roles:

- Strategy role: NEDs have the right and responsibility to contribute to strategic success, challenging strategy and offering advice on direction.

- Scrutinising role: NEDs are required to hold executive colleagues to account for decisions taken and results obtained.

- Risk role: NEDs ensure the company has an adequate system of internal controls and system of risk management in place.

- People role: NEDs oversee a range of responsibilities with regard to the appointment and remuneration of executives and will be involved in contractual and disciplinary issues.

If NEDs were appointed to EMEA, and these directors were truly independent and carried out their role in monitoring the conduct of the executive directors effectively, they should ensure that the board acts in the best interests of all shareholders. They should also help to resolve conflicts between directors. They should also bring additional management expertise to the board which the executive directors do not have.

In order that the NEDs are truly independent they should not have any family ties with the company or any financial interest such as a significant shareholding or income from the business (other than their director's fee).

5   IDAN

Key answer tips

Part (b) asks you to suggest controls to minimise risk exposure. Questions like this one may require you to draw on your personal and work experience in addition to your studies – for example by considering the controls introduced by your own bank which you have experienced as a customer, such as PIN numbers.

(a)   Main categories of risk

Credit risk

Credit risk is the risk that a borrower may not be able to either make interest payments on a loan or repay the capital amount due at the termination of a loan agreement. Banks normally have a mixture of secured and unsecured loans. Secured loans by definition have some form of security against default. IDAN will be most exposed from unsecured loans from commercial or residential customers and needs to monitor repayments on these closely to identify credit risk.

Operational risk

Operational risk relates to the possibility of errors in transaction systems having a negative effect on income or profits. For example, IDAN has experienced a significant increase in online transactions. If customer payments are directed to incorrect payees as a result of faults in processing, then IDAN may be liable to reimburse those customers for the errors made.

Market risk

Market risk is the risk that a bank's earnings or capital will be adversely affected by changes in market prices. For example, IDAN may invest in equity trading either as a long term investment or for short term gain. If the value of equities falls, then expected capital repayments will also decrease and the bank will incur a loss.

Compliance risk

This is the risk that the bank will not comply with relevant legislation. This will be a complex area for IDAN as many different types of legislation affect the bank, e.g. Anti-Money Laundering through to Companies Act requirements. The bank also operates in 35 different countries so the legislation requirements in each country will also have to be adhered to. Failure to comply will result in financial penalties and additional reputation risk.

Business risk

Business risk relates to changes in the economic, political or competitive environment. For example, as customers prefer use of the Internet for banking purposes, IDAN must ensure that its website is continually updated and offers at least the same services as other banks. If this is not carried out, then the ease of switching banks on the Internet will mean that IDAN loses customers.

Reputation risk

Reputation risk arises from the adverse impact of other risks. For example, if IDAN is seen to be breaking Anti-Money Laundering regulations such as regulations on electronic funds transfer, then not only has the regulation been breached, but customers may not want to bank with IDAN due to the belief that IDAN is not keeping their money securely.

Advantages of risk categorisation in design of a risk management system

Advantages include:

Identification of risks

Forces a company to identify the risks that affect its business. The list is likely to be quite long, so placing similar risks into categories allows a common approach to risk management to take place.

Formal approach

Identifying and writing down risks also forces a formal approach to risk management. This can be contrasted with situations where companies take an ad hoc approach, with the result that risks are excluded from the analysis and not adequately guarded against.

Control systems

Placing risks into categories means that specific people can be designated as being in charge of each risk and appropriate control systems put in place to manage those risks. The impact of corporate governance regulations means it is important that companies do have appropriate internal control systems in place to manage risks.

Update

Having a risk management system in place means it is easy and cost-effective to add new risks into the system when they become apparent. Provision of existing systems means new systems do not have to be developed each time a new risk is identified.

(b)   Controls to reduce exposure to risks

New European Union Law

The new law provides compliance risk to IDAN as well as reputation risk if the law is not followed correctly.

Controls that could be implemented include:

- Ensure a list of non-resident accounts is available, with details of the jurisdiction of each account as one of its fields. Test details on list back to original details provided when account opened.

- Create and then test check withholding tax deduction program, ensuring that the tax due to each jurisdiction is separately identified.

- Test calculation of the total withholding tax due to each jurisdiction.

- Internal audit to test the setting up of the new program and the deduction systems.

Rises in interest rates

This is primarily a market risk as the cost of money will change. The actual controls required depend mainly on the bank's risk appetite to interest rate risk. Depending on this assessment, appropriate financial instruments will be chosen to manage the risk.

Controls that can be implemented include:

- Ensure that the bank is receiving up-to-date information regarding future interest rate changes.

- When interest rates change, ensure that interest rate sensitivity tables are updated to show the new rates on a currency by currency basis.

- Where loans made by the bank are linked to base rate, test check loan agreements to ensure that the rate of interest has been increased and that new interest rate repayment details are sent to the borrower.

- Ensure that revised figures for interest rate sensitivity are available following a rate rise and these are reviewed to ensure they are still within the bank's risk appetite.

Use of PIN numbers rather than signatures

There are various risks affected by this change including credit risk: credit card customer not paying, operational risk of debit card transactions being processed incorrectly and reputation risk if the change is not carried out effectively and efficiently.

Controls that can be implemented include:

- Inform customers of change. Ensure customer details are up-to-date and that mail merge programs produce letters for all customers. Check that customers will be informed of the change before PIN numbers are used. There is likely to be some overlap when both signatures and PIN will be accepted so timing may not be critical.

- Ensure appropriate security for the generation and sending out of new PIN numbers. This may include use of recorded delivery for PIN numbers or telephone verification prior to credit/debit cards being activated for PIN use.

- Where PIN numbers are forgotten or need to be changed, ensure security systems are in place to verify customers (e.g. use of telephone passwords or online identification numbers).

- Check that monitoring programs to identify unusual transactions and/or place holds on the use of credit/debit cards continue to work with the new PIN systems.

Use of Internet and telephone banking

Risks associated with this trend include the operational risk of not being able to process transactions and reputation risk of web sites not offering the appropriate facilities for customers.

Controls that can be implemented include:

- Training for call centre staff to ensure that telephone queries are answered quickly and efficiently. This will help to minimise delays in answering calls and therefore decrease reputation risk of poor service being provided.

- Monitoring of the queue length for telephone calls and expansion of the call centre with additional staff based on trend analysis of calls being made.

- Stress testing of the operational systems of the bank (both via call centre staff and Internet transactions) to ensure that the bank's system can cope with the increased number of transactions.

- Personnel controls in place to ensure that new hires, especially in the Internet division, have integrity and will not amend Internet software inappropriately.

- Monitoring of IDAN's web site compared to competitors' sites to ensure that appropriate customer facilities are being offered. Where amendments are needed, an appropriate test plan is in place to check these prior to going live.

- Ensuring that the level of security on the site is sufficient to protect customer details, and that information is communicated to customers which assures them that their data is safe.

Claims of mis-selling

This is a compliance risk resulting from IDAN not following the banking codes of the jurisdictions it is offering banking services in. Most countries have specific banking codes regarding information that must be provided to customers regarding banking products that are being sold.

Controls that can be implemented include:

- Training of all staff involved in selling banking products so they are aware of what information needs to be provided.

- Use of checklists, either manual or computerised, which must be completed during each customer meeting, to ensure again that all necessary information has been provided.

- Compliance checks on promotional material (for bank loans etc.) to ensure that banking regulations are complied with.

- Ensuring any staff bonus schemes are not linked to the sale of specific financial products – but on good customer service and overall sales volumes achieved.

Anti-money laundering

This again is a compliance risk. The risk is that the bank does not obtain appropriate documentation for new customers or for specific transactions (e.g. electronic money transfers) linked to a customer's account. There is also associated reputation risk should IDAN break any specific anti-money laundering regulations.

Controls that can be implemented include:

- Training of all staff to ensure that anti-money laundering regulations are understood.

- On opening new customer accounts, use of checklists to ensure that all necessary documentation has been obtained and checked.

- Ongoing monitoring of transactions of customer accounts, especially large transactions or transactions with other jurisdictions, to ensure they are bona fide. Where transactions appear to be unusual, additional verification with the customer may be sought.

- Appointment of and training of a Money Laundering Reporting Officer (MLRO). Ensure that this person knows when to file suspicious transaction reports with the police.

(c) In a company, the internal audit department is primarily concerned with checking that the internal control systems are working correctly. Staff in the department will carry out tests on the control systems either by tracing documents through the system or by ensuring controls such as authorisation checks have been performed. They will then prepare internal audit reports, highlighting areas of weakness and proposing amendments to the control systems. To retain their independence, internal audit staff do not actually establish systems; they check what has already been established.

The risk management department provides a similar function in a company. Risk management is concerned with ensuring that risks facing the company are monitored and are subject to an appropriate risk management policy. The department will also advise the board on appropriate control processes to identify risks and determine the company's response to those risks. Part of the response process will be to recommend risk management policies and measure risks against target levels of risk – the targets being defined by the risk appetite of the company. Finally, the department will try and maintain a risk conscious culture so that new risks are identified as soon as possible.

The work of internal audit and risk management is similar in the following respects:

- Both departments will be reviewed by the external audit as part of their job of collecting evidence of the operation of control systems within a company.

- Both departments report to the audit committee, rather than the board, so that an impartial and independent committee can decide on appropriate action arising from those reports. In some situations the risk management department may report to a specialist risk management committee.

- Both departments tend to use a risk-based approach to their work, with more risky areas being reviewed on a more regular basis. They both ensure that risks within IDAN do not exceed the company's risk appetite.

The two departments tend to differ in that:

- Internal audit will review the work of the risk management department as part of the review of controls with a company.

- The risk management department designs control systems; the internal audit checks those systems.

- Risk management reviews all risks in a company (e.g. financial through to reputation); internal audit focuses more on compliance risk.

(d) In considering the nature and effectiveness of internal audit it is helpful to refer to the International Standards for Internal Audit issued by the Internal Auditing Standards Board (IASB) of the Institute of Internal Auditors. These identify three key attributes of internal audit:

- Independence

  The internal audit activity should be independent, and the head of internal audit should report to a level within the organisation that allows the internal audit activity to fulfil its responsibilities. It should be free from interference when deciding on the scope of its assurance work, when carrying out the work and when communicating its opinions.

- Objectivity

  Internal auditors should be objective in carrying out their work. They should have an impartial attitude, and should avoid any conflicts of interest. For example, an internal auditor should not provide assurance services for an operation for which he or she has had management responsibility within the previous year.

- Professional care

  Internal auditors should exercise due professional care and should have the competence to perform their tasks. They should have some knowledge of the key IT risks and controls, and computer-assisted audit techniques.

The international standards also include performance standards which provide criteria against which the internal audit service can be assessed. These cover a number of different areas:

- Managing internal audit

  - The head of internal audit should manage the internal audit activity to ensure that it adds value to the organisation.

  - The head of internal audit should establish risk-based plans to decide the priorities for internal audit work, consistent with the organisation's objectives.

  - The internal audit plan should be reviewed at least annually.

  - The head of internal audit should submit the plan of work to senior management and the board for approval.

- Risk management

    - The internal audit department should identify and evaluate significant risk exposures and contribute to the improvement of risk management and control systems.

    - It should evaluate risk exposures relating to governance, operations and information systems, and the reliability and integrity of financial and operating information, the effectiveness and efficiency of operations, safeguarding of assets, compliance with laws, regulations and contracts.

- Control

    - The internal audit department should help to maintain the organisation's control system by evaluating the effectiveness and efficiency of controls, and by promoting continuous improvement.

- Governance

    - The internal audit department should assess the corporate governance process and make recommendations where appropriate for improvements in achieving the objectives of corporate governance.

- Internal audit work

    - Internal auditors should identify, analyse, evaluate and record sufficient information to achieve the objectives of the engagement.

    - The information identified should be reliable, relevant and useful with regard to the objectives of the engagement.

    - The auditors' conclusions should be based on suitable analysis and evaluation.

    - Information to support the conclusions of the auditors should be recorded.

- Communicating results

    - Internal auditors should communicate the results of their engagement, including conclusions, recommendations and action plans.

    - The results should be communicated to the appropriate persons.

6 KEVIN'S KITCHENS

Key answer tips

In questions such as this one which ask you to consider lack of compliance with good practice it is useful to use a known framework as a basis for your answer. In this case, a comparison is made with the COSO framework for internal control.

(a) Factors threatening general corporate governance principles:

- There is no audit committee.

- There are not enough NEDs.

- There is a lack of understanding of the purpose of NEDs.

- The CEO and chairman are closely related and there is no real separation of roles.

- The company is 'family run' at the top level.

- The CEO and chairman have a 20% shareholding between them.

- The bonus scheme and share-option scheme raise inherent risk of manipulation of the financial statements.

- There is no mention of a remuneration committee or nomination committee.

- The external auditors provide due diligence, tax planning as well as audit – this may be a threat to independence.

- The external auditors also provided systems work last year – this represents a self review threat.

- All of above issues have been made worse by the media attention.

(b) Factors threatening COSO compliance:

The following assessment of the internal control function has been made using the COSO framework.

The control environment

Some of the major concerns in this scenario are to do with the control environment. The major weaknesses include:

- All of the above points on general corporate governance principles mean that KK is unlikely to have a good 'tone at the top'. This means a weak control environment.

- There appears to have been no formal training programme for directors on corporate governance responsibilities.

- The executive directors cannot demonstrate a knowledge of control issues.

- The CEO should not be producing forecasts. Work does not appear to be properly delegated.

Risk assessment

There appear to be some very significant risks in this scenario:

- The finance function does not seem to be integrated with the rest of the business. However, controls should be linked between operations and financial reporting.

- It is likely to be difficult to merge the systems of existing, and newly acquired, business especially with the outsourcing of IT and internal audit.

- If IT4U ceases to provide systems maintenance there is a risk of lost data. There appears to be no disaster recovery plan, and this could ultimately lead to a complete breakdown of the systems.

Control activities

No detail is known of the specific control activities but there are indications that control procedures could not be relied upon:

- The systems manuals are not followed and amendments are verbal. It will be difficult to know what control activities should be in place.

- The IT systems are effectively outsourced – the system will not have been developed with current corporate governance requirements in mind and controls may not be focussed on right areas.

- The accounting manuals are likely to be out of date.

- The accounting processes are unlikely to be understood or followed due to a high level of staff turnover – staff training should be continuous.

- There is limited scope for segregation of duties due to the small size of the finance function.

- There is limited scope for approval and review of work due to the small size of the finance function.

- The FD has recently joined and may not be up to speed on KK's accounting systems.

- The finance function may use manual records to compensate for weaknesses in the computer system. However, manual systems are inherently risky.

- Anything maintained on the manual system may not get incorporated into the general ledgers.

- Following the new acquisition, there is no mention of whether the systems have been integrated with KK's. It is also not clear whether controls have been documented and evaluated, or whether the internal auditor's work will cover the new business. Controls are likely to be very weak due to only having a part time accountant.

- Limited controls are likely to operate over the year end closedown due to the small scale of the finance function.

- There is a tight deadline for accounts preparation and audit – the FD may not have time for proper closedown procedures, especially given the first-time consolidation of Camel Kitchens.

Information and communication

Information flows do not appear to be formal:

- The communication of management accounts and analysis of them appears too informal – there is no documented review and no discussion of the management accounts takes place.

- Questions related to the accounts are only raised on an ad-hoc basis.

- There does not appear to be any real discussion of financial issues at board level – they are concentrating on strategy.

Monitoring

The main monitoring function considered in the scenario is the internal audit function. This seems weak due to a number of factors:

- The CEO and chairman dismiss the findings of internal audit – it therefore has a low status in the organisation structure.

- Delegating the task of dealing with internal audit to the finance director detracts from the independence of the report.

- The internal audit function is outsourced. It is very difficult to evaluate and test controls over outsourced functions.

- • Lack of an audit committee means little scope for an independent review of the company's systems and controls.

- • Internal auditors visit only every six months and only for two days. There is not much scope for comprehensive testing of whether controls have operated throughout the accounting period.

(c)   Benefits of appointing non-executive directors

There are a number of reasons why Kevin and Jack should appoint additional non-executive directors:

- • The current board composition with only two NEDs does not comply with good practice in corporate governance.

- • Appointing NEDs would indicate to the media and other investors that Kevin's Kitchens is committed to good corporate governance. At the moment there is a danger that media attention will highlight poor governance.

- • NEDs would provide an independent, impartial voice on the board. This would counteract any problems (or perception of problems) resulting from the powerful position of the family members.

- • NEDs would contribute to strategic success, challenging strategy and offering advice on direction.

- • The NEDs would be responsible for ensuring the company has an adequate system of internal controls and system of risk management in place.

- • NEDs would oversee a range of responsibilities with regard to the appointment and remuneration of executives and would be involved in contractual and disciplinary issues.

- • If care is taken over the appointment of NEDs they should be able to bring management expertise and an understanding of governance issues which is currently missing from KK's board.

- • Effective NEDs should assist the monitoring and improvement of the company's performance.

7   WATER AGENCY

Key answer tips

As the syllabus does not require knowledge of any particular code, you could answer this question based on any code with which you are familiar. However if you know the detail of the UK's Combined Code this is a very useful basis for answers to questions. You should preface your answer with a reference to the code which you have chosen to use.

(a)   This question has been answered with reference to the UK's Combined Code and Turnbull Guidance.

The Water Agency will be required to change fundamentally the manner in which internal controls are considered. The Turnbull Report adopts a 'risk-based approach to establish appropriate internal controls'. This means that the risks suffered by the organisation will have to be identified, measured and prioritised. As an example, we could consider two very different risks:

- A critical risk associated with the agency is the risk of the flood defences failing. This must be considered as a risk of the highest order in spite of the lower likelihood of it happening. In fact, the whole reason for the Water Agency's existence is the maintenance of such defences.

- On another level, we identify that there is a risk of non-ethical behaviour by the management team. This is of less importance in as much as it is unlikely to lead to the failure of the organisation, but it must still be addressed by an appropriate level of control.

The Turnbull Report specifies four steps:

1   Establish business objectives

2   Identify the associated key risks

3   Decide upon the controls to address the risks

4   Set up a system to implement the required controls, including regular feedback

Turnbull goes further by identifying the roles of the directors and management with regard to risk management.

Directors are required to:

(1)   Set appropriate control policy

(2)   Seek regular assurance that the system is functioning

(3)   Review the effectiveness of internal control using the five categories from the COSO Report (1992)

    (i)   Control environment

    (ii)   Risk assessment

    (iii)   Information systems

    (iv)   Control procedures

    (v)   Monitoring

(4)   Provide sufficient disclosure on internal controls in annual reports

Management are required to:

(1)   Implement policy

(2)   Identify risk

(3)   Evaluate risk

If we adopt the Turnbull Report recommendations, then we are able to take a strategic response to the implementation of risk management. This means that the risks may be assessed in terms of their impact on the organisation and their likelihood of arising. The company is then able to focus resources on those risks that are of most importance, i.e. high-impact/high-likelihood.

A risk strategy may be implemented that attempts to link the risk of an organisation to the risk appetite or level of risk acceptable to the organisation. This level of risk is determined by the risk attitude of the management and how much risk they are willing to accept, and the risk capacity of the organisation, that is the amount of risk it is able to absorb.

We are then able to manage the risk down to the risk appetite. Of the key internal controls that we would use, there are five key elements:

(1)   Structure – an appropriate hierarchy that controls all aspects of the organisation and that ensures a clear delineation of line responsibility with regard to risk.

(2)   Policy and procedure – policy as determined by the board leading to effective procedure followed by line management. Policy is particularly effective as a means of determining and spreading information about the ethical perspective of the organisation.

(3)   Contractual obligation – ensure individuals and companies both within and outside the organisation are clear about their responsibilities and that the ethical principles operated by the organisation are followed.

(4)   Performance evaluation – measurement of the performance of individuals in order that the managers involved are encouraged to perform well.

(5)   Discipline and reward – often linked to performance evaluation, good performance should be rewarded and poor performance should be punished.

Other controls that may be used to deal with risk are outside internal control such as avoiding risk or transferring or pooling risk.

 A detailed discussion of the five categories from the COSO report would have been an equally appropriate alternative answer here.

(b)   *Issue* – Until recently the staff have not had to justify their time whilst at work. This has meant that staff may not be as productive as they could be, leading to excessive labour costs for the WA.

Recommendation – Introduction of the timesheet system should alleviate this problem, especially if someone regularly reviews the timesheet input and output. Regarding the input of information, productivity is hoped to be around 75%. Internal audit could perhaps review this on a regular basis. The computer system should be set up to produce this statistic and report on an exception basis whether this target is being satisfied.

Issue – Timesheet information could be fabricated, either accidentally because a member of staff forgot to record what they were doing, or on purpose to cover the fact that they were not doing a 37-hour week. This has led to abuse of the flexi-time system, which will ultimately cost the WA.

Recommendation – If a staff member forgot to record the odd hour each week or month, this should not be a massive problem. However, staff should be encouraged to record their time in a personal diary at the end of each day in order to assist them at the end of each month.

If, however, the staff member were not doing a 37-hour week, then his or her manager should be watching for this. In the WA's case, the manager is rarely in the office, so this might not be spotted by him, although it should become apparent when that person's projects repeatedly overrun in terms of time and/or costs.

Also, the administrator who has previously watched for this kind of thing is now on sick leave. In this case, either a new member of staff should be charged with this responsibility or some kind of clocking in and out system might be necessary to deter this kind of activity.

Issue – The administrator is on long-term sick leave because of a bad back, but is evidently well enough to go abroad on holiday. It would appear that she is not as unwell as first appeared. She may be defrauding the WA of sick payments.

Recommendation – The personnel department should check that she has been signed off properly by her doctor and for what reason. Telephoning the staff member to discuss the issue might help but the personnel department should check whether they are allowed to contact staff whilst off sick. If the WA can collect sufficient evidence of fraud, then they should take legal advice to recover the money and dismiss the administrator.

Issue – The manager of Flood Defence is often out of the office and uncontactable despite having a company mobile phone.

Recommendation – It may be that he is often in meetings and therefore has his phone switched off. This could be easily checked by looking at his timesheet to see what he was doing and, if it were a meeting, then telephoning others at the meeting to check what it was about, where it was and how long it went on for. This would have to be done confidentially.

However, it may be that he is not at work and therefore defrauding the WA of his salary. (It is not unheard-of for someone to have two jobs!) This again would be spotted via the timesheet and phone call method above. If this were proven, then the manager should be dismissed as untrustworthy. In future, managers should authorise each other's timesheets.

Issue – Line managers at other offices may have to authorise a staff member's timesheet when they may not have been able to see the work that employee has done.

Recommendation – It might be more beneficial for a local manager to authorise timesheets since they will actually see the movements of the staff member. On the other hand, the line manager could use the Internet, intranet (if there is one) or telephone to keep better track of their staff's activities, perhaps speaking to each one daily if this is possible.

(c) There are a number of issues arising with the contracting of consultants.

When considering the control of outsourced staff such as consultants, we must identify that we are giving up key controls over a critical group of staff. We will be less able to control such individuals through use of performance evaluation techniques and internal discipline; and the underlying policies and procedures of the organisation will be less important to a consultant employed on a contract-by-contract basis. Finally, the use of a hierarchy and structure will have little impact on any consultant who lies outside the hierarchy of the organisation.

In replacement to all of the above we will have a contractual obligation laid down between the organisation and the individual consultant. It could be argued that this is the most effective form of control because the individual and the organisation will have a very direct relationship that ensures completion of work as required.

In relation to the company, it appears that the consultants are not being effectively controlled through contractual obligation. This is probably due to poor framing of the contracts, maybe because the consultants do not appear to have specific targets or objectives but instead are pseudo-employed by the organisation.

Strangely this may act as a benefit to the organisation because, the closer the consultants become to employees in their actions, the more we can require them to conform to policies and procedures of the organisation. If they want to continue their consultancy over the medium to long term, then they have a vested interest in adopting the appropriate culture of the organisation.

(d) The internal auditor needs to decide whether the manager is acting ethically, and should collect evidence to prove this either way. His findings should immediately be reported to his manager because of its sensitive nature.

The internal auditor, being new to the job, should find out whether 'sweeteners' are indeed a normal part of the way projects are carried out at the WA.

The auditor should consider the materiality of the amounts involved and whether it is worth investigating further. The 'sweetener' of which there is evidence equates to 5% of that project's costs and this may be deemed large enough to warrant an investigation, especially since other payments are as big as $20,000. Cumulatively they may be material to the Flood Defence Department.

A further issue to consider is the fact that this is a government body and the reputation issues involved if this became common knowledge. The general, tax-paying public may not look on this favourably. However, in this instance the money was used to improve a children's play area so this might not cause too much negative publicity.

A much more serious issue that the auditor should spot is the ability of the manager to drive a Porsche on a salary of $27,000. There may be a perfectly valid reason for this (his wife earns much more than him or he won the lottery, for example). However, the auditor should investigate this because he appears to be living beyond his means. A possibility would be that he was receiving 'backhanders' from the 'sweeteners' he was authorising, or indeed that there were no 'sweeteners' at all, and these amounts were simply bogus payments to the manager.

Subsequent actions for the internal auditor should be taken in line with principles which form the basis of ACCA's Code of Ethics and Conduct.

(1) Integrity: The internal auditor should raise all issues of concern with the internal audit manager.

(2) Objectivity: The internal auditor should ensure that the issues of both the 'sweeteners' and the car are investigated thoroughly, and without bias as to the final outcome.

Steps that could be taken include:

- to find out whether there are a set of guidelines produced in respect of 'sweeteners' by the WA, or to ask the internal audit manager who should already know;

- ask the payroll department for his salary details and tax code – it may be that he has income from other sources that would be reflected in his tax code.

(3) Professional competence: The internal auditor should involve the internal audit manager on any aspects of this investigation that he does not feel experienced in, or capable of investigating fully.

(4) Confidentiality: All enquiries regarding the concerns should be made in such a way that the nature of the concerns is not exposed. For example:

- subtle queries could be made of the staff in his department as to his lifestyle, in order to ascertain how such a car can be afforded;

- speak to the council that received the $5,000 'sweetener' and ask someone to check the value of the receipt, i.e. that it was $5,000 and not, say, $2,500.

(5) Professional behaviour: This should be followed at all times in investigations made by the internal auditor. Actions such as:

- setting up a meeting with the Flood Defence department manager to discuss the situation of 'sweeteners' if he has not followed the WA guidelines;

- investigating further projects to assess the total cost involved of 'sweeteners'

will demonstrate that such standards are being followed.

This is a very difficult case to prove and the auditor will have to tread very carefully. A meeting with the manager is not recommended at this time, until the internal auditors have concrete evidence to prove their findings.

8 FUEL SURCHARGES

(a) (i) Kohlberg theory

Kohlberg's theory relates to cognitive moral development (CMD) – that is theories that attempt to explain cognitive processes and the decisions taken by individuals. Kohlberg's theory of CMD attempts to show the reasoning processes used by individuals, and how those processes change as the individual matured from a 'child' to be an 'adult'.

CMD therefore relates to the different levels of reasoning that an individual can apply to ethical issues and problems.

Kohlbert identified three levels of moral development, with two sub-stages within each level – giving six stages in total.

Level one:

The individual is focused on self-interest, external rewards and punishment. Decisions are likely to be unethical because the person makes decisions entirely in accordance with expected rewards and punishment protecting their own interests.

The two sub-levels are:

1.1 Right and wrong are defined according to expected rewards and/or punishment from figures of authority.

1.2 Right is defined according to whether there is fairness in exchanges – individuals are concerned therefore with their own immediate interests.

Level two:

The individual tends to do what is expected of them by others. 'Others' in this situation relates to work colleagues initially but is broadened to society in general in the second sub-stage of this level. In other words the person is starting to think about their actions and society as a whole rather than focusing on just their immediate peers.

The two sub-levels are:

2.1 Actions are defined by what is expected of individuals by their peers and those close to them.

2.2 The consideration of the expectations of others is broadened to social accord in general terms rather than immediate peers.

Level three:

The individual starts to develop autonomous decision making which is based on internal perspectives of right/wrong ethics etc. rather than based on any external influences.

The two sub-levels are:

3.1 Right and wrong are determined by reference to basic rights, values and contracts of society.

3.2 Individuals make decisions based on self-chosen ethical principles which they believe everyone should follow. Individuals therefore have a strong ethical stance, meaning that ethical decisions are made, even when they mean harm is incurred to the individual from making those decisions

As individuals move through the stages then they are moving onto higher levels of moral reasoning – with higher levels in general terms providing more 'ethical' methods of reasoning. Most individuals operate at level two reasoning – so decisions are made in accordance with what an individual perceives others to believe and in accordance with what is therefore expected of that individual by others.

(ii) The initial decision by TY and JK to collude on the fuel surcharge appears to meet the interests of both companies to maximise profits. In this sense, it appears they were acting at level 1.2 – there was fairness in the exchange in that both companies benefited from the increased prices being charged. The collusion meant that there was fairness in the exchanges   both airlines benefited.

It is unlikely that the price fixing could be explained as level two of Kohlberg. While airline customers would expect TY and JK to make some profit (else they would go out of business) that profit would not be 'excessive'. It is possibly reasonable to expect an airline to charge a fuel surcharge, placing the decision at level 2.1. However, the fact that there was collusion means there was an attempt to raise prices artificially, which would not be expected by customers. Level 2.1 action is therefore not appropriate.

Regarding the decision by JK to disclose that there had been a price fixing agreement, it appears that the directors are attempting to justify the company's initial lack of disclosure. The argument that disclosure is now 'in the public interest' appears to be focused on Kohlberg stage 3.1. In other words, disclosure was expected by society and therefore disclosure was made. This reasoning obviously ignores the initial issue of collusion and lack of disclosure. The disclosure could therefore simply be stated as being at level 2.1; disclosure would be expected by their customers.

Given the rivalry between TY and JK another aspect of disclosure can be considered. Given that either company could have disclosed the price fixing, there could be an element of JK attempting to gain moral superiority over TY; disclosure could also be explained as JK being 'better' morally than TY. In this case JK was therefore attempting again to achieve level 2.2 or even 3.1 by acting in the interests of society. However, disclosure could also have been prompted by level 1.1 – if disclosure was not made then JK would have been punished by the imposition of a fine as TY was.

In conclusion, disclosure was probably prompted by the necessity of avoiding a large fine – but with the intention of making JK appear to be more morally superior to TY.

(b) (i) **Public interest**

There is no overall definition or agreement on the term 'public interest'. However, the public interest is normally seen to refer to the 'common well-being' or 'general welfare.'

An action is usually thought to be in the public interest where it benefits society in some way. It is unclear though how many members of society must benefit before the action can be declared to be in the public interest. Some people would argue an action has to benefit every single member of society in order to be truly in the public interest. At the other extreme, any action can be in the public interest as long as it benefits some of the population and harms no one.

The extent to which an individual will make a disclosure 'in the public interest' depends on their moral stance. In terms of Kohlberg this means that the individual will be at level three and is prepared to 'blow the whistle' on unethical conduct.

(ii) In terms of the disclosure, JK is attempting to show a better moral stance than TY. In other words, disclosure was in the public interest because customers of TY and JK were being overcharged. However, only a limited number of 'members of society' would benefit from the disclosure – that is customers of TY and JK. If public interest disclosure means that all members of society must benefit, this argument cannot be used by JK. However, the argument that disclosure has benefited some members of society and has not harmed anyone else would mean disclosure was in the public interest.

(c) **Evaluation of remuneration**

Remuneration for directors is normally based on two elements:

- Firstly a basic annual salary to compensate directors for their normal work in attending board meetings and running the company, and

- Secondly, a performance related component to provide compensation for good decision making in ensuring that the company is successful and profitable.

This means that whatever remuneration package is determined, it is essential to ensure that the directors have a stake in doing a good job for the shareholder. Each element of a remuneration package should therefore be designed to ensure that the director remains focused on the company and motivated to improve performance.

A balance must be struck between offering a package:

- that is too small and hence demotivating and leading to potential underachievement, and

- that is too easily earned.

This implies that there is a mix of salary and performance related pay as noted above. Corporate governance guidelines do not provide a precise 'mix' but indicate that the performance related element should be substantial.

In terms of TY and JK, there is a performance related element of remuneration. At 40% and 30% it could be argued that the fixed salary percentage is too low – there is a risk that directors will not be sufficiently well compensated if their company does not perform well. A company needs to attract and retain directors with sufficient knowledge and skill to run the company and 30% specifically may be too low an amount to meet this objective. Marks & Spencer, for example, have 55% of remuneration from fixed salary etc.

Role of remuneration committee

Remuneration will be set by the remuneration committee taking into account the amount of compensation being paid by comparable companies. No information is provided in the scenario regarding other companies; however, it is not clear whether the board of TY are actually meeting governance regulations in this area. The directors appear to be discussing methods of increasing their remuneration following the fall in profits with the fine. This decision should be taken by the remuneration committee, ensuring that no director is also responsible for setting their own remuneration. The committee removes any conflict of interest in this area.

Performance-related elements of remuneration

Performance related remuneration is defined as those elements of remuneration dependent on the achievement of some form of performance-measurement criteria. Care must be taken in determining the elements of performance related remuneration. For example, if the market goes down as a whole, then this could potentially penalise directors for an outcome that has nothing to do with their performance. In other words, the performance related element should be linked to the performance of the company and not to the stock markets as a whole.

TY and JK have chosen different methods of doing this.

TY Company – proportion of profit

Part of remuneration is based on the profit for the year. At 40%, this is a relatively high amount as it tends to focus the directors on achieving a high profit in absolute terms, and could lead to attempts to amend the financial statements to increase profit. The imposition of the fine on TY has had the immediate effect of making the directors try to amend their remuneration package, again indicating that reliance on profit may be too high.

TY and JK Companies – share options

The granting of share options means that the directors have the right to buy shares at the current price in a number of years' time. If the price of shares has increased, then the directors will make a profit based on the difference between the two share prices (current and the future price). Options appear to be a good method of rewarding long term performance as they are normally granted for periods in excess of three years. However, there remains the issue that directors may attempt to increase share price near the option date.

Having 20% of remuneration as options is probably acceptable. Many companies even require directors to purchase company shares to show their long-term commitment to the company. Forty per cent may be excessive as this does focus longer-term remuneration on one measure. If there is a declining market overall, then the value of JK's shares may also be falling through no fault of the directors. Use of share options in this situation is unlikely to be particularly motivating.

JK Company – change in share price

Basing incentive on movement in share price again forces directors to look to improvement in the company as part of their compensation package. However, as the movement is based on the price at two specific points in time, then again there is the incentive to try and maximise the share price at these times to provide the highest possible level of remuneration. The only benefit of using the share price is that 'inflating' the value in one year means that next year's bonus is likely to be reduced as it will be difficult to obtain a similar increase in price.

(d) **Reasons for providing a CSR report**

Accountability:

Disclosure is the dominant philosophy of the modern system and the essential aspect of corporate accountability. Providing appropriate disclosure shows the company to be a good 'corporate citizen'.

Information asymmetry:

Disclosure provides an attempt to deal with information asymmetry between managers and owners in terms of agency theory. The managers or directors have more information about the company than the owners – the shareholders. Provision of a CSR helps to minimise this information imbalance.

Attracts investment:

Institutional investors are likely to be attracted by increased disclosure and transparency provided by the CSR.

Compliance:

Although not a precise listing requirement, it is possible that non-compliance would threaten listing in the future. Provision of information now helps to ensure that JK will be able to meet any future requirements regarding CSR. For example, Marks & Spencer and other UK listed companies already provide information over and above statutory and listing requirements as a sign of good governance and to show that information can be provided should listing rules change.

Stakeholders:

The amount of voluntary disclosure helps in discharging the multiple accountabilities of various stakeholder groups. For example, shareholders obtain a better picture of the company (as noted above) but other interested parties such as pressure groups can see progress being made on the ethical stance of the company, for example.

9 AEI

(a) **Ethical codes and ethical dilemmas**

Ethical codes may assist in resolving ethical dilemmas for the following reasons:

Provision of a framework

Ethical codes provide a framework within which ethical dilemmas can be resolved. The codes set the basic standards of ethics as well as the structures that can be applied. For example, most codes provide a general sequence of steps to be taken to resolve dilemmas. That sequence can then be applied to any specific dilemma.

Provision of example methods of resolution

Ethical codes also provide examples of ethical situations and how those example situations were expected to be resolved. Specific ethical dilemmas can be compared to those situations for guidance on how to resolve them.

Establishes boundaries

Ethical codes provide boundaries which ethically it will be incorrect to cross. For example, many accountants prepare personal taxation returns for their clients. However, it is also known that ethically, it is incorrect to suggest illegal methods of saving tax or to knowingly prepare incorrect tax returns. Maintenance of ethical conduct in this situation ensures that the accountant continues to be trusted by both his clients and by the taxation authorities.

Ethical codes do not always assist in resolving ethical dilemmas for the following reasons:

Codes only

Ethical codes are literally what they say – they are 'only' a code. As a general code it may not fit the precise ethical dilemma and therefore the code will be limited in use.

Interpretation of code

As a code, it is subject to interpretation. This means that two different people could form two entirely different but potentially correct views on the same element of the code. For example, terms such as 'incorrect' will mean that an action should not be attempted at all by some people, while others will interpret this as a warning that the action may be attempted, as long as good reasons are given for the attempt.

Lack of enforcement provisions

Many codes have limited or inadequate penalties and/or enforcement provisions. Breach of the code may result in fines, or simply a warning not to breach the code again. Again, a code is subject to interpretation making a 'breach' of the code difficult to identify anyway.

(b) (i) **Ethical threats and safeguards**

An *ethical threat* is a situation where a person or corporation is tempted not to follow their code of ethics.

An *ethical safeguard* provides guidance or a course of action which attempts to remove the ethical threat.

(ii) **Attempting 'bribery' of P**

P, an audit junior, has been offered a free re-fitting of his kitchen with AEI goods. The manager in charge of the department mentioned that this was standard practice each year as a 'thank you' to the member assigned to carry out the inventory checking and subsequent valuation of that inventory. P has also discovered that the inventory is materially overvalued.

There appears to be a threat to P's objectivity. P needs to ensure that audit work is being carried out correctly, while at the same time ensuring there are no factors influencing judgment in this respect. The offer of a free kitchen could influence that judgment as P may be being asked to ignore the over-valuation of inventory and consequent over-statement of profits in AEI. However, it is also concerning that this situation appears to be 'normal' and has therefore been the practice for some years.

To remove the threat P needs to:

- Inform you, the audit manager, of the situation and ask for advice. As a junior member of staff P would be expected to refer the issue to senior management for advice.

Actions that the audit manager should then take include:

- Ascertaining the situation from previous years, including contacting the previous audit manager and juniors to determine action taken in previous years.

- Inform the manager of the warehouse that P is concerned about the situation and ask the manager to confirm this is standard practice.

- Inform the audit partner and ask for his or her advice.

- Inform P not to accept any free goods until the situation has been resolved.

It is possible, albeit unlikely, that this is standard practice. However, this does not assist in resolving the objectivity issue. It is more likely that P will have to decline the offer and also recommend the inventory valuation adjustment. At this stage, actions will include:

- The audit partner explaining the need for the adjustment to AEI's directors.

- Where the adjustment is carried out, no further action will be required.

- Where the adjustment is refused, then there will be the requirement for further discussion with the possibility of the audit report being modified, even if this leads to the loss of the audit client.

Q and disclosure requirements, holding of shares in AEI

Q has two ethical issues to resolve:

- Firstly, to determine whether or not disclosure of directors' remuneration is complete

- Secondly, the issue of holding shares in the audit client.

Regarding disclosure of remuneration, statute requires the disclosure of the different elements of remuneration, including share options. The fact that the total remuneration payable cannot be determined when options are granted is not a reason for non-disclosure. In this situation Q appears to be being pressured into disclosing incorrect information. The ethical threat is therefore not behaving with integrity – Q understands what should be disclosed and integrity would be threatened if this disclosure was not made.

The argument from the chair of the audit committee is not valid. While disclosure of information between an audit client and the auditor attracts confidential status, this confidentiality cannot hold where statutory requirements have not been fulfilled. To maintain integrity, Q must recommend that share option information is disclosed.

However, the situation is made more complicated by the fact that Q holds shares in AEI. The ethical threat here is that Q's objectivity may be compromised. Q may overlook issues which would adversely affect the profit of AEI as this would also affect the share price and dividend that would be obtained as a shareholder.

Furthermore, it is not clear whether Q has disclosed this information to his employer. The 2.5% holding is below the disclosure limit (currently 3% in the UK) for the financial statements, so it is also possible the audit firm is unaware of this conflict. To resolve the conflict, Q should dispose of the audit shares and inform his employer.

The situation is made more complex by the fact that the share price of Q is likely to fall when the results for the year are announced. It could therefore be argued that Q is using inside information and in breach of insider trading rules if shares were sold now. It therefore appears that Q must resign from the audit immediately and make full disclosure of the share holding and the lack of information in the directors' remuneration statement.

Finally, by resigning now, Q may well face disciplinary action from the employer and/or from the institute for not disclosing the conflict of interest earlier. There is therefore still the temptation to 'keep quiet' about the directors' remuneration disclosure and trust that the chair of the audit committee will not disclose information about Q's shareholding to any third party.

Cross-directorships

The ethical threat here appears to be a lack of independence and self-interest regarding the setting of remuneration for these directors. The chair of the remuneration committee of AEI will be voting on the remuneration of directors in AEI; similarly, one of those directors as chair of the remuneration committee of IEA would be voting on remuneration of that executive director in IEA. There would be a temptation to vote for high remuneration levels in AEI in the knowledge that reciprocal high levels of remuneration would be voted for in IEA.

In corporate governance terms, one ethical safeguard is to ban these cross-directorships. The ban would be enforceable as the directors of companies must be stated in annual accounts; hence it would be easy to identify cross-directorships. The ban would also be effective as the conflict of interest would be removed. However, in principles based jurisdictions, the fact that the rule had been broken would only lead to disclosure of this fact; the actual directorships could continue. It is only by making corporate governance regulations enforceable by statute (as in the USA) that the situation could be removed.

In professional terms, the directors clearly have a conflict of interest. While their professional code of ethics may mention this precisely as an ethical threat. Both directors should follow the spirit of the code and resign their non-executive directorships. This again would remove the threat.

Bank reconciliation

R has not carried out work on the bank reconciliation correctly. Ethically accountants must have the correct level of knowledge to perform their duties, otherwise audit and other clients will not receive the standard of service they are paying for. It would be unethical therefore to imply knowledge was available when this was not the case.

However, in this situation, it appears that R has simply followed the instructions given; there was no indication that the timing of clearance of cheques was an issue to be identified as an error. The problem, if anything, is therefore lack of appropriate training of R and/or supervision of R by the audit manager. The 'real' ethical threat is that the audit firm are not training their staff correctly decreasing the standard of service provided to their clients.

Actions to be taken to resolve the situation include:

- Ensuring that training within the audit firm does include appropriate knowledge on audit procedures for all levels of staff.

- Contacting the client to determine why the cheques were presented for payment late. If 'window dressing' has taken place then ask the client to amend the financial statements. Lack of amendment may again result in a modification of the audit report.

(c)   NEDs – advantages and disadvantages of:

Advantages of NEDs

Monitoring

They offer a clear monitoring role on the executive directors of a company. For example, on the remuneration committees they provide a check on the level of remuneration to prevent adverse publicity that executives are being paid excessive amounts.

Expertise

They provide external expertise in general terms of managing companies or specific skills such as finance and audit to complement and expand the knowledge and skills of executive directors.

Perception

The presence of NEDs provides evidence to third parties that executive directors are being monitored. NEDs also provide 'whistle-blowing' opportunities to employees and third parties, again providing the perception of good corporate governance.

Communication

There is an implied improvement in communication between shareholders' interests and the company. The senior non-independent director, for example, will normally try and maintain a dialogue with major institutional investors.

Disadvantages

Unity

There is a risk that the presence of NEDs on a board will undermine the working of the board. There can be a lack of trust as the executives and NEDs may not know each other and find it different to work together. Similarly, there may be resentment against the NEDs if they provide needless input during board meetings.

Quality

There may be a poor gene pool for NEDs willing to serve on boards. This issue is particularly relevant as the liability for NEDs for default is the same as that for executive directors, although NED time and commitment is a lot less than for executive directors. Few potential NEDs may be willing to take this risk.

Remuneration

NED remuneration is basic salary only, there is no reward linked to company performance. While this does help ensure independence, the lack of significant remuneration may again deter potential NEDs from accepting the position.

(d)   Roles of NEDs in AEI Co

Strategy role

NEDs have the right and responsibility to contribute to strategic success of AEI, challenging strategy and offering advice on direction to the executive directors.

The NEDs should be able to offer this advice, as they have the appropriate qualifications and experience to provide this input. However, the potential to provide input will be limited by the fact that all NEDs were appointed this year and they have not had any contact with the executive directors before. There is a danger of the board becoming focused on conflict between the executives and non-executives rather than working together.

Scrutinising role

NEDs are required to hold executive colleagues to account for decisions taken and results obtained.

Again, the NEDs have the ability to provide this checking role. Whether this will be accepted by the executive directors is another matter. Previous NEDs did not appear to be carrying out a particularly good job, hence their removal and appointment of the new NEDs. It is possible that the executives will resent their actions being queried, limiting the effectiveness of the NEDs.

Risk role

NEDs ensure the company has an adequate system of internal controls and system of risk management in place.

The new NEDs may find this role difficult. There is no indication that any NED has experience in this area – many companies appoint a senior NED with relevant financial and or audit experience (e.g. member of ACCA or similar institution). There is a risk that controls in AEI will not be sufficiently well monitored.

People role

NEDs oversee a range of responsibilities with regard to the appointment and remuneration of executives and will be involved in contractual and disciplinary issues.

The NEDs will be able to provide this role, although again effectiveness will be limited by their relative 'newness' to AEI. The NEDs need to discuss their roles with the executive directors initially, and then ensure that appropriate amendments are made within AEI. One area for consideration is the contracts of executive directors which are currently the same in length as NEDs. Listing requirements normally provide for a one year contract length.

10   BMB

(a)   Risk is the 'chance of exposure to the adverse consequences of uncertain future events'. If and when those risks actually occur, they can have an adverse impact on the organisation's objectives.

Risk management is therefore the process of reducing the possibility of adverse consequences either by reducing the likelihood of an event or its impact. Reducing the likelihood involves putting into place procedures to try and stop the risk actually occurring. For example, the risk of key staff leaving an organisation can be reduced by ensuring those staff are being paid at or above the industry average wage. Reducing the impact involves risk mitigation procedures such as taking out insurance or an organisation withdrawing from a risky area of business.

Historically, the focus of risk management has been on preventing loss. However, recently, organisations have begun to view risk management in a different way, so that risks are also seen as opportunities to be seized. Organisations are accepting some uncertainty in order to benefit from higher rewards associated with higher risk. Risk management is being seen as a way to identify risks associated with new opportunities and to increase the probability of positive outcomes and maximise returns. Effective risk management is then seen as a way of enhancing shareholder value by improving performance.

Management are responsible for establishing a risk management system in an organisation. There are four elements to that system:

1.   **Risk identification**

      Risks are identified by key stakeholders. Risks must obviously be identified before they can be managed. Key stakeholders normally include directors, managers and employees within a company and may also include other external stakeholders (Mendelow's matrix is useful in determining the power and interests of external stakeholders and therefore their involvement in risk identification).

2.   **Risk analysis**

      Risks are evaluated according to the likelihood of occurrence and impact on the organisation. This analysis provides a prioritised risk list identifying those risks that need the most urgent attention.

3.   **Risk planning**

Planning involves establishing appropriate risk avoidance policies. Policies include ceasing risky activities through to obtaining insurance against unfavourable events. Contingency planning involves establishing procedures to recover from adverse events, should they occur.

4.   **Risk monitoring**

Risks are monitored on an ongoing basis. Where risks change or new risks are identified then those risks are added to the risk analysis for appropriate categorisation and action.

(b)   **Product/market risk**

This is the risk that customers will not buy new products (or services) provided by the organisation, or that the sales demand for current products and services will decline unexpectedly.

For BMB there is the risk that lack of investment in railways will mean that customers turn to other modes of transport; BMB's forecast income may therefore be overstated. This risk is made worse by government policies focusing on road building at the expense of investment in the rail network. At worse, BMB may not be able to pay the lease amount to the government, jeopardising the going concern status of the company.

Commodity price risk

Businesses might be exposed to risks from unexpected increases (or falls) in the price of a key commodity.

The new trains that BMB want to run assume that sufficient quantities of bio-diesel will be available to power the trains. It will be extremely difficult to backward engineer these trains to run on 'ordinary' diesel; lack of supply of bio-diesel will increase the price of this resource forcing BMB to increase train ticket prices. Too large an increase in prices will have the effect of forcing more customers back onto the roads.

Product reputation risk

Some companies rely heavily on brand image and product reputation, and an adverse event could put its reputation (and so future sales) at risk.

The reputation of BMB is based on the company's ability to use innovative and new products as well as being able to advertise those products effectively. The use of the bio-diesel train is a case in point here. However, the bio-diesel has not been fully tested and it could therefore still fail or have unforeseen side-effects (e.g. increase in pollution).

Credit risk

Credit risk is the possibility of losses due to non-payment by debtors or the company not being able to pay its creditors, which will adversely affect the company's credit rating.

Train tickets are always purchased in advance – this means that BMB does not have any debtors removing this credit risk.

However, BMB is committed to significant expenditure in terms of the purchase of new trains and lease payments to the government to provide rail services. If income is less than expected (see market risk above) then BMB may require short term loans to pay its expenses; late payment will also decrease the credit rating of the company.

Currency risk

Currency risk, or foreign exchange risk, arises from the possibility of movements in foreign exchange rates, and the value of one currency in relation to another.

BMB is exposed to currency risk with respect to the sourcing of new trains. The trains are being manufactured in a country with a volatile exchange rate, with the sale being denominated in the second country's currency. Adverse movements will affect BMB as the amount payable will increase. Obtaining some form of hedging against this risk would be appropriate.

Interest rate risk

Interest rate risk is the risk of unexpected gains or losses arising as a consequence of a rise or fall in interest rates. Exposures to interest rate risk arise from borrowing and investing.

BMB already has significant bank loans, making the company very exposed to this risk. As interest rates are expected to rise in the future then BMB would be advised to consider methods of hedging against this risk.

Gearing risk

Gearing risk for non-bank companies is the risk arising from exposures to high financial gearing and large amounts of borrowing.

Again, BMB has significant amounts of bank loans. This increases the amount of interest that must be repaid each year. In the short term BMB cannot affect this risk as the bank loans are a necessary part of its operations.

Political risk

Political risk depends to a large extent on the political stability in the country or countries in which an organisation operates, and the political institutions.

Although BMB operates in a politically stable country, there is still political risk in terms of government policy towards the rail network. If the current lack of investment in rail infrastructure continues, then this will have an adverse impact on BMB, as noted above.

Legal risk or litigation risk

The risk arises from the possibility of legal action being taken against an organisation.

There is a risk from the government that if BMB does not provide the rail services in its lease then fines can be imposed on the company. BMB therefore needs to work with the government to ensure that lack of service provision is not caused by under-funding of the rail network by the government.

Regulatory risk

This is the possibility that regulations will affect the way an organisation has to operate.

The rail industry appears to be highly regulated, with areas such as safety being very important. Situations in the UK where customer safety has been compromised have normally led to fines on the train provider. BMB needs to ensure that its trains do meet safety and other standards imposed on it.

Technology risk

Technology risk arises from the possibility that technological change will occur or that new technology will not work.

There remains the risk that bio-diesel does not work, or works less efficiently than first considered. The risk occurs because bio-diesel has not been fully tested for use on railways. To mitigate this risk, BMB must ensure that investment continues in its new trains.

Economic risk

This risk refers to the risks facing organisations from changes in economic conditions, such as economic growth or recession, government spending policy and taxation policy, unemployment levels and international trading conditions.

Demand for rail travel has increased during the last five years and is forecast to keep on increasing. However, forecasts can be inaccurate, particularly regarding the ability of the rail network to take more trains and whether customers will move to other modes of transport. The risk is made worse by government policy, as noted above. Risk mitigation must focus on ensuring that the government continues to invest in the rail network.

Environmental risk

This risk arises from changes to the environment over which an organisation has no direct control, such as global warming for which the organisation might be responsible, such as oil spillages and other pollution.

BMB are subject to this risk in terms of emissions from its current petrol and diesel powered trains. Investment in bio-diesel alternatives is a method of mitigating this risk.

Business probity

This is the risk that a company does not follow rules of good corporate governance or show appropriate ethical awareness.

In BMB, the provision of large bonuses to directors based on annual profits provides an element of short-terminism; directors may attempt to increase profit to obtain more bonus. Given the possibility of reduced profits in the future, there remains the risk that profits will be overstated this year in an attempt to gain more income now. Whether this is ethical when other workers will not obtain this increase could be queried with the board.

(c) **Risk mapping**

A risk map identifies whether a risk will have a significant impact on the organisation and links that into the likelihood of the risk occurring. The aim of the approach can provide a framework for prioritising risks in the business.

A risk map shows the likelihood and consequence as either Hi or Lo. Risks with a significant impact and a high likelihood of occurrence need more urgent attention than risks with a low impact and low likelihood of occurrence.

The actual significance and impact of each risk will vary depending on the organisation and the industry sector that organisation operates in. This means a risk map must be drawn for each individual company.

For example, an increase in the price of oil will be significant for an airline company but will have almost no impact on a financial services company offering investment advice over the Internet.

The severity of risk can also be explained in terms of 'hazard'. The higher the impact or hazard of the risk, the more severe it is.

A risk map for BMB is shown below.

Consequences (impact or hazard)

Likelihood	Low	High
Low		• Passenger demand falls • Bio-diesel train fails trials • Breach of regulatory requirements (e.g. health and safety • Brand image of BMB declines (bio-diesel fails)
High	• Government continues low investment in rail infrastructure	• Government rejects lease for BMB

The most 'damaging' risk for BMB is that the government rejects the lease for BMB – which effectively means that BMB would not be able to provide passenger rail services.

Many risks have a potentially high consequence although they are unlikely to occur. For example, passenger demand has continued to increase for the last five years which means it is unlikely to fall in the near future. However, if demand does fall then this will have a significant impact on BMB in terms of being able to pay the lease, meet bank repayment terms and pay for its fixed operating costs.

There remains a high likelihood that the government will continue to provide low investment in the rail infrastructure. It is, however, unclear what consequence this will have for BMB. As investment has been low but rail services continue to operate, then the consequence of low investment can be deemed to be low – it is also possible that continued low investment will eventually have a high consequence if the rail network becomes unsafe.

There are no points in the Low:Low category because all the factors affecting BMB appear to be significant in some way.

11 ROWLANDS & MEDELEEV

Key answer tips

This question has been broken down into many small sections to assist you in structuring your answer. A couple of sections ((a)(i) and (c)) ask for a specific number of points – do not exceed this number, since you will gain no additional marks.

Part (a) commences with some definitions, so it is always useful to ensure you have practiced these in your revision. It goes on to ask you to identify four stakeholders and their claims – ensure that you only refer to external stakeholders.

In drawing the diagram of a risk map in part (b) use a ruler and pencil, labelling the diagram in pen. This will ensure you gain all marks available. The assessment of risks in (c) is highly subjective, so marks will be awarded for any well justified assessment that you make.

In Part (d) it is critical to ensure that your answer is a statement that can be read out. Focus on the audience and insert some opening and closing phrases to assist you in gaining the four professional marks.

Part (e) requires a common sense approach to the difficulties of working with external sub-contractors, and why this enhances the need for sound internal controls. Do not take this as an opportunity to write all you know about sound internal control systems.

(a) (i) **Stakeholders**

A stakeholder can be defined as any person or group that can affect or be affected by an entity. In this case, stakeholders are those that can affect or be affected by the building of the Giant Dam Project. Stakeholding is thus bi-directional. Stakeholders can be those (voluntarily or involuntarily) affected by the activities of an organisation or the stakeholder may be seeking to influence the organisation in some way.

All stakeholding is characterised by the making of 'claims' upon an organisation. Put simply, stakeholders 'want something' although in some cases, the 'want' may not be known by the stakeholder (such as future generations). It is the task of management to decide on the strengths of each stakeholder's claim in formulating strategy and in making decisions. In most situations it is likely that some stakeholder claims will be privileged over others.

R&M's external stakeholders include:

– The client (the government of the East Asian country)

– Stop-the-dam pressure group

– First Nation (the indigenous people group)

– The banks that will be financing R&M's initial working capital

– Shareholders

(ii) **Stakeholder claims**

Four external stakeholders in the case and their claims are as follows.

The client, i.e. the government of the East Asian country. This stakeholder wants the project completed to budget and on time. It may also be concerned to minimise negative publicity in respect of the construction of the dam and the possible negative environmental consequences.

Stop-the-dam, the vocal and well organised pressure group. This stakeholder wants the project stopped completely, seemingly and slightly paradoxically, for environmental and social footprint reasons.

First Nation, the indigenous people group currently resident on the land behind the dam that would be flooded after its construction. This stakeholder also wants the project stopped so they can continue to live on and farm the land.

The banks (identified as a single group). These seem happy to lend to the project and will want it to proceed so they make a return on their loans commensurate with the risk of the loan. They do not want to be publicly identified as being associated with the Giant Dam Project.

Shareholders. The shareholders have the right to have their investment in the company managed in such a way as to maximise the value of their shareholding. The shareholders seek projects providing positive NPVs within the normal constraints of sound risk management.

*(**Tutorial note**: only four stakeholders need to be identified. Marks will be given for up to four relevant stakeholders only)*

(b)   **Framework for assessing risk**

Risk is assessed by considering each identified risk in terms of two variables:

–   its hazard (or consequences or impact) and,

–   its probability of happening (or being realised or 'crystallising').

The most material risks are those identified as having high impact/hazard and the highest probability of happening. Risks with low hazard and low probability will have low priority whilst between these two extremes are situations where judgement is required on how to manage the risk.

In practice, it is difficult to measure both variables with any degree of certainty and so if is often sufficient to consider each in terms of relative crude metrics such as 'high/medium/low' or even 'high/low'. The framework can be represented as a 'map' of two intersecting continuums with each variable being plotted along a continuum.

Consequences (impact or hazard)

	Low	High
Low		
High		

(with "Likelihood/probability" labelled along the vertical axis)

*(**Tutorial note:** other relevant risk assessment frameworks are valid)*

(c)   **Assessment of three risks**

Disruption and resistance by Stop-the-dam. Stop-the-dam seems very determined to delay and disrupt progress as much as possible. The impact of its activity can be seen on two levels. It is likely that the tunnelling and other 'human' disruption will cause a short-term delay but the more significant impact is that of exposing the lenders. In terms of probability, the case says that it 'would definitely be attempting to resist the Giant Dam Project when it started' but the probability of exposing the lenders is a much lower probability event if the syndicate membership is not disclosed.

Impact/hazard: low

Probability/likelihood: high

The risk to progress offered by First Nation can probably be considered to be low impact/hazard but high probability. The case says that it 'would be unlikely to disrupt the building of the dam', meaning low impact/hazard, but that 'it was highly likely that they would protest', meaning a high level of probability that the risk event would occur.

Impact: low

Probability: high

There are financing risks as banks seems to be hesitant when it comes to lending to R&M for the project. Such a risk event, if realised, would have a high potential for disruption to progress as it may leave R&M with working capital financing difficulties. The impact would be high because the bank may refuse to grant or extend loans if exposed (subject to existing contractual terms). It is difficult to estimate the probability. Perhaps there will be a range of attitudes by the lending banks with some more reticent than others (perhaps making it a 'medium' probability event).

Impact: medium to high (depending on the reaction of the bank)

Probability: low to medium (depending on how easy it would be to discover the lender)

(d) **Chairman's statement at AGM**

Thank you for coming to the annual general meeting of Rowlands & Medeleev. I would like to make a statement in response to the concerns that a number of our investors have made in respect to our appointment as the principal contractor for the prestigious and internationally important Giant Dam Project. We are very pleased and honoured to have won the contract but as several have observed, this does leave us in a position of having a number of issues and risks to manage.

As a project with obvious environmental implications, the board and I wish to reassure investors that we are aware of these implications and have taken them into account in our overall assessment of risks associated with the project.

(i) **A definition of 'sustainable development'**

One investor asked if we could explain the sustainability issues and I begin with addressing that issue. According to the well-established Brundtland definition, sustainable development is development that meets the needs of the present without compromising the ability of future generations to meet their own needs.

This definition has implications for energy, land use, natural resources and waste emissions. In a sustainable development, all of these should be consumed or produced at the same rate they can be renewed or absorbed so as to prevent leaving future generations with an unwanted legacy of today's economic activity. We believe that our involvement in the Giant Dam Project has implications for environmental sustainability and it is to these matters that I now turn.

*(**Tutorial note:** other relevant definitions of sustainability will be equally acceptable.*

(ii) **Environmental and sustainability implications of the Giant Dam Project**

In our preparation for the bid to act as principal contractor for the Giant Dam Project, we established that there were two prominent negative implications of the project but these are, in our view, more than offset by two major environmental positives.

The environmental arguments against the Giant Dam Project both concern the flooding of the valley behind the dam. Regrettably, it seems that there will be some loss of important habitats. This, in turn, may mean the removal of balanced environmental conditions for certain animal and plant species. In addition, the flooding of the valley will result in the loss of productive farmland. This will mean reduced capacity for the host country to grow food and thus support citizens such as the members of First Nation. From our point of view, as the board of R&M, however, we would remind shareholders and other observers that the decisions involving the size and positioning of the Giant Dam were taken by the client, the government. It is R&M's job, having won the contract as principal contractor, to now carry out the plans, regardless of our own views.

Happily, however, there are two very powerful environmental arguments in favour of the Giant Dam Project. It will create a large source of clean energy for economic development that will be sustainable, as it will create no carbon emissions nor will it consume any non-renewable resources as it does so (compared to, for example, fossil fuels).

At a time when people are becoming very concerned about greenhouse gases produced from conventional power generation, the Giant Dam Project will contribute to the East Asian country's internationally agreed carbon reduction targets. This, in turn, will contribute to the reduction of greenhouse gases in the environment.

It is clear that the construction of the Giant Dam Project is an environmental conundrum with strong arguments on both sides. The deciding factor may be the opinion that we each have of the desirability of economic growth in the East Asian country (which the energy from the dam is intended to support). It seems that Stop-the-dam values the preservation of the original environment more than the economic growth that the energy from the dam would support. The client does not agree with this assessment and we are happy to be involved with a project that will create such a useful source of renewable and non-polluting energy.

(iii) **Importance of confidentiality in the financing of the project and the normal duty of transparency.**

I have been asked to include a statement in my remarks on the balance between our duty to be transparent whenever possible and the need for discretion and confidentiality in some situations. In the case of our initial working capital needs for the Giant Dam Project, the importance of confidentiality in financing is due to the potential for adverse publicity that may arise for the lender. It is important that R&M have the project adequately financed, especially in the early stages before the interim payments from the client become fully effective.

In general, of course, we at R&M attempt to observe the highest standards of corporate governance and this involves adopting a default position of transparency rather than concealment wherever possible. We recognise that transparency is important to underpin investor confidence and to provide investors with the information they need to make fund allocation decisions.

Whilst it is normal to disclose the amount of debt we carry at any given point (on the balance sheet), it is rarely normal practice to disclose the exact sources of those loans. In the case of the financing of initial working capital for the Giant Dam Project, I'm sure you will realise that in this unique situation, disclosure of the lender's identity could threaten the progress of the project. For this reason we must resist any attempts to release this into the public domain. We are aware of one pressure group that is actively seeking to discover this information in order to disrupt the project's progress and we shall be taking all internal measures necessary to ensure they do not obtain the information.

Thank you for listening.

(e) **Control and sub-contractors**

Specifically in regard to the maintenance of internal controls when working with sub-contractors, the prominent difficulties are likely to be in the following areas:

Configuring and co-ordinating the many activities of sub-contractors so as to keep progress on track. This may involve taking the different cultures of sub-contractor organisations into account.

Loss of direct control over activities as tasks are performed by people outside R&M's direct employment and hence its management structure.

Monitoring the quality of work produced by the sub-contractors. Monitoring costs will be incurred and any quality problems will be potentially costly.

Budget 'creep' and cost control. Keeping control of budgets can be a problem in any large civil engineering project (such the construction of the new Wembley Stadium in the UK) and problems are likely to be made worse when the principal contractor does not have direct control over all activities.

Time limit over-runs. Many projects (again, such as the new Wembley Stadium, but others also) over-run significantly on time.

(*Tutorial note:* only four difficulties need to be described)

Examiner's Report

Introduction

The rubric for the P1 paper was the same as for the pilot paper and for the December 07 paper. Section A thus contained a case study of about a page followed a number of requirements that sampled the syllabus so as to draw content from several areas of the study guide. The case study described a large civil engineering project ('the Giant Dam Project') that had a large environmental impact and also finance issues associated with the fact that some banks wanted to remain confidential as lenders. The case was designed to underpin several questions from across the P1 study guide.

Part (a) was about the stakeholders in R&M, the principal contractor building the Giant Dam. Part (a)(i) required candidates to define the terms 'stakeholder' and 'stakeholder claim' and then to identify four external stakeholders in R&M. Most candidates performed well on this although there was some confusion over internal and external (R&M's employees are not 'external' stakeholders). Part (a)(ii) was a little more ambitious as candidates were required to analyse the case to establish what each of the four identified stakeholders' claims were on R&M. What this meant was what each of the stakeholders wanted R&M to do in respect of the project. Candidates who performed well on this were able to point to what each stakeholder's objectives were for the project. This meant, for example, that First Nation's claim was not that hydroelectric power represented 'misery and cruelty' but that they wanted to project to be discontinued.

Part (b) asked candidates to describe a framework to assess risks and to include a diagram as part of the answer. The correct answer was, of course, the intersecting continua of probability and impact. Markers allowed for a latitude of ways of expressing these variables, allowing, for example for terms such as 'likelihood' and 'hazard', both of which are completely correct terms. Some candidates incorrectly thought that this question might be referring to the Mendelow framework. The Mendelow map is a way of understanding the sources of influence of various stakeholders, not necessarily of risk assessment, although understanding the extent of influence and power of particular stakeholders may in some circumstances have some use in mitigating or avoiding some potential risks.

Part (c) invited candidates to use the risk assessment framework they had just described to actually assess three risks. The question specifically asked candidates to use 'information from the case' and to assess 'three risks to the Giant Dam Project'. Some candidates failed to address the specific risks in the case and described risks in more general terms, perhaps describing risks such as 'exchange rate risk', 'environmental risk' and 'reputation risk', which were not necessarily related to the case. The case contained three specific risks to the project with enough information to make an assessment of each. In order to gain maximum marks, therefore, candidates had to identify those three specific risks and, using information from the case, describe each one's impact and probability. Any other risks the candidates mentioned in their answers could not be assessed as there was no information in the case to do so.

It was thus crucial to adequately analyse the case. If a requirement asks candidates specifically to use information from the case as this one did, then they will not be awarded the best marks unless they do what the question requires.

Part (d) was a multi-part question containing professional marks for the drafting of a statement for Mr Markivnikoff to read out at the annual general meeting. All P1 papers will contain between 4 and 6 professional marks and candidates are well-advised to note that these can make the difference between a marginal fail and a pass. The time budget for 4 marks in a three hour paper is about 7 minutes and some of this time should have been spent on planning how to draft answers in line with the requirements of the question. In December 2007, professional marks were awarded for the drafting of a letter and in this paper, they were for the drafting of a formal statement.

If a senior company director were to address shareholders in a formal meeting, how would it sound? It would begin with a formal introduction, provide an overview of what he was going to cover and, as he spoke, the sections would be connected with narrative designed to make the speech sound convincing, logical and persuasive. It would, obviously, not contain bullet points (how would they be delivered in a speech?).

The actual content of Mr Markovnikoff's statement should have contained three elements, as set out in the three requirements of Q1(d). The majority of candidates were able to define and briefly explain what 'sustainable development' is although (incorrectly) some seemed to think that 'sustainability' referred to the continuance of R&M as a going concern!

Part (d) (ii) required an evaluation of the environmental and sustainability implication of the project. In one sense, the whole point of using a big civil engineering project as the basis for Q1 in this paper was to probe the environmental implication of such a project. In an evaluation, candidates are required to present both sides of the argument – explaining the environmental negatives and also the positives. Importantly, this question was about environmental and sustainability implications and therefore was not concerned with 'social' matters such as the fate of First Nation nor the unfortunate fate of the important archaeological sites.

Part (d) (iii), for 6 marks, invited candidates to wrestle with one of the conundrums raised by the situation of R&M in the case. Again, this involved applying prior learning to the case. It concerned two seemingly conflicting themes with relevance to the case: the duty of transparency and the importance of confidentiality in respect of the lenders.

In **part (e)**, for 4 marks, candidates were invited to bring in prior learning on internal controls and to apply this to a particular situation when a sub-contractor carries out activities over which R&M would not have direct control. Whereas R&M could manage its own internal controls directly, sub-contractors may compromise the project's progress through having inadequate internal controls. Many candidates correctly picked up on issues such as the sub-contractors having different corporate cultures, structures and control regimes to R&M whilst others struggled to make any coherent points.

ACCA marking scheme				
				Marks
(a)	(i)	1 mark for each relevant point made on definition of stakeholder up to a maximum of 2 1 mark for each relevant point made on definition of stakeholder claim up to a maximum of 2 0·5 marks for each stakeholder correctly identified up to a maximum of 2 marks		
				6
	(ii)	1 mark for a brief description of each claim up to a maximum of 4 marks		
				4
(b)		1 mark each for recognition of impact and probability as the two variables up to a maximum of 2 (alternative terms may be used to mean the same thing) 1 mark each for explanation of each variable in context. Up to a maximum of 2 2 marks for a correct diagram (axis labelling may vary)		
				6
(c)		1 mark for identification of each risk up to a maximum of 3 2 marks for assessment of each risk up to a maximum of 6 (1 for impact, 1 for probability)		
				9
(d)	(i)	1 mark for each relevant point made Total 3 marks		3
	(ii)	1 mark for each environmental impact identified up to a maximum of 4 (2 positive, 2 negative factors) 1 mark for description of each up to a maximum of 4 Total 8 marks		8
	(iii)	1 mark for each relevant point on the 'normal duty of transparency' up to a maximum of 3 1 mark for each relevant point on the importance of confidentiality in the case up to a maximum of 4 Maximum 6 marks		6
		Professional marks for layout, logical flow and persuasiveness of the answer (i.e. the professionalism of the statement) Total 4 marks		4
				21
(e)		1 mark for each difficulty briefly identified and explained (half mark for mention only)		
				4
Total				50

12   POOL PUBLISHING

(a)   (i)   Diversification can reduce risk. This is because the actual long-run average outcome from an event or series of events is likely to be close to the expected average outcome. For example, if a company invests in a large number of independent projects, each expected to earn a return of 10%, the actual return from any individual investment might be higher or lower than 10%, but the average return from the entire portfolio of investments is likely to be close to 10%.

The ability of an investor or company to reduce risk by diversifying investments and holding a varied portfolio of independent investments or businesses can be demonstrated statistically. The standard deviation of returns from the portfolio (a measure of risk) will be lower for the portfolio as a whole than for individual investments within it.

However, certain conditions need to apply for diversification to be successful in reducing risks.

- The expected returns from each investment in a portfolio need to be independent. When the returns from two investments have positive correlation, this means that when one investment performs well ,the other will perform well, and when one performs badly, the other will also perform badly. To reduce risk by building up a portfolio, the correlation between returns from investments in the portfolio should not be strongly positive and ideally the correlation of returns should be negative.

- There is also an argument that management should diversify within areas of their own competence. In a business context, a company that seeks to diversify should have the management skills to manage the diversification successfully. For example, POOL Publishing might diversify successfully by publishing more books or acquiring more book rights through takeovers of other book publishing companies. However, it would be more risky to diversify into areas where management do not have demonstrable management skills and experience.

(ii)   The diversification strategy of the board might be inappropriate for several reasons.

- The management of POOL Publishing might not have the skills or experience to take the company into completely different areas of business. There are no similarities between book publishing and operating internet cafes or a chain of restaurants. If management do not have the skills to manage new businesses, diversification will add to the business risk rather than reduce it.

- The same argument probably applies to the proposal to acquire the business of a magazine publisher. Magazine publishing is very different in character from book publishing.

- Even a proposal to acquire a book publishing company in another country could be risky, if POOL Publishing cannot rely on good local management to operate the business after an acquisition. However, in terms of management skills and experience, this acquisition prospect is possibly appropriate.

- There is also an argument that to a certain extent, shareholders can make their own decisions to diversify, and do not need companies to diversify on their behalf. For example, if a shareholder wants to invest in a book publisher, internet cafes and a restaurant business, he can buy shares in three different companies, each specialising in its own particular area of operations. Nothing is gained by the company making investments to create a similar portfolio, and it can be argued that the companies will perform better by concentrating on their core competences.

If stock market investors believe that companies should concentrate on core competences, they are likely to 'punish' conglomerate companies that have a widely-diversified portfolio of investments by under-valuing their shares. In such a situation, the conglomerate can become a target for a takeover bid, with the bidder intending to make a profit by acquiring the conglomerate and 'spinning off' its separate businesses at their 'true' value in order to make a profit.

(b) A significant risk in switching from one service provider for accounting services to another is the risk of loss or corruption to data during the change. ITW will be required to supply up-to-date and accurate files at the end of its contract, either to POOL or to the new service provider. During this handover process, records might be lost from files, or entire files might be corrupted. For example, ITW might hand over out-of-date files, missing some recent transactions. POOL needs to be able to check that all the information has been properly transferred.

One way of dealing with this problem might be to arrange for a short period during which both ITW and the new service provider are maintaining accounting records for POOL. An internal (or external) audit can then carry out a check on the files in the two systems, to ensure that they appear identical (eg with the same total number of records and same control totals).

There might be technological or software difficulties if the accounts are moved from ITW's computer system to the system of another provider, and there might be difficulties in getting the system to operate properly on the system of the new service provider. The solution to this problem is also to have a period of time during which the two systems are running in parallel, so that any technical problems can be identified and resolved.

There is also a risk of unauthorised retention of files. An individual within the ITW organisation might retain copies of the accounts files of POOL. This would create a risk of file data about customers getting into the possession of another organisation. Alternatively, the individual retaining the file copies might subsequently use the information they contain for fraudulent purposes. POOL needs to check, if possible, that there are no duplicate copies of files that have been retained within ITW without authorisation.

This risk is difficult to deal with. However, ITW should be asked to demonstrate that after the handover of the files, copies have not been retained in ITW's computer system. If ITW is an ethical organisation, it should be willing to comply with this request, and demonstrate that it no longer holds files for POOL.

There could be operational difficulties in changing from ITW to a new service provider, particularly if ITW is unwilling to be helpful. ITW might have no incentive to give assistance to another company that has taken their contract with POOL. Inevitably, operational problems will arise, and the new service provider might need to ask questions. Unless ITW is willing to provide assistance, operating difficulties might arise.

The efficiency and success of the change to the new service provider depends on the goodwill of ITW for a number of reasons, and POOL might wish to consider offering a bonus payment to ITW after the change has taken place, provided this has happened in a satisfactory way, and with the full co-operation and assistance of ITW's staff.

It has been assumed that the same system operated on behalf of POOL by ITW will be used by the new service provider. This is not necessarily the case, and it might be the intention of POOL to switch its accounting system to a different accounting system that is better able to handle the growing volume of transactions and data. If a new system is required, all the risks associated with new system design, development and implementation will arise.

(c) Internal audit is a management control. It is an independent activity established within an organisation to reviews the effectiveness of other controls within the company in order to ensure that they are working properly. In some situations, it is a statutory requirement to have internal audit; in others codes of corporate governance strongly suggest that an internal audit department is necessary. For example the Turnbull Report on corporate governance in the UK notes that 'in the absence of an internal audit function, management needs to apply other monitoring processes in order to assure itself and the board that the system of internal control is functioning as intended. In these circumstances, the board will need to assess whether such procedures provide sufficient and objective assurance'. Effective internal audit is particularly important for large, diverse companies which are going through major strategic change, as is the case for POOL.

The role of internal audit

The work of internal audit is varied and the focus will depend on the specific situation and characteristics of the organisation. Activities which are covered include:

- Reviewing accounting and internal control systems

    This is the traditional view of internal audit. The internal auditor checks the financial controls in the company and comments on whether appropriate controls exist as well as whether they are working correctly.

- Assisting with the identification of significant risks

    The auditor may be asked to investigate areas of risk management, with specific reference on how the company identifies, assesses and controls significant risks from both internal and external sources. This aspect of the role is particularly important at the moment for POOL as it is considering a major strategic change involving a number of significant risks which need to be managed effectively.

- Reviewing the economy, efficiency and effectiveness of operations

    This is also called a value for money (VFM) audit. The auditor checks whether a particular activity is cost effective (economical), uses the minimum inputs for a given output (efficient) and meets its stated objectives (effective).

- Examining financial and operating information

    Internal auditors ensure that reporting of financial information is made on a timely basis and that the information in the reports is factually accurate.

- Special investigations

    Investigations into other areas of the company's business, e.g. checking the cost estimates for a new factory.

- Reviewing compliance with laws and other external regulations

    This objective is particularly relevant regarding SOX where the internal auditor will be carrying out detailed work to ensure that internal control systems and financial reports meet stock exchange requirements.

Reviewing the effectiveness of internal audit

Reviewing the effectiveness of internal audit is the responsibility of the audit committee. Such a review will normally involve four key areas, as outlined below. The review should examine the activities undertaken by internal audit to ensure that they meet the requirements for effectiveness as described below in each area.

- Organisational status

  The internal auditor needs to be objective and independent. This means that internal audit can report to senior management (or the audit committee) so that their reports are considered and the internal auditor is not in fear of being reprimanded in any way for presenting adverse reports.

- Scope of function

  Any report and recommendations made by internal audit should be acted on, or management should state why the report has not been actioned. Any review on effectiveness of the department would therefore ensure that their reports were heard and actioned.

- Technical competence

  Internal audit work should be carried out by persons who have had appropriate technical training. Any lack of training implies that the internal auditor will not be able to carry out their duties to the necessary standard.

- Due professional care

  The work of the internal audit department should be properly planned, supervised, reviewed and documented. Any review would therefore ensure that adequate working papers were produced and work programmes reflected the audit work that had to be carried out.

13   COMPLETE COMPUTER CARE

(a)   **Lack of experience of board members**

In any business which is run by owner-managers it is always a possibility that these individuals could hold the position of director due to their membership of the family, rather than because of their ability to manage the business. This may create a board which is unable to manage the business in the best interests of its stakeholders. There is no evidence that any of the four board members had any skills other than in IT before forming the company such as finance or marketing.

Family relationships between individuals

The closeness of the relationship between the married couple Janet and John may mean that they communicate well with one another, frequently on an informal basis, but not with the shareholders. This could lead to problems if essential information and concerns are not discussed by the board as a whole.

There is also potential for problems in the future if the relationship between the couple deteriorates. Married couples and families have greater emotional ties to one another and to the business and this adds complexity to the culture of the business. In addition if the situation became so bad that Janet and John could no longer work together this could be costly in terms of buying out their shareholdings and restructuring.

An aspect of this family involvement which could improve the governance of the company is that there is likely to be less short-termism as long-term growth is usually particularly important to a family.

Different views

Some members of the board could pursue their own agenda at the expense of others. As executive directors all four shareholders have a high degree of power to influence the business to their own benefit at the expense of the other shareholders, employees and other stakeholders.

It is already clear that the board are not unanimous in their desire for expansion and that Henry and James are putting pressure on Janet and John to agree. If the company does go ahead with the expansion despite this there is potential for conflict in the future, particularly if the expansion is not successful.

In the absence of any executive directors who are not shareholders or non-executive directors there is no one to bring an impartial view to the board.

Remuneration

The directors may be inclined to reward themselves excessively via both salary and bonuses if they are allowed to decide such matters for themselves, as is presumably the case in 3C. Good corporate governance says that no director or manager should be involved in any decisions as to their own remuneration.

(b)   There are a number of reasons why the venture capital company would want to appoint non-executive directors (NEDs):

- The current board composition with no NEDs does not comply with good practice in corporate governance. For example, the UK's Combined Code suggests that there should be a balance between the executive and non-executive directors (excluding the Chair) which would be achieved by appointing three non-executives as has been suggested.

- NEDs who have no financial interest in the business would provide an independent, impartial voice on the board. This would counteract any problems (or perception of problems) resulting from the current composition of the board as discussed in (a) above.

- NEDs would contribute to strategic success, challenging strategy and offering advice on direction. This is a key role of independent NEDs.

- The NEDs would be responsible for ensuring the company has an adequate system of internal controls and system of risk management in place, something which is clearly lacking in 3C at the moment.

- NEDs would oversee a range of responsibilities with regard to the appointment and remuneration of executives and would be involved in contractual and disciplinary issues. This would avoid any problems associated with directors deciding their own remuneration as is likely to be the case at the moment.

- If care is taken over the appointment of NEDs they should be able to bring management expertise and an understanding of governance issues which is currently missing from 3C's board. Katy would obviously bring financial expertise, and although she has not worked in the IT industry there will be similarities between a two companies which both provide home servicing of equipment. When appointing the other directors the company should look for directors with complementary expertise such as marketing and human resource management.

- Effective NEDs should assist the monitoring and improvement of the company's performance. NEDs are required to hold executive colleagues to account for decisions taken and results obtained.

If NEDs were appointed to 3C, were truly independent and carried out their role in monitoring the conduct of the executive directors effectively they should ensure that the board acts in the best interests of all the shareholders. They should also help to resolve conflicts between directors. They should also bring additional management expertise to the board which the executive directors do not have.

In order that the NEDs are truly independent they should not have any family ties with the company or any financial interest such as a significant shareholding or income from the business (other than their director's fee).

There are a number of possible problems which could arise:

- There is a risk that the presence of NEDs on a board will undermine the working of the board. There can be a lack of trust as the executives and NEDs may not know each other and find it different to work together. Similarly, there may be resentment against the NEDs if they provide needless input during board meetings.

- There may be a poor gene pool for NEDs willing to serve on boards. This issue is particularly relevant as the liability for NEDs for default is the same as that for executive directors, although NED time and commitment is a lot less than for executive directors. Few potential NEDs may be willing to take this risk.

- NED remuneration is basic salary only, there is no reward linked to company performance. While this does help ensure independence, the lack of significant remuneration may again deter potential NEDs from accepting the position.

(c) Why does 3C need to manage risk?

The issue of corporate governance and how to manage risk has become an important area of concern across the world. Reviews such as that carried out by the Turnbull Committee in the UK have identified risk management as key to effective internal control.

Risk is the chance of exposure to the adverse consequences of uncertain future events. Risks can have an adverse impact on the organisation's objectives. Risk management is the process of reducing the possibility of adverse consequences either by reducing the likelihood of an event or its impact. The venture capital company will be particularly concerned about the lack of risk management in 3C as there are significant strategic risks involved in the expansion plan which could threaten the future of the business and the security of their investment. The board of 3C need to monitor risk on an ongoing basis to:

- identify new risks that may affect the company so an appropriate risk management strategy can be determined.

- identify changes to existing or known risks so amendments to the risk management strategy can be made. For example, where there is an increased likelihood of occurrence of a known risk, strategy may be amended from ignoring the risk to possibly insuring against it.

- ensure that the best use is made of opportunities

Historically, the focus of risk management has been on preventing loss. However, recently, organizations are viewing risk management in a different way, so that risks are seen as opportunities to be seized. The venture capital companies is probably used to investing in high risk companies to gain high rewards and this is likely to be the reason why they are asking for a 40% share in the business.

What does 3C need to do?

There are a number of steps involved in managing risk

Risk identification

Risks are identified by key stakeholders. Risks must obviously be identified before they can be managed.

Risk analysis

Risks are evaluated according to the likelihood of occurrence and impact on the organisation. This analysis provides a prioritised risk list identifying those risks that need the most urgent attention.

Risk planning

Planning involves establishing appropriate risk management policies. Policies include ceasing risky activities through to obtaining insurance against unfavourable events. Contingency planning involves establishing procedures to recover from adverse events, should they occur.

Risk monitoring

Risks are monitored on an ongoing basis. Where risks change or new risks are identified then those risks are added to the risk analysis for appropriate categorisation and action.

Risk management is the responsibility of the board. However in order to be truly effective, risk management should become 'embedded' in the company. Embedding risk management is the process of ensuring that risk management becomes an integral part of the systems and culture of the organisation. In this way, risk management is no longer seen as a separate activity but part of the way in which the organisation does business.

Embedding risk in control systems

The aim of embedding risk management in the control systems of the organisation is to ensure that the processes required for risk management are incorporated in the everyday activities of the business. For example, to ensure that the use of contract staff does not damage the service offered by the company 3C's systems could be set up to prevent a new contractor being taken on until full checks have been carried out into the contractor's experience and references with acceptable results and fully documented on the system.

The process of embedding risk management within an organisation's systems and procedures involves:

- identifying the controls that are already operating within the organisation

- identifying the controls required for risk management

- monitoring those controls to ensure that they work

- improving and refining the controls as required in order to incorporate risk management activities

- documenting evidence of monitoring and control operations.

In addition, the system needs to be:

- supported by the board and communicated to all managers and employees within the organisation

- supported by experts in risk management

- incorporated into the whole organisation, i.e. not part of a separate department seen as 'responsible' for risk

- linked to strategic and operational objectives

- supported by existing processes such as strategy reviews,

- planned and budgeted, e.g. again not seen as an entirely separate process

- supported by existing committees, e.g. audit committee and board meetings rather than simply the remit of one 'risk management' committee

- given sufficient time by management to provide reports to the board.

Embedding risk in the culture of the organisation

Even if risk management controls are incorporated in the systems and activities of the organisation, risk management may still not be effective unless staff at all levels in the business recognise its importance and the need to carry out the activities required of them. This demands that risk management is embedded in the culture and values of the organisation so that it is seen as 'normal' for the organisation.

The first prerequisite for this is a high level of risk awareness. This means an understanding by all staff of the importance of risk and risk management, the way risks impact on the all aspects of the business and in particular on their department and activities, and their role in the management of risks faced by the organisation. It is essential for effective identification, assessment and monitoring of risks. A high level of risk awareness ensures that:

- All staff understand the risk management policy and processes and take responsibility for the management of risk in their particular area

- Staff are able to identify risks, particularly at the operational level which senior managers are not aware of

- The organisation identifies, assesses and monitors risks effectively across all functions and at all levels, strategic, technical and operational.

- The recognition and management of risk becomes part of the culture and everyday activities of the business.

Various cultural factors will affect the extent to which risk management can be embedded into an organisation:

- whether the culture is open or closed

- the overall commitment to risk management policies at all levels in the organisation

- the attitude to internal controls

- governance.

There are various methods of including risk management in culture, some of which also form part of the process of embedding risk in the systems:

- aligning individual goals with those of the organisation

- including risk management responsibilities within job descriptions

- establishing reward systems that recognise that risks have to be taken in practice

- establishing metrics and performance indicators

- publishing success stories.

Section 4

ANSWERS TO PRACTICE QUESTIONS – SECTION B

GOVERNANCE AND RESPONSIBILITY

14 STAKEHOLDERS

(a)   Stakeholders in a company include: shareholders, directors/managers, lenders, employees, suppliers and customers. These groups are likely to share in the wealth and risk generated by a company in different ways and thus conflicts of interest are likely to exist. Conflicts also exist not just between groups but within stakeholder groups. This might be because sub-groups exist, for example preference shareholders and equity shareholders within the overall category of shareholders. Alternatively individuals within a stakeholder group might have different preferences (e.g. to risk and return, short term and long term returns). Good corporate governance is partly about the resolution of such conflicts. Financial and other objectives of stakeholder groups may be identified as follows:

Shareholders

Shareholders are normally assumed to be interested in wealth maximisation. This, however, involves consideration of potential return and risk. For a listed company, this can be viewed in terms of the changes in the share price and other market-based ratios using share price (e.g. price/earnings ratio, dividend yield, earnings yield).

Where a company is not listed, financial objectives need to be set in terms of other financial measures, such as return on capital employed, earnings per share, gearing, growth, profit margin, asset utilisation, and market share. Many other measures also exist which may collectively capture the objectives of return and risk.

Shareholders may have other objectives for the company and these can be identified in terms of the interests of other stakeholder groups. Thus, shareholders as a group may be interested in profit maximisation; they may also be interested in the welfare of their employees, or the environmental impact of the company's operations.

Directors and managers

While executive directors and managers should attempt to promote and balance the interests of shareholders and other stakeholder groups, it has been argued that they also promote their own individual interests and should be seen as a separate stakeholder group.

This problem arises from the divorce between ownership and control. The behaviour of managers cannot be fully observed by the shareholders, giving them the capacity to take decisions which are consistent with their own reward structures and risk preferences. Directors may therefore be interested in their own remuneration package.

They may also be interested in building empires, exercising greater control, or positioning themselves for their next promotion. Non-financial objectives of managers are sometimes inconsistent with what the financial objectives of the company ought to be.

Lenders

Lenders are concerned to receive payment of interest and eventually re-payment of the capital at maturity. Unlike the ordinary shareholders, they do not share in the upside (profitability) of successful organisational strategies. They are therefore likely to be more risk averse than shareholders, with an emphasis on financial objectives that promote liquidity and solvency with low risk (e.g. low gearing, high interest cover, security, strong cash flow).

Employees

The primary interests of employees are their salary/wage and their security of employment. To an extent there is a direct conflict between employees and shareholders as wages are a cost to the company and income to employees.

Performance-related pay based on financial or other quantitative objectives may, however, go some way toward drawing the divergent interests together.

Suppliers and customers

Suppliers and customers are external stakeholders with their own set of objectives (profit for the supplier and, possibly, customer satisfaction with the good or service from the customer) that, within a portfolio of businesses, are only partly dependent on the company in question. Nevertheless it is important to consider and measure the relationship in term of financial objectives relating to quality, lead times, volume of business, price and a range of other variables in considering any organisational strategy.

(b)   This question has been answered with reference to the corporate governance system in the UK.

Corporate governance is the system by which organisations are directed and controlled.

Where the power to direct and control an organisation is given, a duty of accountability exists to those who have devolved that power. Part of that duty of accountability is discharged by disclosure of both performance in the annual report and accounts and also the governance procedures themselves.

Corporate governance codes in the UK are voluntary, and operate on a comply or explain basis. Thus, any requirements are to disclose governance procedures in relation to best practice, rather than comply with best practice, and to explain/justify any divergence from best practice.

The decision-making powers in a company rest mainly with the board of directors. Much of the corporate governance regulation in the UK has therefore focused on governance principles and best practice relating to this stakeholder group. The principles and guidelines in the Combined Code are aimed largely at trying to ensure that the directors act responsibly and in the interests of the other stakeholder groups, particularly the shareholders, rather than themselves. Ideally, the interests of directors and other stakeholders should be aligned and consistent with each other.

A feature of UK companies is a unitary board structure, with one board consisting of both executive and non-executive directors. This contrasts with the two-tier board structure in Germany for instance where there is more independence between the two groups of directors. In a two-tier structure, non-executives will be on a supervisory board and executive directors on a management board which reports to the supervisory board.

Particular corporate governance proposals in the UK written into the Combined Code include:

(1)   Independence of the board with no covert financial reward.

(2)   Adequate quality and quantity of non-executive directors to act as a counterbalance to the power of executive directors.

(3)   Remuneration committee controlled by non-executives, to decide the remuneration of the executive directors.

(4)   Appointments committee consisting of non-executives, to recommend new appointments to the board.

(5)   Audit committee consisting of non-executives, with responsibilities for audit matters, including negotiating the fee of the external auditors.

(6)   Separation of the roles of chairman and chief executive to prevent concentration of power in one person.

(7)   Full disclosure of all forms of director remuneration including shares and share options.

(8)   Better communication between the board of directors and the shareholders, particularly institutional investors.

(9)   Greater prominence for risk management, which is specified as a particular board responsibility.

Overall, the visibility given by corporate governance procedures goes some way toward discharging the directors' duty of accountability to stakeholders and makes more transparent the underlying incentive systems of directors.

15   CORPORATE GOVERNANCE GUIDELINES

Key answer tips

The suggested answer focuses on the UK Combined Code. However, the question does not specifically ask about corporate governance in the UK, and a well-prepared answer can refer to the governance rules in any other country. Answers which included comments on how points (i) – (vi) might comply with other corporate governance systems are equally acceptable.

(a)   Many aspects of the extracts in the question would not comply with corporate governance systems such as the UK Combined Code guidelines.

    (i)   Audit fees and auditor independence. In the UK, it is a requirement of company law that all audit fees and fees for other services provided by auditors should be fully disclosed. Non-audit fees include fees for tax advice, management consultancy and general accountancy services.

        It has been argued that the partner(s) responsible for the audit should be changed regularly so that the audit is perceived to be more objective, and there is less chance of missing important anomalies in the audit process. However, there are no provisions about audit partner rotation in the Combined Code. It should be the responsibility of the audit committee to ensure the independence of the auditors, and to review the appointment/re-appointment and make suitable recommendations to the full board.

(ii)   The UK Combined Code states that the remuneration committee should consist of at least three (or two, in the case of smaller companies) members, and these should all be independent non-executive directors. The committee should objectively determine the remuneration and individual packages for each executive director and also the chairman and 'senior management' (but consult with the chairman and/or CEO about the remuneration of the other executive directors).

(iii) The UK Combined Code states that the roles of chairman and chief executive should not be exercised by the same individual. The division of responsibilities between the chairman and chief executive should also be clearly established, agreed by the board and set out in writing. The chairman should be independent, and the CEO should not go on to become chairman in the same company.

(iv)   The disclosure of whether principles of good corporate governance have been applied is not normally enough; companies should also fully explain how such principles have been applied. The requirements for preparing a corporate governance report (and 'comply or explain' in this report) are contained in the UK Listing Rules for listed companies.

(v)   There is a requirement for directors to meet regularly and to retain full and effective control over the company. In practice, it is doubtful if anyone holding so many directorships, whether executive or non-executive, could devote sufficient time to each company to effectively fulfil their responsibilities. However, the Combined Code makes no specific reference to the number of directorships any individual may hold. The Code merely states that the letter of appointment of a NED should set out the expected time commitment, and the individual should also make a disclosure to the board, before his or her appointment, of his or her other time commitments. There is also a requirement in the Code for individual directors to undergo a performance appraisal annually. Presumably, any director who does not have the time to perform his or her duties properly will be identified and asked either to commit more time or to resign.

(vi)   This is likely to comply with the Combined Code, although the board should also review risk management generally, not just the system of internal controls. The Combined Code states that the directors should maintain a sound system of internal control and, at least annually, conduct a review of the effectiveness of the group's system of internal controls and they should report to the shareholders that they have done so. The review should cover all material controls. These include not just financial controls, but also operational controls, compliance controls and the risk management system.

This question – and solution – does not cover every aspect of the UK Combined Code. Similarly, corporate governance codes in other countries will address other issues, in addition to those covered by this question. Perhaps a significant item to remember in the UK is that it is recommended that at least one half of the board of directors in large listed companies (and at least two directors in smaller companies) should be independent non-executive directors. A further item to note for the UK is the introduction of the Directors' Remuneration Disclosure Regulations in 2002, amending the Companies Act 1985 and requiring detailed disclosures about directors' remuneration and remuneration policy.

(b)   (i)   **Report on Corporate Governance in a rules-based system**

The broad principles of corporate governance are similar in the UK and the USA, but there are significant differences in how they are applied. In particular, whereas the UK has a voluntary corporate governance code, the US system is based on legislation which sets statutory requirements for publicly-traded companies which are imposed through the Sarbanes-Oxley Act (SOX). The Act is relevant to directors of subsidiaries of US-listed businesses and auditors who are working on US-listed businesses.

Advantages are that there is clarity in terms of the requirements for companies and standardisation for all companies. However, this also means that there is no room for flexibility or to improve governance beyond the level set by the law. Non-compliance with the law is a criminal offence.

These requirements include the certification of published financial statements by the CEO and the chief financial officer (finance director), faster public disclosures by companies, legal protection for whistleblowers, a requirement for an annual report on internal controls, and requirements relating to the audit committee, auditor conduct and avoiding 'improper' influence of auditors.

The Act also requires the Securities and Exchange Commission and the main stock exchanges to introduce further rules, relating to matters such as the disclosure of critical accounting policies, the composition of the board and the number of independent directors. The Act has also established an independent body to oversee the accounting firms. (This is called the Public company Accounting Oversight Board, or 'Peek-a-Boo'). Managers must be careful to comply with regulations to avoid possible legal action against the company or themselves individually.

(ii)   **Two-tier boards**

Germany is an example of a country with two-tier boards for companies. This contrasts with the UK where the board structure is a unitary board (consisting of executive and non-executive directors together).

The supervisory board of non-executives (Aufsichrat) has responsibility for corporate policy and strategy, and the management board of executive directors (Vorstand) has responsibility primarily for the day to day operations of the company. The supervisory board typically includes representatives from major banks that have historically been large providers of long-term finance to German companies (and are often major shareholders). The supervisory board does not have full access to financial information, is meant to take an unbiased overview of the company, and is the main body responsible for safeguarding the external stakeholders' interests. The presence on the supervisory board of representatives from banks and employees (trade unions) may introduce perspectives that are not present in some UK boards. In particular, many members of the supervisory board would not meet the criteria under UK Combined Code guidelines for being considered independent.

16   INFLUENCE ON OBJECTIVES

(a)   Non-financial issues, ethical and environmental issues in many cases overlap, and have become of increasing significance to the achievement of primary financial objectives such as the maximisation of shareholder wealth. Most companies have a series of secondary objectives that encompass many of these issues.

Traditional **non-financial issues** affecting companies include:

(i) **Measures that increase the welfare of employees** such as the provision of housing, good and safe working conditions, social and recreational facilities. These might also relate to managers and encompass generous perquisites.

(ii) **Welfare of the local community and society as a whole**. This has become of increasing significance, with companies accepting that they have some responsibility beyond their normal stakeholders in that their actions may impact on the environment and the quality of life of third parties.

(iii) **Provision of, or fulfilment of, a service**. Many organisations, both in the public sector and private sector provide a service, for example to remote communities, which would not be provided on purely economic grounds.

(iv) **Growth of an organisation**, which might bring more power, prestige, and a larger market share, but might adversely affect shareholder wealth.

(v) **Quality**. Many engineering companies have been accused of focusing upon quality rather than cost effective solutions.

(vi) **Survival**. Although to some extent linked to financial objectives, managers might place corporate survival (and hence retaining their jobs) ahead of wealth maximisation. An obvious effect might be to avoid undertaking risky investments.

Ethical issues of companies were brought into sharp focus by the actions of Enron and others. There is a trade-off between applying a high standard of ethics and increasing cash flow or maximisation of shareholder wealth. A company might face ethical dilemmas with respect to the amount and accuracy of information it provides to its stakeholders. An ethical issue attracting much attention is the possible payment of excessive remuneration to senior directors, including very large bonuses and 'golden parachutes'.

 Other areas that could be considered include:

Should bribes be paid in order to facilitate the company's long-term aims? Are wages being paid in some countries below subsistence levels? Should they be? Are working conditions of an acceptable standard? Do the company's activities involve experiments on animals, genetic modifications etc? Should the company deal with or operate in countries that have a poor record of human rights? What is the impact of the company's actions on pollution or other aspects of the local environment?

Environmental issues might have very direct effects on companies. If natural resources become depleted the company may not be able to sustain its activities. Weather and climatic factors can influence the achievement of corporate objectives through their impact on crops, the availability of water etc. Extreme environmental disasters such as typhoons, floods, earthquakes, and volcanic eruptions will also impact on companies' cash flow, as will obvious environmental considerations such as the location of mountains, deserts, or communications facilities. Should companies develop new technologies that will improve the environment, such as cleaner petrol or alternative fuels? Such developments might not be the cheapest alternative.

Environmental legislation is a major influence in many countries. This includes limitations on where operations may be located and in what form, and regulations regarding waste products, noise and physical pollutants.

All of these issues have received considerable publicity and attention in recent years. *Environmental pressure groups* are prominent in many countries; companies are now producing social and environmental accounting reports, and/or corporate social responsibility reports. Companies increasingly have multiple objectives that address some or all of these three issues. In the short-term non-financial, ethical and environmental issues might result in a reduction in shareholder wealth; in the longer term it is argued that only companies that address these issues will succeed.

(b) Corporate citizenship suggests that companies have responsibilities which go beyond its direct stakeholder relationships. It is linked to the idea of corporate accountability which suggests that organisations are answerable for the wider consequences of their actions on society. This goes well beyond the provision of charitable donations to the local community and extends to the management of environmental and social issues.

The implication of this idea is that when setting objectives and strategy organisations should consider the impact of their decisions on society as a whole, and look for ways in which they can influence and improve the community, for example by local investments and local initiatives.

The demands for corporations to be more accountable as members of society is a response to the recognition that companies have power and the view that they can affect society in a number of different ways, for example:

- Companies create wealth and jobs, and have a direct impact on the well-being of their employees

- The products and services of companies have the potential to improve or damage society.

- Companies have a responsibility to consider not only their own action but those of their suppliers and customers.

- Countries struggle with unemployment and yet the decision to locate and support societies is often not theirs but that of corporations.

- Liberalisation and deregulation of markets increase market power and restrict the ability of governments to intervene.

- Privatisation of many previous state monopolies places greater power in the corporate hand.

- Complex cross-border legal agreement is very difficult and so corporations are encouraged to self-regulate.

- Governments have failed to address the risks and consequences of rapidly-changing modern economies and the availability of more and more products and services – companies are seen to have the power to act where governments have failed in their duty.

The implication of this idea is that when setting objectives and strategy organisations should consider the impact of their decisions on society as a whole, and look for ways in which they can influence and improve the community, for example by local investments and local initiatives.

17   MULTI-JURISDICTIONAL GOVERNANCE

Key answer tips

This question focuses in parts (a) & (b) on one of the key concepts of corporate governance: the separation of roles of chairman and chief executive. For part (a) you will need to find five separate roles to earn full marks, so make sure you don't put two roles into one sentence.

To earn the marks for 'assess' in part (b) you will need to describe each benefit, then go on to say something additional about it – how big is the benefit or what problem can it help with. Ensure that you separate your answer into two parts, and focus on the idea of accountability to shareholders in the second part of the answer. Planning your answer before writing up will ensure that you don't talk about accountability as a benefit in the first part of (b).

Part (c) requires you to critically evaluate. To answer this requirement you will need to consider arguments for and against the idea, but giving more emphasis to the points against this statement, i.e. in favour of a single set of governance provisions. There is no need to go into the detail of the OECD or ICGN codes since the question requires you to consider the overall concept of a single set of governance codes.

(a)   **Roles of the chairman in corporate governance**

The chairman is the leader of the board of directors in a private or public company although other organisations are often run on similar governance lines. In this role, he or she is responsible for *ensuring the board's effectiveness* as a unit, in the service of the shareholders. This means agreeing and, if necessary, *setting the board's agenda* and ensuring that board meetings take place on a regular basis.

The chairman represents the *company to investors* and other outside stakeholders/ constituents. He or she is often the 'public face' of the organisation, especially if the organisation must account for itself in a public manner. Linked to this, the chairman's roles include *communication with shareholders*. This occurs in a statutory sense in the annual report (where, in many jurisdictions, the chairman must write to shareholders each year in the form of a chairman's statement) and at annual and extraordinary general meetings.

Internally, the chairman ensures that directors receive relevant information in advance of board meetings so that all discussions and decisions are made by directors fully apprised of the situation under discussion. Finally, his or her role extends to *co-ordinating the contributions of non-executive directors* (NEDs) and *facilitating good relationships between executive and non-executive directors.*

(b)   **Separation of the roles of CEO and chairman**

Benefits of separation of roles

The separation of the roles of chief executive and chairman was first provided for in the UK by the 1992 Cadbury provisions although it has been included in all codes since. Most relevant to the case is the terms of the ICGN clause s.11 and OECD VI (E) both of which provide for the separation of these roles. In the UK it is covered in the combined code section A2.

The separation of roles offers the benefit that it frees up the chief executive to *fully concentrate on the management of the organisation* without the necessity to report to shareholders or otherwise become distracted from his or her executive responsibilities. The arrangement provides a position (that of chairman) that is *expected to represent shareholders' interests* and that is the point of contact into the company for shareholders. Some codes also require the chairman to represent the interests of other stakeholders such as employees.

Having two people rather than one at the head of a large organisation *removes the risks of 'unfettered powers'* being concentrated in a single individual and this is an important safeguard for investors concerned with excessive secrecy or lack of transparency and accountability. The case of Robert Maxwell is a good illustration of a single dominating executive chairman operating unchallenged and, in so doing, acting illegally. Having the two roles separated *reduces the risk of a conflict of interest* in a single person being responsible for company performance whilst also reporting on that performance to markets. Finally, the chairman provides a *conduit for the concerns of non-executive directors* who, in turn, provide an important external representation of external concerns on boards of directors.

*(**Tutorial note:** Reference to codes other than the UK is also acceptable. In all cases, detailed (clause number) knowledge of code provisions is not required)*

Accountability and separation of roles

In terms of the separation of roles assisting in the accountability to shareholders, four points can be made.

The chairman scrutinises the chief executive's management performance on behalf of the shareholders and will be involved in approving the design of the chief executive's reward package. It is the responsibility of the chairman to hold the chief executive to account on shareholders' behalf.

Shareholders have an identified person (chairman) to hold accountable for the performance of their investment. Whilst day-to-day contact will normally be with the investor relations department (or its equivalent) they can ultimately hold the chairman to account.

The presence of a separate chairman ensures that a system is in place to ensure NEDs have a person to report to outside the executive structure. This encourages the freedom of expression of NEDs to the chairman and this, in turn, enables issues to be raised and acted upon when necessary.

The chairman is legally accountable and, in most cases, an experienced person. He/she can be independent and more dispassionate because he or she is not intimately involved with day-to-day management issues.

(c) **Corporate governance provisions varying by country**

There is a debate about the extent to which corporate governance provisions (in the form of either written codes, laws or general acceptances) should be global or whether they should vary to account for local differences. In this answer, Vincent Viola's view is critically evaluated.

In general terms, corporate governance provisions vary depending on such factors as local business culture, businesses' capital structures, the extent of development of capital funding of businesses and the openness of stock markets. In Germany, for example, companies have traditionally drawn much of their funding from banks thereby reducing their dependence on shareholders' equity. Stock markets in the Soviet Union are less open and less liquid than those in the West. In many developing countries, business activity is concentrated among family-owned enterprises.

Against Vincent's view

Although business cultures vary around the world, all business financed by private capital have private shareholders. Any dilution of the robustness of provisions may *ignore the needs of local investors* to have their interests adequately represented. This dilution, in turn, may *allow bad practice*, when present, to exist and proliferate.

Some countries suffer from a poor reputation in terms of endemic corruption and fraud and any reduction in the rigour with which corporate governance provisions are implemented fail to address these shortcomings, notwithstanding the fact that they might be culturally unexpected or difficult to implement.

In terms of the effects of macroeconomic systems, Vincent's views *ignore the need for sound governance systems to underpin confidence in economic systems*. This is especially important when inward investment needs are considered as the economic wealth of affected countries are partly underpinned by the robustness, or not, of their corporate governance systems.

Supporting Vincent's view

In favour of Vincent's view are a number of arguments. Where local economies are driven more by small family businesses and less by public companies, *accountability relationships are quite different* (perhaps the 'family reasons' referred to in the case) and require a different type of accounting and governance.

There is a high *compliance and monitoring cost* to highly structured governance regimes that some developing countries may deem unnecessary to incur.

There is, to some extent, a link between the stage of economic development and the adoption of formal governance codes. It is generally accepted that developing countries need not necessarily observe the same levels of formality in governance as more mature, developed economies.

Some countries' governments may feel that they can use the laxity of their corporate governance regimes as a *source of international comparative advantage*. In a 'race to the bottom', some international companies seeking to minimise the effects of structured governance regimes on some parts of their operations may seek countries with less tight structures for some operations.

Examiner's Report

Introduction

This question drew from the main corporate governance sections of the study guide. The answers to the question showed that whilst most had a basic knowledge of the content area in question, the less-prepared candidates struggled when it came to responding to the higher level verbs used in parts (b) and (c).

Part (a) was, at first sight, a fairly simple task to explain the roles of a chairman in corporate governance. It is when answering questions like this one that candidates have to pay special attention to the cognitive level of the verb in the question. The question specifically asked candidates to 'explain' the roles. Accordingly, answers that merely 'identified' the roles did not receive good marks. Short bullet lists of 'identified' roles received less than a pass (i.e. less than 3 out of 5) because they did not answer at the required cognitive level. An 'explanation' differs from an 'identification' in that it offers some evidence of understanding of the role over and above a mere identification. This need not be a long explanation but something rather more than a brief bullet list.

Part (b) was the most substantive part in Question 3 and asked two questions about the separation of the roles of chairman and chief executive. The first task was to assess the benefits of separating the roles. The idea of separating the roles was formally proposed in the UK by the Cadbury code back in 1992. Although there are other reasons for the separation of roles, Cadbury's proposals took place in the wake of a number of 'scandals' in which the abuse of power at the top of a company was a major cause. The report said (s. 4.9):

'If the two roles are combined in one person, it represents a considerable concentration of power. We recommend, therefore, that there should be a clearly accepted division of responsibilities at the head of a company, which will ensure a balance of power and authority, such that no one individual has unfettered powers of decision.'

Good answers usually contained a clear statement on the increased accountability arising from the separation of roles reducing the 'unfettered power' of a single, powerful individual. In order to score highly on part (b), however, a second task was to explain how the separation of roles led to increased accountability to shareholders. Fewer candidates did as well on this as on the first task, perhaps because it was a little unexpected. Candidates should be aware, though, the questions on Paper P1 will often ask candidates to think about something in the exam that they may not have read directly in the study guides or been taught in class. The structure of Q3 (b) is one that candidates should expect in future P1 papers.

ACCA marking scheme		Marks
(a)	1 mark for each relevant role clearly identified.	5
(b)	'Cross mark' points made in these answers. Benefits of separation of roles: Up to 2 marks for each point identified and assessed as an argument. (Up to a maximum of 10 marks) Accountability and separation of roles: 1 mark for each point made explaining the comment up to a maximum of 4 marks. (Up to a maximum of 12 marks)	12
(c)	'Cross mark' points made/issues raised in the two parts of this answer. 1 mark for each relevant point made on why corporate governance provisions should not vary by country, up to a maximum of 5 marks. 1 mark for each relevant point made on why corporate governance provisions might vary by country up to a maximum of 5 marks. (Up to a maximum of 8 marks)	8
Total		25

18 FOOTBALL CLUB

Key answer tips

This question focuses on the areas of stakeholders and Corporate Social Responsibility which are important topics for this paper.

Part (a) begins with a definition of a stakeholder, which is something that you need to ensure you can produce in two sentences. It goes onto discuss why it is important to identify all stakeholders. This is **not** asking you to identify the stakeholders in this scenario, but to discuss **why** a business would need to carry out such an exercise. Think of what would happen if they ignored all stakeholders – this may give you some thoughts as to why it is important to identify them.

The first part of the requirement for part (b) is to compare and contrast. This can be done either by highlighting similarities and differences between the two positions, or simply by describing them in a couple of sentences each. There is no need to describe the other five positions that Gray, Owens and Adams discussed.

A simple structure for your answer would be to describe the position and then go onto the second part of the question and explain how a company operating from this perspective would respond to stakeholder concerns. Then repeat for the other position.

Fiduciary responsibility (part (c)) is generally discussed in the context of agency theory. 'Construct the case' requires you to highlight the benefits of broadening the responsibility in this situation. There is no need to bring any problems with doing this into your answer.

(a) **Stakeholders**

Definition

There are a number of definitions of a stakeholder. Freeman (1984), for example, defined a stakeholder in terms of any organisation or person that can affect or be affected by the policies or activities of an entity. Hence stakeholding can result from one of two directions: being able to affect and possibly influence an organisation or, conversely, being influenced by it. Any engagement with an organisation in whom a stake is held may be voluntary or involuntary in nature.

 Any definition of a stakeholder that identifies bi-directional influence will be equally valid.

Importance of identifying all stakeholders

Knowledge of the stakeholders in the stadium project is important for a number of reasons. This will involve surveying stakeholders that can either affect or be affected by the building of the stadium. In some cases, stakeholders will be bi-directional in their stakeholding (claim) upon the stadium project. Stakeholders in the stadium project include the local government authority, the local residents, the wildlife centre, the local school and the football club's fans.

Stakeholder identification is necessary to gain an understanding of the sources of risks and disruption. Some external stakeholders, such as the local government authority, offer a risk to the project and knowledge of the nature of the claim made upon the football club by the stakeholder will be important in risk assessment.

Stakeholder identification is important in terms of assessing the *sources of influence* over the objectives and outcomes for the project (such as identified in the Mendelow model). In strategic analysis, stakeholder influence is assessed in terms of each stakeholder's power and interest, with higher power and higher interest combining to generate the highest influence. In the case, it is likely that the fans are more influential on the club's objectives than, say, the local wildlife centre, as they have more economic power over the club.

It is necessary in order to identify *areas of conflict and tension* between stakeholders, especially relevant when it is likely that stakeholders of influence will be in disagreement over the outcomes for the project. In this case, for example, the claims of the football club board and the local residents are in conflict.

There is a *moral case* for knowledge of how decisions affect people both inside the organisation or (as is the case with the stadium project) externally.

(b) **Pristine capitalist and social contract approaches**

Definitions

The *pristine capitalist* position sees economic performance as the primary and only legitimate goal of all business organisations, especially those publicly owned by private shareholders. The *agency relationship is viewed as monofiduciary*. Any claim upon the organisation that would threaten the optimal profitability of the organisation is viewed as morally unacceptable as it would be an *effective theft of shareholder wealth*. It would also introduce economic inefficiencies that lead to the misallocation of capital resources. All such claims are therefore dismissed. The position is sometimes put as 'the business of business is business'.

The *social contractarian* position sees a business organisation as a citizen of society bound by society's norms and beliefs. Accordingly, organisations exist and thrive *only with a societal 'licence' to operate* in the same way that democratic governments only exist with the explicit consent of the governed. Discordance between organisational and societal values can result in the *withdrawal of support by society*. Accordingly, organisations seek to align themselves with social values, norms and expectations so as to maximise their social legitimacy. This sometimes necessitates modifying business objectives to take account of certain stakeholders' concerns.

Application to case

The pristine capitalist position *would recommend proceeding with the stadium project* notwithstanding local concerns. The reason is that the building of the stadium *offered the club the best way of maximising its primary strategic goals* by gaining larger crowds and thereby increasing revenues and obtaining more funds for players and other improvements.

Conversely, the social contractarian position would suggest that *the club only exists with the permission of its local stakeholders* (that could, collectively, harm the club) and accordingly, the *club needs to align its values with those of its key stakeholders* to continue to enjoy its 'licence' to exist. It may, therefore, need to amend its plans to continue to enjoy ongoing social support. It would be against the interests of the club to be seen to harm the interests of the school or the wildlife centre, for example, and so stadium plans may need to be amended accordingly to take their concerns into account.

(c) **Fiduciary responsibility**

Definition of 'fiduciary responsibility'

A fiduciary responsibility is a duty of trust and care towards one or more constituencies. It describes direction of accountability in that one party has a fiduciary duty to another. In terms of the case, the question refers to whose interests the directors of the football club should act in. Traditionally, the fiduciary duty of directors in public companies is to act in the economic interests of shareholders who invest in the company but are unable to manage the company directly. The case raises a number of issues concerning broadening the fiduciary duties of the directors of the football club with regard to the building of the new stadium, to other stakeholder groups.

The case for extending fiduciary responsibility

Although the primary fiduciary duty of directors in large public companies will be to shareholders, directors in businesses such as the football club described in the case may have good reason to broaden their views on fiduciary responsibility. This would involve taking into account, and acting in the interests of, the local wildlife centre, the residents, the school, the local government authority and the fans. The stakeholders in the case are not in agreement on the outcome for the new stadium and the club will need to privilege some stakeholders over others, which is a common situation whenever a proposal involving multiple impacts is considered. The specific arguments for broadening the fiduciary duties in this case include the following:

Such an acceptance of claims made on the football club would clearly demonstrate that the *club values the community* of which it considers itself a part.

It would help to maintain and manage its *local reputation*, which is important in progressing the stadium project.

To broaden the fiduciary responsibility in this case would be to an important part of the *risk management strategy*, especially with regard to risks that could arise from the actions of local stakeholders.

It could be argued that there is a moral case for all organisations to include other stakeholders' claims in their strategies as it *enfranchises and captures the views* of those affected by an organisation's policies and actions.

Examiner's Report

Introduction

This was the section B question that caused candidates the most problems. The content of the question was drawn from parts of the study guide concerned with stakeholders, ethical perspectives and the arguments about extending corporate responsibility beyond the duties to shareholders. In each case, the reason why candidates underperformed was, again, because they failed to answer the question as it was actually set. It may be tempting to answer the question you wish was being set but unfortunately that will sometimes not achieve very many marks.

Part (a) asked candidates to define stakeholder (which most candidates got right) and then to 'explain the importance of identifying stakeholders...'. It was the second task that confused many candidates. It might be worth noting what this part did NOT ask candidates to do. It did NOT ask candidates to:

Identify the stakeholders (so lists of stakeholders did not attract marks)

Describe the Mendelow framework

Describe each stakeholder's position on the Mendelow matrix

Explain each stakeholder's claim on the stadium project.

Most poor answers followed one or more of these paths.

Some marks would have been available for stating that one of the main purposes of identifying all stakeholders is to take into account the relative power and influence of stakeholder groups when planning for and communicating about the stadium project. However this was not specifically a 'Mendelow' question. The correct approach required candidates to 'take a step back' and place themselves in the position of the board of the football club, considering all the benefits of knowing who the stakeholders and their different claims were? That is what the question was probing.

Part (b) invited candidates to apply an important area of ethical theory to the case. Gray et al.'s 'seven positions' describe the possible perspectives that people can adopt in respect of the ethical role of business. The question specifically mentioned two of these – the pristine capitalist position and the social contractarian position. Again, it is worth noting that the question did not ask candidates to list the seven positions nor to explain any of the other five.

There were two tasks in part (b). The first was to compare and contrast the two positions. This involved recognising that the pristine capitalist position recognised only a responsibility to shareholders whilst the social contractarian position sees a 'deal' being done between an organisation and the society in which it operates. In the 'social contract', the organisation agrees to act in line with the norms of the society in which it operates in exchange for the support of that society in allowing it to survive and prosper. The second part was to explain how adopting each position as an ethical stance would affect how the football club responded to the stakeholder concerns. The way that many candidates answered this question was to correctly describe the two ethical positions but then to fail to adequately apply them to the situation facing the football club. It was this failure to apply, both in this question and elsewhere in the paper, that explains why many candidates did not achieve higher marks than they did. Again, it is not enough to rely on the 'book knowledge' learned from the study texts or classes. An ability to apply that knowledge to the case is essential in achieving higher marks.

The final part of question 4, **part (c)**, also asked for some evidence of understanding and then some application. In addition to explaining what 'fiduciary responsibility' meant, candidates were also invited to 'construct' a case for something. To 'construct', or 'synthesise', is a level 3 verb alongside others like assess or evaluate. It requires candidates to prepare an argument in favour of a particular position or course of action (or against, of course, depending on the question). Candidates do not need to personally believe in that position, of course, but to prepare the main points of a convincing case in support of the position stated.

In this case, the task was to prepare a case in favour of extending the fiduciary responsibility toward stakeholders other than the club's shareholders. The limit of accountability of a business organisation is one of the key arguments in the debate over the social responsibility of business and this case probed some of the issues involved in that debate. This part was not done well overall. For many candidates it was the final part of the examination itself and there was evidence in some exam papers of time pressure compromising the quality of the answers but it was also true that many candidates struggled with the task of constructing an argument. This should represent a challenge to candidates sitting the P1 paper in future.

ACCA marking scheme		Marks
(a)	1 mark for each relevant point made on definition of 'stakeholder' up to a maximum of 2 marks. Up to 2 marks for each relevant point on the importance of stakeholder identification up to a maximum of 8 marks.	10
(b)	2 marks for description of pristine capitalist position. 2 marks for description of social contractarian position. 1 mark for each relevant point made applying the theories to the case up to a maximum of 4.	8
(c)	1 mark for each relevant point made defining 'fiduciary responsibility' up to a maximum of 3 marks. 1 mark for each relevant point made in favour of extending fiduciarity up to a maximum of 4 marks.	7
Total		25

19   DELCOM

Key answer tips

This question tackles a number of the less popular parts of the governance section of the syllabus. Ensure that you try all sections, and use the solution as a learning tool to recap these topics.

(a)   **Insider governance**

Insider structure refers to a company that is majority owned by individuals who have substantial influence over the executive operations at the organisation. This means that major shareholders are also directors. In this instance, Mr Kumas is both a majority shareholder and the CEO of the enterprise. Further, he effectively runs the company since the rest of the directors do not seem to have input to major strategy decision making.

Insider structures are very common as a global form of governance, being associated with the German and Asian model. Governments and financial institutions may be insiders although family structures are the most common form of insider model. Mr Kumas's involvement could be generalised as a family form of insider governance since it is run in his interests and therefore presumably those of his siblings and dependents.

Evaluation of insider governance structure

An evaluation should consider positive and negative aspects to this form of governance.

As identified in the scenario by Mr Kumas, there are potentially less agency costs in the form of directorial salaries and substantial disclosure since, as the majority shareholder, the major owner is well aware of how the company is performing and has little need for high paid executives to act for him.

The negative side of this is the lack of independence between decisions in the best interests of the company and his own individual shareholder needs. These may be at odds with other shareholders. There is clearly a lack of transparency in disclosure and this has been the cause of complaint by other shareholders at the AGM.

A lack of minority protection is often associated with insider structures and, through the above, can been seen to be at least a potential problem here. The poor local stock exchange regulatory regime may not highlight the importance of not disadvantaging the minority, and legal systems may offer little recourse. This subsequently becomes the focus for action in global governance standards discussed below.

Mr Kumas demonstrates that he has a tight control over company operations. This can be seen through taking sole responsibility for many decisions. Tight control can however lead to a lack of scope of skills in decision making. This insider failing can also be associated with governance theory and considered as a problem in transaction cost theory.

The personal nature of ownership and executive control coupled with the potential lack of transparency and threat to minority protection often restrict the flow of capital into such companies.

(b)   **Transaction cost theory**

Transaction cost theory is a framework for managerial decision making. It has its roots in management accounting but can be adapted to consider governance and strategic control.

Strategic transactions are often complex and risky involving large scale resources. The growth of this organisation highlights the importance of acquisitive decisions in order to build the company portfolio. Such decisions require close consideration of the costs involved in the transaction and its outcomes.

Transaction cost theory identifies potential problems in such decisions arising from the bounded rationality of the decision maker and problems in opportunistic behaviour. Mr Kumas's failure to adequately consider due diligence in recent acquisitions and his reliance on intuition is an example of the former. The lack of any other board members involvement simply reinforces the problem of bounded rationality.

Opportunism is essential for growth and Mr Kumas has shown great skill in this area. The problem within opportunism is the personal nature of the perception of gain and thus consideration as to whether the decision maker is acting in the company's or his/her best interests. This issue is of concern to shareholders who require better information in order to understand the reasoning behind decisions made.

The greater the extent to which these two problems exist, the greater the need for change through improvements in the governance of the enterprise. This can be seen in shareholders requests for improvements in disclosure and accountability of Mr Kumas.

Governance measures taken are however about balancing increased governance measures with the potential to restrict entrepreneurial flair. The greater the external control the weaker the innovative response and motivation within. This can have a detrimental effect on shareholders returns.

Ultimately, through transaction cost theory, we see governance as a balance between the need to control and monitor whilst allowing a degree of professional freedom that is the very basis for the investment decision in the first place.

(c)   **Disclosure improvements**

There are a wide range of measures that can be taken in order to improve the level of disclosure made by the organisation in its annual report in order to appease the shareholders.

More information regarding strategic rationale would seem an obvious and immediate area where improvement is required. This should be accompanied by information regarding objectives and performance measures for future strategies. In general shareholders would like to see more information concerning future rather than current operations since the latter only provides comfort in previous performance and no real information relating to the security of their investment or the need to increase their investment in the company.

Stakeholder information is considered a prerequisite in order to satisfy the growing ethical standpoint of investors. They would like, especially under ICGN regulation, to see the company taking its responsibilities as a corporate citizen seriously. Stakeholder information may relate to direct and indirect stakeholders, narrow and wide, national and global. This does not seen from the scenario to be an area that Mr Kumas is likely to dramatically improve in the short term but may be a long term aspiration.

Specific rather than general information is a final important consideration. Annual accounts can be plagued with meaningless management speak and rhetoric rather than attempt to communicate anything meaningful to shareholders. There has recently been a backlash against this marketing fuelled use of jargon, hence the greater emphasis on such issues in governance such as Combined Code reference C1 in the UK.

(d) **Focus for action within global governance standards**

The focus for action should relate to the major issues raised in previous sections of the question. Shareholder rights and protection of the minority is the most important concern in stimulating global investment. This should be enshrined in law as well as in governance standards.

Directorial responsibility to act in shareholder interests or more specifically to develop and monitor strategy is also important as is the need to improve disclosure in order to communicate the nature of decision made and their reasons. This should be coupled with the need to consider the need for control and risk management with governance structures in place to address these issues or at least the need to report on them.

Finally, as mentioned, corporate citizenship or stakeholder analysis and consideration in strategy is often considered a facilitator to attracting investment in organisations.

20 VESTEL

Key answer tips

Your answer to parts (b) and (c) of this question can pull upon your own experience and business knowledge. The recruitment of a board member will have many similarities to the process that you will have been through to get your current job. And, similarly, to earn marks for the content of an induction process consider the things that you do, or are shown, in the first few days in a new job.

(a) **Nomination committee**

Committees form an important part of board operations and, as stated, are generally included within principles laid down by regulatory bodies in order to advise as to appropriate governance structures. In the UK the role of nomination committees is outlined in section A4 of the Combined Code.

Committees allow the expertise and skills of a focused group of individuals to be used in order to form advisory opinion for the board of directors. They usually consist of non-executive directors who have specialist skills in areas such as environmentalism or ethics. The non-executive nature of membership creates a degree of independence from executive management and this in turn suggests that no undue influence has been placed upon them in relation to conclusions drawn.

Skill provision, appropriate balance to membership and the independence of thought suggested will be important for a nomination committee. Their decisions will affect board composition and the independence of non-executives selected will be vital to ensure that shareholder needs are paramount in the decision making process of the board.

The committee structure offers a channel of communication for both executives and external consultants to ensure all relevant views are canvassed. At the same time they allow the board to off load responsibility for some key areas of decision making so allowing them to focus on other considerations such as strategy definition.

Nomination committees are essential for effective board operations because of the results they produce. The provision of new directors refreshes the board and ensures succession into roles, promoting stability and loyalty of senior management given a route through which promotion on merit can be achieved.

(b) **Director recruitment**

There is no set approach to recruitment of new non-executive directors although certain issues in the case highlight the need for thoughtful and exacting methodology in order to subsequently ensure quality in the outcome.

The scenario suggests there may be a shortage of suitable local candidates for the job. It draws this conclusion through an analysis of the size of the corporate skill base available locally. This raises a number of issues.

Firstly, candidates will need to be carefully sought out and selected possibly through the use of search firms to act as intermediaries, approaching those in senior roles within other companies with a degree of confidentiality.

Secondly, candidates from outside the private sector should be considered, particularly in areas such as ethics and environmentalism. Academics and activists may be a part of the gene pool trawled in this respect.

Thirdly, overseas or foreign candidates should not be excluded, particularly when a large part of the company's business is in the export market. This will require a benchmarking exercise in order to ensure the company can afford the costs of drawing individuals from their home country in order to serve.

The Chairman's and CEO's view should be canvassed as part of the process. It may be the case that the Chairman takes overall responsibility for the committee. Since it has such a vital role to perform this is likely to be the case.

Standard background checks and interviews should be used as part of the selection process prior to selection of the best candidate and the negotiation over terms and contracts. Critically, the most important aspect of committee operations takes place following selection. The committee must ensure that their operations are appropriately disclosed to shareholders in the form of a separate section within the annual report. This ensures a degree of transparency exists in order to deal with the agency issue.

Performance appraisal is a final aspect to any board operation. The nomination committee must critically appraise the success and failures within the recruitment process used and ensure it continually evolves and improves over time.

(c) **Business case for induction**

Induction for UK governance is included in section A5 of the Combined Code. This highlights the need for the process to occur, managed by the Company Secretary, as well as the need for ongoing CPD arrangements to be available to all board members.

The business case for induction is partially discussed in the scenario as to the need to ensure individuals are able to be active members of board decision making as quickly as possible. This rapid assimilation assists in ensuring the board continues to be effective and able to deal with the operational and market challenges detailed in the scenario.

A high quality induction process also ensure individuals feel they have been given the right knowledge and support to ensure they are effective. This has ramifications in terms of ensuring retention of non-executives over time.

The business case can be considered in terms of what is delivered through induction. In this way the process ensures individuals are knowledgeable concerning the vision, objectives, customer base, operational value chain and ethics at the centre of board decision deliberations. Induction gives individuals the skills to do their job.

This can be extended to information concerning the legal and procedural framework within which the board operates so ensuring shareholders needs are continually met and risks reduced coupled with improved efficiency and effectiveness of board meetings.

Induction is an accepted part of human resource management for all employees and so there is no reason why it should not be a part of operations at the highest level. In fact, the gravity and consequence of decisions made suggests a greater needs to ensure skills exist at this level and that individuals are fully aware of their roles and responsibilities.

Induction process

The content of induction should vary according to need and ability, especially at this level when dealing with executive status management. Information provision concerning legal duties may include provision of standard text on responsibilities such as that provided by the Institute of Directors in the UK. Company specific information would embrace data on markets and competitors, key customers, product portfolio and strategy.

Induction must include introducing the new non-executive to shareholders. This may be restricted initially to a meeting with key institutional shareholders and a pseudo induction meeting at the AGM when the candidate is introduced to shareholders in general meeting as they are given the opportunity to vote the person onto the board or reject them.

Visits to key corporate sites and even suppliers would be very useful as well as the need to meet key personnel below the board level as part of familiarisation or to open communication channels for future use by the non-executive.

Induction is really the start of a continuous learning process that occurs at each board meeting and which should be formalised through CPD. The induction process itself offers an opportunity to identify future training needs for non-executives.

21 CORPORATE GOVERNANCE

Key answer tips

In part (b) the question asks about the principles of corporate governance – however there is no method of underpinning corporate governance regulations. The question has therefore to be taken as actually asking for a summary of the key points of each part of the corporate governance code.

Overall, this is a factual question – if you know the material you can score high marks, otherwise it is a question to avoid as there is no scenario or other hints as to the content required in your answer.

Don't forget to tell the examiner which corporate governance code you have based your answer on.

(a)   Key reasons for the emergence of corporate governance regulations include:

- Concern in the ways in which organisations are run, with particular focus on corporate scandals such as Maxwell (UK), Holtzman (Germany), Enron (USA) and OneTel (Australia).

- The need to provide some form of enforcement mechanism to try to stop company failures such as those noted above, occurring again in the future.

- The desire of many institutional investors to become more involved with the companies in which they have invested.

- The need for stability and security in the equities markets as investment from areas such as pension schemes expands. Private individuals as well as corporate investors are looking for similar stability in equities as in, say, government stocks to protect their investments and eventually their financial security in old age.

- The need to raise the standard of corporate reporting, particularly when auditors appear to 'miss' important control failures or window dressing of financial statements.

(b) The main areas of corporate governance included in typical requirements such as the UK's Combined Code are:

- Directors

- Remuneration of directors

- Accountability and audit

- Relations with shareholders

- Institutional investors

- Disclosure.

Core principles underpin each of these areas.

Directors

A company should be led by an effective board which is also responsible for the success of the company.

To limit the power of any one individual, there should be a division of responsibilities between the person running the board (the chair) and the person running the company (the CEO). One person should not therefore hold both posts at the same time.

To ensure that the board focuses attention on the best interests of the company, and no group of directors can exert too much power, the board should comprise of a mix of executive and non-executive directors.

So shareholders and other interested parties have confidence in the abilities of board members, the appointment procedure for directors should be transparent.

To ensure that directors can carry out decision making effectively, they should be provided with information in a timely manner.

To check that the board is working effectively and efficiently, an annual evaluation should take place of the performance of the board against agreed standards and targets.

To ensure that board members do not become too blinkered in their decision making, new board members should be introduced on a regular basis to question the decisions and philosophy of the board.

Remuneration

To attract directors with the necessary skills, remuneration levels should be adequate but not excessive compared to other companies. Some elements of the reward systems should also be linked to company performance so as not to reward 'failure'.

The way in which remuneration is decided should be transparent so that third parties can see clearly how much remuneration each director is receiving.

Accountability and audit

So investors and other interested parties can check on how their investment is being managed, the directors are charged with presenting an understandable assessment of the company's financial position.

Similarly, the board has to maintain a sound system of internal control to protect the assets of the company and therefore the investment of the shareholders.

To provide confidence in the financial statements, the method of preparation of those statements should be transparent and understandable.

Relations with shareholders

Shareholders, particularly institutional shareholders, require input into how their investment in the company is being managed; the board has the responsibility of ensuring that this input is received.

Additional input should also be obtained from investors at the Annual General Meeting.

Institutional investors

Institutional investors are recommended to use their votes carefully. They should also ensure that the objectives of the company fit their objectives (e.g. perhaps regarding ethical trading) to ensure there is no conflict of interest between their objectives and the company.

Disclosure

The core principle here relates to the information which should be provided in the annual report. In overview, the report should provide investors with all the information that they need to confirm that the directors are managing their company effectively without any conflicts of interest. The reports will therefore include information such as:

- a statement of how the board operates;

- details of all board members;

- details of board sub-committees and their work (e.g. remuneration and audit committees);

- details of remuneration;

- how the board conducts its activities.

(c) This answer has been based on the UK's Combined Code.

According to the UK's Combined Code, the board of a company should establish an audit committee of at least three or, in the case of smaller companies, two members who should all be independent non-executive directors. The board should satisfy itself that at least one member of the audit committee has recent and relevant financial experience.

The audit committee is therefore a formal sub-committee of the board of a company. Its main role is to assist the board in fulfilling its stewardship responsibilities by reviewing the system of internal control, the external audit process, the work of internal audit and the financial information that is provided to shareholders. The overall role is therefore supporting the board by providing an independent check on the process of production and review of financial information in the company.

At a more detailed level, specific responsibilities of the audit committee include:

- Checking the integrity of the company's financial statements. The committee will review the judgments made by the board in preparing the financial statements, ensuring these are appropriate to the company. The committee will also check stock exchange announcements to confirm those announcements accurately reflect the situation of the company.

- Reviewing the company's internal control and risk management systems (unless the latter is undertaken by a separate risk management committee). The committee will ensure that the directors establish suitable systems of internal control including internal audit. Reports from internal audit will also be received by the committee which will then ensure that appropriate action is taken on those reports.

- Reviewing the work of the external auditor, with specific responsibility to recommend to the board the re-appointment of existing auditors, or their removal and appointment of a different firm. Making this decision helps maintain the external auditor's independence from the board of directors, improving the effectiveness of the external audit function. The audit committee will also recommend the remuneration level of the external auditor.

- Producing and implementing a policy regarding the provision of non-audit services to be provided by the external auditor (where specific country legislation or corporate governance guidance allows this). Again, this process helps to protect the independence of the external auditor while demonstrating that the company itself does not automatically appoint the same external audit firm to provide all financial services.

- Finally, the audit committee has the responsibility of reporting to the board regarding matters such as recommending amendments to internal control systems. The committee may also be available to receive confidential reports from staff regarding financial irregularities in the company.

22 MANAGERS AND SHAREHOLDERS

Key answer tips

In your answer to part (a) ensure that you distinguish between agency theory and the agency relationship. This will assist you in scoring more marks in this area.

(a) **Agency theory**

Agency theory considers the duties and conflicts that occur between parties who have an agency relationship.

Agency relationships occur when one party, **the principal**, employs another party, **the agent**, to perform a task on their behalf. In the case of companies, one example of the agency relationship is that between directors and shareholders.

Historically, companies were owned and managed by one or a small number of individuals. However in order to raise finance for expansion to enable companies and economies to grow it was necessary for owners to find external investors. This led to the development of stock markets for a wide number of investors to buy and sell shares without taking a direct interest in the management of the business. This also resulted in the development of the concept of limited liability of directors, who now had limited personal risk and therefore less interest in the company. Responsibility for running the business is delegated by shareholders to directors.

As the agent, the director has a **fiduciary responsibility** to the shareholders, which is generally expressed in law as the director operating in the best interests of shareholders. Fiduciary responsibilities are those which arise within a trusting relationship. This only applies to the directors of a company as they are directly responsible for the activities of their staff. The responsibility of shareholders is to monitor this relationship closely and act if problems arise.

Directors are in turn accountable to shareholders. This means that they need to:

- act in shareholders' interests

- provide good information such as audited accounts and annual reports in order to prove that they are carrying out their responsibilities to shareholders in line with expectations

- operate within a defined legal structure.

(b) **Non-executive directors and conflicts of interest**

This separation of ownership and control and the different goals of shareholders concerned with wealth maximisation and managers with personal objectives gives rise to conflicts of interest and agency problems, such as the conflict between the short-term perspective of managers and the need to maximise long-term shareholder wealth.

Without controls, executive directors are in a position to neglect their fiduciary duties and manage the business with too much regard for their own interests.

The major areas of conflict, all of which are addressed in the latest version of the UK's Combined Code, are as follows:

(i) Remuneration. Directors may be inclined to reward themselves excessively via both salary and bonuses if they are allowed to decide such matters for themselves. The Combined Code says that no director or manager should be involved in any decisions as to their own remuneration.

(ii) Nominations to the board. Executive directors would typically prefer to appoint people who share their own views about the management of the business or can be manipulated. The Combined Code says that a nomination committee should lead the process for board appointments and make recommendations to the board, and that a majority of members of the committee should be independent non-executive directors.

(iii) Audit. The danger here is that executive directors could appoint 'friendly' auditors, who will turn a blind eye to misuse of company assets for the directors' benefit or to misreporting of the company's financial position. The Combined Code says that an audit committee should include at least three members, and all should be independent non-executive directors.

(iv) In many areas of board level decision making executive directors may be inclined to make decisions that enhance their own position and may not be in the best interests of the company. Examples could range from major investment in an executive director's 'pet' project to rejecting a takeover bid, irrespective of its merit, simply to preserve their own jobs. Non-executive directors will not have these personal issues and can take a more objective view. The Combined Code says that the board should include a balance of executive and non-executive directors (and in particular independent non-executive directors) such that no individual or small group of individuals can dominate the board's decision taking.

23 ANDROM

Key answer tips

Always follow the instructions in questions like this which ask for the answer to be structured in a certain way – to use a different format for your answer will mean losing marks unnecessarily.

REPORT

To: Board of Androm

From: Management accountant

Subject: Corporate Governance requirements

Date: 2 August 200X

As requested at the board meeting of 23 July, I summarise below the implications of applying corporate governance provisions to Androm.

Board of directors

An effective board of directors is essential for good corporate governance, with the board providing entrepreneurial leadership of the company.

There are three specific activities affecting the board of a company:

- It should meet regularly to discharge its duties effectively. Unless the board meets regularly, control of the company will effectively be placed in the hands of the executive management.

- There must be a clear list of responsibilities for the board, and decisions that the board should take. These decisions should not be delegated to the executive management team.

- The chairman should hold meetings with the non-executive directors without the executive directors present. The non-executives should also meet at least once a year without the chairman (and led by the senior independent director) to review the performance of the chairman.

The roles of chairman of the board and chief executive officer

To maintain good corporate governance, the chairman of the board is responsible for managing the board of directors. The chief executive officer (CEO) is responsible for the executive management team (and as executives, the executive directors' report to the CEO). There should also be a division of responsibilities between running the board (the role of the chairman) and the executive responsibility for the running of the company's business (the role of the CEO).

Within Androm, Mr Hunt is currently both chairman and CEO. Appointing another individual to the role of CEO will satisfy corporate governance requirements as well as allowing Mr Hunt to limit any perceived abuse of power in the company.

Composition of the board

According to corporate governance guidelines, the board should include a balance of executive and non-executive directors (and in particular independent non-executive directors), such that no individual or small group of individuals can dominate the board's decision making.

In the case of Androm, there appears to be only one non-executive director. Whilst that individual is correctly attempting to provide external guidance to the board on the decision regarding listing, currently this is by recommending an independent report. Provision of more non-executive directors may help to bring appropriate experience in-house. Small listed companies normally have at least two non-executive directors, while larger listed companies have half of the board (excluding the chairman) as non-executive directors.

Position of non-executive directors

Codes on corporate governance usually set out circumstances in which a non-executive director is normally assumed not to be independent. For example, an individual is normally assumed not to be independent when he or she:

* has been an employee of the company within the past five years

* receives additional remuneration from the company other than his or her fee as a non-executive director, or is a member of a share option or pension scheme of the company

* has significant links with other directors through involvement in other companies (eg holds cross-directorships)

* has served on the board for more than nine years since first election.

As Mr Tyr was recently chairman of the company, and still retains his share options, then he cannot be considered 'independent'. To ensure corporate governance principles are followed, Mr Tyr should resign from the board and at least two new non-executive directors should be appointed.

Appointments to the board

In most corporate governance regulations, it is stated that there should be a formal, rigorous and transparent procedure for the appointment of new directors to the board. The process should be led by a nomination committee of board directors, which should make its recommendations to the main board for approval.

However, within Androm, the board chairman still appoints directors, although the shareholders could still disagree with this appointment in general meeting. Again, this is indicative of the power of the chairman, already noted above. To meet corporate governance regulations, Androm needs to form a nominations committee with specific remit to:

* identify gaps in board skills

* seek out and appoint appropriate individuals

* prepare a succession plan.

Other committees that will also be required include the remuneration committee and the audit committee, both of which will require additional non-executive directors on the board.

Information and professional development

It is normal to supply board members with suitable information in a timely manner to enable them to fulfil their duties properly. It is the responsibility of the board chairman to make sure that all the board members are suitably informed.

This has not happened with the most recent board meeting. Provision of an agenda and supporting documentation prior to the meeting is appropriate. The issue of secrecy is important; sending documents in private and confidential envelopes should overcome this issue.

The chairman is also responsible for ensuring that all directors continually update their skills and knowledge to enable them to carry out their work properly. It appears that the directors are keen to update their skills, but lack of time (particularly with reference to the point on listing) prevents this.

An appropriate plan for training should be implemented for board members as soon as possible.

Summary

Some amendments are needed to Androm should the company wish to proceed to listing.

Please let me know if you require any additional information at this stage.

Presented by:

Management Accountant

24   GISTC

Key answer tips

Part (a) of the question is **not** asking for the threats to independence of auditors. However these threats (which you should ensure you know for the exam) may help you in identifying **how** this independence can be maintained. Make sure that you are describing the 'how' and not the threat to demonstrate that you have read the question properly.

(a)   **Auditor independence**

The independence of external auditors within a large entity can be maintained in various ways.

Auditor appointment

The external auditors are appointed by the members in general meeting. However, members normally accept the recommendation of the directors in this respect. To ensure some independence, the initial recommendation for appointment should be made by the audit committee. This helps to ensure that the executive directors and auditors maintain a professional relationship and are not influenced by personal relationships which may build up over the years.

In the case of GISTC, this control will be ineffective. The audit committee normally comprises non-executive directors to provide some independence from the executive directors. However, in GISTC, the committee is made up from executive directors only.

Work

The work of the external auditor will be reviewed by the audit committee, partly to ensure it has been carried out correctly and partly to ensure that there are no ongoing independence issues.

In the case of GISTC, the external auditors have been asked to carry out a review of the internal control systems within the company. This may affect their independence in two areas:

- Firstly, regarding remuneration. The external auditors may find a significant amount of fee income is being derived from the client for non-audit services. This may adversely affect their ability to provide an unbiased opinion on the financial statements.

- Secondly, there is a possibility that the external auditors will effectively audit their own work. Any amendments to the internal control system proposed will then be audited by the same firm, losing any element of independence. This can be avoided either by using two different firms of auditors, or by the one firm splitting to provide different services using different staff.

Duration of appointment

There is an argument that independence is lost through increasing familiarity over time. The auditors effectively get to know the directors of the company and the activities of the company very well, meaning that mistakes and errors are less likely to be identified.

In the case of GISTC, TMC have been external auditors for the last 14 years. This raises the issue of independence problems through familiarity with the company. It may be possible to limit this problem by rotating audit staff, including the audit partner so 'new' staff are auditing GISTC.

(b)   **Corporate governance/board of directors**

Introduction

In the UK, the Combined Code provides guidance regarding good corporate governance and the board of directors. In overview, the board is to provide entrepreneurial leadership of the company within a framework of prudent and effective controls. To do this the board should:

- Meet regularly to discharge its duties.

- Have a clear list of responsibilities for each board member and of the decisions that the board is expected to take.

- Ensure that the chairman holds meetings with the non-executive directors without the executive directors being present to review the performance of the board.

Specific issues affecting the board include the following:

Chairman and CEO

The positions of chairman of the board and the chief executive officer (the person in charge of running the company) should be separated. This is to ensure that no one individual has too much power in the company. This is not the case in GISTC, and there is a danger that the board chairman will dominate the company. These roles should be split.

Non-executive directors

To provide some review and check on the executive directors, each board should have at least 50% of its membership (excluding the chairman) as non-executive directors. This appears to be the case in GISTC.

However, non-executive directors should have the appropriate experience and training to be able to make an active contribution to board discussions. The experience of the non-executive directors relates to financial services, not provision of goods. It is unclear how effective they will be given lack of knowledge in this area. Similarly, there is no mention of any training being provided, which again will limit their effectiveness.

Appointments to the board

Appointments to the board should be made via an appointments committee. This is to provide some independence from the current board members and ensure that appointments are based on merit and not on familiarity with other board members.

Audit committee

The board should establish an audit committee of non-executive directors to liaise with the external auditors, recommend the external auditor appointment and review audit reports prior to the board receiving this information.

In GISTC, the audit committee comprises executive directors. This will limit the effectiveness of the committee because the executive directors will lack independence in reviewing audit reports – they will be concerned with achieving company objectives and not necessarily want to change financial information where this adversely affects the company.

Use of the AGM

The board should use the AGM to construct a dialogue with the shareholders – it appears that the chairman wants this to happen.

However, the issue of directors' service contracts needs clarification. Good corporate governance indicates these should not last more than three years; having contracts for five years is therefore not acceptable. The longer service contract may encourage directors to be complacent, as well as providing potentially large payments for loss of office should their service contracts be broken.

25   SYKES ENGINEERING GROUP

(a)   The situation at the Sykes Engineering Group should never have been allowed to reach this unfortunate state of affairs. There are several actions that could have been taken to avoid this situation. Firstly **it is usually not appropriate for one person to hold both offices of chairman and chief executive officer (managing director).** This is recommended practice by the UK Combined Code on corporate governance. There is too much concentration of power and it is difficult for lesser managers/directors to challenge someone in Jerome Sykes' position. The UK Combined Code also warns of the dangers of centralising power in too few hands and proposed a **stronger role for non-executive directors** of the board. Sykes should have had to surrender one of his posts, allowing a director with similar powers to be appointed so that he or she could challenge/question Sykes' decision-making.

The **non-executive directors have failed in their responsibilities**. Action should have been taken before such an unfortunate situation arose. What have they been doing?

The **embracing culture of the organisation is tainted**. Managers have been able to ride roughshod over employees – sexual and racial **harassment**. Part of corporate governance requires that companies are answerable to other stakeholders and not just to shareholders. It would appear that managers have been breaking the law. Why are there no systems in place to prevent this? What has happened to supervisory management?

Bribery is a more contentious issue. It is often difficult to define and circumstances in different countries do require different approaches. However hints of bribery can harm the reputation of a company and can have adverse effects on a company's performance. *[The following is for information only and is not expected in the answer. The World Bank has reported that '. . . higher levels of corruption are associated with lower levels of growth'. Admittedly this refers to macro level corruption (country-wide) and not corruption at a local, business level, but a general perception is that bribery is not beneficial in the long run. The USA has a Foreign Corrupt Practices Act and there is an organisation, Transparency International, which has an integrity pact, requiring bidders in international tenders to reject bribery.]* Bribery should not be tolerated within organisations.

It is worrying that **the auditors** have not uncovered the irregularities within the company's accounts. Is this another example of an audit company being too closely involved in the strategy of the firm or just its failure to do a competent job? Furthermore it is of concern that the **main institutional shareholders** have only acted when share prices have fallen. They have a stronger duty to monitor all activities of the company and if they were aware of unsavoury activities, action should have been taken earlier, not now when the share price is falling.

(b) **Legal rights and responsibilities**

The legal duties of a director provide a baseline for the responsibilities of directors. Breaching these duties can leave a director open to criminal prosecution and imprisonment.

The law is there to protect the owners of the company. It exists because of the nature of a fiduciary relationship where one person acts on behalf of another. The law provides a framework for directors' actions in upholding the best principles in this owner/manager relationship. The fiduciary responsibilities are:

- The duty to act in good faith: as long as directors' motives are honest and they genuinely believe they are acting in the best interests of the company they are normally safe from claims that they should have acted otherwise.

- The duty of skill and care: this care is a specific fiduciary duty. The law requires a director to use reasonable skill and care in carrying out their tasks.

Directors do not have unlimited power. There are a number of ways in which the law defines the limits to the power of directors:

- Articles of association: the articles of association provide a framework for how directors operate such as the need to be re-elected on a three-year rotation.

- Shareholder resolution: this curtails director action in a legal sense.

- Provisions of law: these could be health and safety or the duty of care.

- Board decisions: legally it is the board that makes decisions in the interests of shareholders – not individual directors, but rather a collective view.

The company may be able to take civil action against a director who is in breach of his or her duties:

- any contract made by the director may be void

- they may be held personally liable for damages payable to the company in compensation for negligence

- they may be forced to restore company property at their own expense.

(c) There are a number of potential causes of disqualification, following which an individual is not permitted to hold any directorships.

Potential causes of disqualification include:

- allowing the company to trade while insolvent (wrongful trading or fraudulent trading)

- not keeping proper accounting records

- failing to prepare and file accounts

- being guilty of three or more defaults in complying with companies' legislation regarding the filing of documents with Companies House during the preceding five years

- failing to send tax returns and pay tax

- taking actions that are deemed to be unfit in the management of a company.

26 ROSH AND COMPANY *Walk in the footsteps of a top tutor*

Key answer tips

All parts of this question can be separated into two sections, so ensure that your answer reflects this (use headings for each section).

The second half of part (a) only requires criticisms of the situation at Rosh and Company – so do not waste time commenting on anything that it is doing well.

Careful planning should ensure that you can separate out the theory of the roles of the nominations committee in (b) from the application in the case given.

The definition in part (c) should be of a couple of sentences, with your emphasis going on how this may assist in this situation. There are some clear hints in the scenario about longstanding directors and family members. Ensure that your answer states these points clearly.

The highlighted words are key phrases that markers are looking for.

(a) **Defining and explaining agency**

Agency is defined in relation to a principal. A principal appoints an agent to act on his or her behalf. In the case of corporate governance, the principal is a shareholder in a joint stock company and the agents (that have an agency relationship with principals) are the directors. The directors remain accountable to the principals for the stewardship of their investment in the company. In the case of Rosh, 60% of the shares are owned by shareholders external to the Rosh family and the board has agency responsibility to those shareholders.

Criticisms of Rosh's CG arrangements

The corporate governance arrangements at Rosh and Company are far from ideal. Five points can be made based on the evidence in the case.

There are several issues associated with the non-executive directors (NEDs) at Rosh. It is doubtful whether two NEDs are enough to bring sufficient scrutiny to the executive board. Some corporate governance codes require half of the board of larger companies to be non-executive and Rosh would clearly be in breach of such a requirement. Perhaps of equal concern, there is significant doubt over the independence of the current NEDs as they were recruited from retired executive members of the board and presumably have relationships with existing executives going back many years. Some corporate governance codes (such as the UK Combined Code) specify that NEDs should not have worked for the company within the last five years. Again, Rosh would be in breach of this provision.

Succession planning for senior positions in the company seems to be based on Rosh family membership rather than any meritocratic approach to appointments (there doesn't appear to be a nominations committee). Whilst this may have been acceptable before the flotation when the Rosh family owned all of the shares, the flotation introduced an important need for external scrutiny of this arrangement. The lack of NED independence makes this difficult.

There is a poor (very narrow) diversity of backgrounds among board members. Whilst diversity can bring increased conflict, it is generally assumed that it can also stimulate discussion and debate that is often helpful.

There is a somewhat entrenched executive board and Mary is the first new appointment to the board in many years (and is the first woman). Whilst experience is very important on a board, the appointment of new members, in addition to seeding the board with talent for the future, can also bring fresh ideas and helpful scrutiny of existing policies.

There is no discussion of strategy and there is evidence of a lack of preparation of strategic notes to the board. The assumption seems to be that the 'best' option is obvious and so there is no need for discussion and debate. Procedures for preparing briefing notes on strategy for board meetings appear to be absent. Most corporate governance codes place the discussion and setting of strategy as a high priority for boards and Rosh would be in breach of such a provision.

There is no evidence of training for Mary to facilitate her introduction into the organisation and its systems. Thorough training of new members and ongoing professional development of existing members is an important component of good governance.

(b) **Nominations committees**

General roles of a nominations committee.

It advises on the balance between executives and independent non-executive directors and establishes the appropriate number and type of NEDs on the board. The nominations committee is usually made up of NEDs.

It establishes the skills, knowledge and experience possessed by current board and notes any gaps that will need to be filled.

It acts to meet the needs for continuity and succession planning, especially among the most senior members of the board.

It establishes the desirable and optimal size of the board, bearing in mind the current size and complexity of existing and planned activities and strategies.

It seeks to ensure that the board is balanced in terms of it having board members from a diversity of backgrounds so as to reflect its main constituencies and ensure a flow of new ideas and the scrutiny of existing strategies.

In the case of Rosh, the needs that a nominations committee could address are:

To recommend how many directors would be needed to run the business and plan for recruitment accordingly. The perceived similarity of skills and interests of existing directors is also likely to be an issue.

To resolve the issues over numbers of NEDs. It seems likely that the current number is inadequate and would put Rosh in a position of non-compliance with many of the corporate governance guidelines pertaining to NEDs.

To resolve the issues over the independence of NEDs. The closeness that the NEDs have to existing executive board members potentially undermines their independence and a nominations committee should be able to identify this as an issue and make recommendations to rectify it.

To make recommendations over the succession of the chairmanship. It may not be in the interests of Rosh for family members to always occupy senior positions in the business.

(c)   **Retirement by rotation.**

Definition

Retirement by rotation is an arrangement in a director's contract that specifies his or her contract to be limited to a specific period (typically three years) after which he or she must retire from the board or offer himself (being eligible) for re-election. The director must be actively re-elected back onto the board to serve another term. The default is that the director retires unless re-elected.

Importance of

Retirement by rotation reduces the cost of contract termination for underperforming directors. They can simply not be re-elected after their term of office expires and they will be required to leave the service of the board as a retiree (depending on contract terms).

It encourages directors' performance (they know they are assessed by shareholders and reconsidered every three years) and focuses their minds upon the importance of meeting objectives in line with shareholders' aims.

It is an opportunity, over time, to replace the board membership whilst maintaining medium term stability of membership (one or two at a time).

Applied to Rosh

Retirement by rotation would enable the board of Rosh to be changed over time. There is evidence that some directors may have stayed longer than is ideal because of links with other board members going back many years.

Examiner's Report

Introduction

This was the most popular question in section B with most candidates attempting it. The case describes a company with a number of poor practices in its corporate governance.

In the first task, **(part a)**, candidates were required to explain one of the key themes in corporate governance, agency, and then, using their knowledge of best practice, to criticise the company in the case. 'Criticise' is a level 3 verb (along with assess, evaluate, construct, etc.) because a certain amount of understanding is necessary before the criticism can be undertaken. There was plenty to criticise in the case and most candidates did well in this task.

Part (b) was done well by some but poorly by others. Where candidates weren't sure they often wrote what they thought might be the roles of a nominations committee. These were sometimes right but sometimes they confused the nominations committee with the roles of the HR department (appraisals, induction, etc.). The second part, typical of a P1 task, was to apply the knowledge to the case. This involved an assessment of how a nominations committee would be useful to the company in the case which does, of course, require a close study of the case.

There was some confusion over the meaning of the term 'retirement by rotation' which was asked for in **part (c)**. Again, there was some evidence that candidates had not fully revised the whole syllabus for P1. The form of this question again shows the importance of not only knowing the whole of the P1 syllabus but also being prepared to apply the knowledge to the case.

ACCA marking scheme		Marks
(a)	1 mark for each relevant point made up to a max of 4 marks 1 mark for identification of each criticism up to a max of 5 1 mark for brief discussion of each criticism of each up to a max of 5 (Maximum 12 marks)	12
(b)	1 mark for each relevant role of the nominations committee up to a max of 5 marks 1 mark for each relevant point on the usefulness of a nominations committee to Rosh up to a max of 4 marks (Maximum 8 marks)	8
(c)	1 mark for each relevant point made for definition up to a max of 2 marks 1 mark for each relevant point made on importance up to a max of 3 marks 1 mark for each relevant point made on applying to Rosh up to a max of 2 marks (Maximum 5 marks)	5
Total		25

27   CORPORATE GOVERNANCE DEBATE

Key answer tips

Be very careful with the requirements for part (a) (ii) and ensure that your answer keeps to this point. When you have a long requirement like this one you may find it helpful to paraphrase it and write out the simple version on your question paper to avoid confusion. Ensure that all points you make are applied to developing countries since this will be key to earning the marks.

Part (b) requires details of a report to be published by the company about internal controls. This is a not a request to write all you know about internal controls, nor internal control systems, but to provide details of the requirements under Sarbanes-Oxley for reporting on such controls. You will need to have the relevant knowledge at hand to score well in this part.

(a)   (i)   Describe rules-based

In a rules-based jurisdiction, corporate governance provisions are legally binding and enforceable in law. Non-compliance is punishable by fines or ultimately (*in extremis*) by delisting and director prosecutions.

There is limited latitude for interpretation of the provisions to match individual circumstances ('one size fits all'). Some have described this as a 'box ticking' exercise as companies seek to comply despite some provisions applying to their individual circumstances more than others.

Investor confidence is underpinned by the quality of the legislation rather than the degree of compliance (which will be total for the most part).

(ii) Principles-based approach

Advantages of a principles-based approach

The rigour with which governance systems are applied can be varied according to size, situation, stage of development of business, etc. Organisations (in legal terms) have a choice to the extent to which they wish to comply, although they will usually have to 'comply or explain'. Explanations are more accepted by shareholders and stock markets for smaller companies.

Obeying the spirit of the law is better than 'box ticking' ('sort of business you are' rather than 'obeying rules'). Being aware of overall responsibilities is more important than going through a compliance exercise merely to demonstrate conformance.

Avoids the 'regulation overload' of rules based (and associated increased business costs). The costs of compliance have been a cause of considerable concern in the United States.

Self-regulation (e.g. by Financial Services Authority in the UK) rather than legal control has proven itself to underpin investor confidence in several jurisdictions and the mechanisms are self-tightening (quicker and cheaper than legislation) if initial public offering (IPO) volumes fall or capital flows elsewhere.

Context of developing countries

Developing countries' economies tend to be dominated by small and medium sized organisations (SMEs). It would be very costly and probably futile, to attempt to burden small businesses with regulatory requirements comparable to larger concerns.

Having the flexibility to 'comply or explain' allows for those seeking foreign equity to increase compliance whilst those with different priorities can delay full compliance. In low-liquidity stock markets (such as those in some developing countries) where share prices are not seen as strategically important for businesses, adopting a more flexible approach might be a better use of management talent rather than 'jumping through hoops' to comply with legally-binding constraints.

The state needs to have an enforcement mechanism in place to deal with non-compliance and this itself represents a cost to taxpayers and the corporate sector. Developing countries may not have the full infrastructure in place to enable compliance (auditors, pool of NEDs, professional accountants, internal auditors, etc) and a principles-based approach goes some way to recognise this.

(b) Internal control statement

The United States Securities and Exchange Commission (SEC) guidelines are to disclose in the annual report as follows:

A statement of management's responsibility for establishing and maintaining adequate internal control over financial reporting for the company. This will always include the nature and extent of involvement by the chairman and chief executive, but may also specify the other members of the board involved in the internal controls over financial reporting. The purpose is for shareholders to be clear about who is accountable for the controls.

A statement identifying the framework used by management to evaluate the effectiveness of this internal control. This will usually involve a description of the key metrics, measurement methods (e.g. rates of compliance, fair value measures, etc) and tolerances allowed within these. Within a rules-based environment, these are likely to be underpinned by law.

Management's assessment of the effectiveness of this internal control as at the end of the company's most recent fiscal year. This may involve reporting on rates of compliance, failures, costs, resources committed and outputs (if measurable) achieved.

A statement that its auditor has issued an attestation report on management's assessment. Any qualification to the attestation should be reported in this statement.

*(**Tutorial note:** guidance from other corporate governance codes is also acceptable)*

(c)   The external reporting requirements (from the Sarbanes-Oxley section 404) being 'too ambitious' for small and medium companies

There are several arguments to support Professor Leroi's remark.

Fewer spare resources to carry out internal control. SMEs tend to operate with lower levels of spare resource than larger businesses and conducting internal reviews would be more of a challenge for them.

The extra attestation fee (over and above normal audit fee) for the attestation of the internal control report could be a constraint for many SMEs.

Lack of expertise from within existing employees (to internally audit/police as well as carry out internal activities) would be a likely constraint.

SMEs will have fewer activities and less complexity, hence less need for shareholders to require the information (less to go wrong).

Examiner's Report

Introduction

This was the least well done question in section B. Although the case scenario mentioned Sarbanes Oxley, none of the tasks actually required a knowledge of Sarbanes Oxley.

The first part **(part a(i))** was well done on the whole, asking as it did for the essential features of a rules-based approach to corporate governance.

Part (a)(ii) was not so well done overall. The question required candidates to construct an argument in favour of applying a principles-based approach to developing countries. The question assumed that candidates were aware of the features of, and argument for, principles rather than rules. If candidates were not aware of these, then obviously it would be very hard to get a good mark. Then, candidates were required to consider these advantages in the specific context of developing economies and to construct an argument accordingly.

Similarly, many candidates were confused in answering **part (c)**. The question asked candidates to 'describe the typical contents of an external report on internal controls' this being the nature of the content of section 404 of Sarbanes Oxley. This is not a uniquely Sarbanes Oxley issue, however as other codes have similar provisions. The question tended to be misinterpreted in two ways: that it was about external reporting in general (it wasn't) and it was about internal controls in general (it wasn't). This question highlights the importance of knowledge of the whole syllabus (this is from section B3b and C3d) and not just hoping that what has been revised will come up in the exam.

Part (c) was about external reporting requirements rather than about (as some candidates wrongly believed) principles based approaches in developing countries. One of the criticisms of rigid reporting requirements is that they are burdensome for smaller companies and this question sought to explore some of those issues..

ACCA marking scheme			
			Marks
(a)	(i)	1 mark for each essential feature briefly described (total 3 marks)	
(a)	(ii)	1 mark for each relevant point made on the advantages of principles-based up to a max of 4 marks 2 marks for each relevant point on developing countries up to a max of 6 marks	
			13
(b)		2 marks for each relevant area of content identified and briefly described	
			8
(c)		1 mark for each relevant valid argument put forward	
			4
Total			25

28 BERT BROWN

(a) Bert is right to be concerned. As finance director of the business he has a responsibility to all the shareholders of the business and not just the three active shareholders. The circumstances suggest that these three shareholders are hoping that the 'sleeping' partner will sell his share to the others at a price which does not reflect the true value of the business and are asking Bert to play a part in misleading this shareholder.

As a qualified accountant Bert also has a professional responsibility to ensure that the information which he provides should be as timely and accurate as possible. Not including the potential impact in the forecasts being prepared for the strategic planning board meeting would mean that the decision making would be based on information which Bert and the three active shareholders know is incomplete. The decision made will not then reflect the best information available.

(b) There are a number of governance issues which could arise in a small, family-owned company such as Bert's employer:

- With a small number of shareholders who know each other very well and work full-time in the company it is possible that there will be a large amount of informal communication about what is happening in the business but a lack of transparency in the reporting. This could exclude the 'sleeping' partner and make it difficult for Bert to know what is happening in the company.

- Some members of the family could pursue their own agenda at the expense of others. The active shareholders have a high degree of power to influence the business to their own benefit at the expense of the other shareholder, employees and other stakeholders.

- In a small private firm it is unlikely that there will be non-executive directors to bring balance and impartiality.

- There is a potential for problems in the event of a falling-out among the family members. This can add complexity or result in costly restructuring if shareholders need to be bought out.

- The fact that people working in the business are family members does not mean that they are capable of running the business – this could lead to skills shortages.

There may also be ways in which the structure of the company could have a positive effect on governance.

- Threats to the reputation of the business could be seen as threats to family honour; this could increase the likely level of ethical behaviour.

- There are fewer short-term decisions made – the longevity of the company and the wealth already inherent in such families suggest long-term growth is a bigger issue.

- There will be fewer agency costs since most of the shareholders are also involved in the running of the business.

(c)   As a small private company there are limited external requirements related to governance for this business. However, this does not mean that the company has no need to consider corporate governance:

- All organisations, whatever their size, need to operate within the law.

- All businesses should act with transparency, openness and integrity. Good governance is not just about reporting requirements – it is also about ensuring that the company acts responsibly and ethically towards its employees, customers and suppliers. This is important for all businesses.

- Depending on the size of the business, they may be required to produce audited accounts.

- The company has a fiduciary responsibility towards all the shareholders, including the fourth shareholder who does not take part in the running of the company.

- Good governance plays a part in protecting the interests of employees.

- Risk management is part of governance and needs to be carried out by all businesses.

29   CODES OF GOVERNANCE

Key answer tips

You are only asked to give details of one international convergence code in part (b) – this answer includes both for completeness.

(a)   There are two different approaches to the communication, management and monitoring of codes, a principles-based approach and a rules-based approach, such as the US model enshrined in law through the Sarbanes-Oxley Act (SOX).

A rules-based approach instills the code into law with appropriate penalties for transgression. For example SOX includes criminal penalties for non-compliance with specific requirements. In contrast a principles-based approach requires the company to adhere to the spirit rather than the letter of the code. The company must either comply with the code or explain why it has not through reports to the appropriate body and its shareholders.

Decisions as to which approach to use can be governed by many factors:

- The dominant ownership structure (bank, family or multiple shareholder)

- The legal system and its power/ability

- The government structure and policies

- The state of the economy

- The national culture and history

- The levels of capital inflow or investment coming into the country

- The global economic and political climate.

There are a number of advantages of a rules-based approach:

- There is clarity in terms of what companies must do since the rules are a legal requirement.

- There is standardisation for all companies – there is no choice as to complying or explaining and this creates a standardised and it could be argued that this is a fairer approach for all businesses.

- As the sanctions are criminal they are likely to be a greater deterrent to transgression.

However there are also a number of disadvantages:

- Rules-based systems are rigid and the exacting nature of the law lends itself to the existence of loopholes ripe for exploitation.

- There is an underlying belief that you must only play by the rules set. There is no suggestion that you should want to play by the rules.

- There are limits enshrined in the law with no room to manoeuvre, or improve, or go beyond the minimum level set.

In general rules-based codes cover the same areas of governance as principles-based codes – the difference is in the way in which the code operates.

SOX, which is extremely detailed and carries the full force of the law includes requirements for the Securities and Exchange Commission (SEC) to issue certain rules on corporate governance. It is relevant to UK companies, directors of subsidiaries of US-listed businesses and auditors who are working on US-listed businesses.

Measures introduced by SOX include:

- All companies with a listing for their shares in the US must provide a signed certificate to the SEC vouching for the accuracy of their financial statements.

- If a company's financial statements are restated due to material non-compliance with accounting rules and standards, the CEO and chief finance officer (CFO) must forfeit bonuses awarded in the previous 12 months.

- Restrictions are placed on the type of non-audit work that can be performed for a company by its firm of auditors.

- The senior audit partner working on a client's audit must be changed at least every five years (i.e. audit partner rotation is compulsory).

- An independent five-man board called the Public Company Oversight Board has been established, with responsibilities for enforcing professional standards in accounting and auditing.

- Regulations on the disclosure of off balance sheet transactions have been tightened up.

- Directors are prohibited from dealing in the shares of their company at 'sensitive times'.

Key effects of SOX are:

- personal liability of directors for mismanagement with criminal punishment

- improved communication of material issues to shareholders

- improved investor and public confidence in corporate US

- improved internal control and external audit of companies

- greater arm's length relationships between companies and audit firms

- improved governance through audit committees.

There has been some negative reaction to the law, which in part relate to the disadvantages outlines above:

- A doubling of audit fee costs to organisations.

- Onerous documentation and internal control costs.

- Reduced flexibility and responsiveness of companies.

- Reduced risk taking and competitiveness of organisations.

- A limited impact on the ability to stop corporate abuse.

- Criticism that the legislation defines a legal minimum standard and little more.

(b) Many individual countries and governments have introduced governance codes applicable to corporations registered or listed within their jurisdictions. However, as globalisation has intensified and there has been an increase in international investment there has been a drive towards international standards. Two organisations have published corporate governance codes intended to apply to multiple national jurisdictions. These organisations are the Organisation for Economic Cooperation and Development (OECD) and the International Corporate Governance Network (ICGN).

There are limitations to such codes. The main limitations are that:

- All codes are voluntary and are not legally enforceable unless enshrined in statute by individual countries.

- Local differences in company ownership models may mean parts of the codes are not applicable.

However they do useful tools and guidance for good practice in governance.

The OECD Principles of Corporate Governance

The OECD is an international organisation composed of the industrialised market economy countries, as well as some developing countries, and provides a forum in which to establish and co-ordinate policies. The OECD Principles of Corporate Governance were updated and republished in 2004. They represent the first initiative by an intergovernmental organisation to develop the core elements of a good corporate governance regime.

Objectives of the OECD Principles of Corporate Governance

- The Principles are intended to assist OECD and non-OECD governments in their efforts to evaluate and improve the legal, institutional and regulatory framework for corporate governance in their countries, and to provide guidance and suggestions for stock exchanges, investors, corporations, and other parties that have a role in the process of developing good corporate governance.

- The Principles focus on publicly-traded companies, both financial and non-financial. However, to the extent that they are deemed applicable, they might also be a useful tool for improving corporate governance in non-traded companies, e.g. privately-held and state-owned enterprises.

- The Principles represent a common basis that OECD member countries consider essential for the development of good governance practices.

- The Principles are intended to be concise, understandable and accessible to the international community.

- The Principles are not intended to be a substitute for government, semi-government or private sector initiatives to develop more detailed 'best practice' in corporate governance.

Content of the Principles:

- ensuring the basis for an effective corporate governance framework

- the rights of shareholders and key ownership functions

- the equitable treatment of shareholders

- the role of stakeholders in corporate governance

- disclosure and transparency

- the responsibilities of the board.

The ICGN Statement on Global Corporate Governance Principles

ICGN was founded in 1995 at the instigation of major institutional investors and represents investors, companies, financial intermediaries, academics and other parties interested in the development of global corporate governance practices. The ICGN believes that improved governance should be the objective of all participants in the corporate governance process, including investors, boards of directors, corporate officers and other stakeholders as well as legislative bodies and regulators. Therefore, the ICGN intends to address these Principles to all participants in the governance process.

Objectives of the ICGN Statement on Global Corporate Governance Principles

- The ICGN Principles highlight corporate governance elements that ICGN-investing members take into account when making asset allocations and investment decisions.

- The ICGN Principles mainly focus on the governance of corporations whose securities are traded in the market – but in many instances the Principles may also be applicable to private or closely-held companies committed to good governance.

- The ICGN Principles also encourage jurisdictions to address certain broader corporate and regulatory policies in areas which are beyond the authority of a corporation.

- The ICGN Principles are drafted to be compatible with other recognised codes of corporate governance, although in some circumstances, the ICGN Principles may be more rigorous.

Content of the ICGN Principles:

- the main corporate objective is shareholder returns

- disclosure and transparency

- audit

- shareholders' ownership, responsibilities, voting rights and remedies

- corporate boards

- corporate remuneration policies

- corporate citizenship, stakeholder relations and the ethical conduct of business

- corporate governance implementation.

30 ROLES AND RELEVANCE

(a) It is generally regarded as best practice in corporate governance that the roles of chairman of the board and chief executive officer should be held by different individuals. The chairman of the board has the responsibility for managing the board of directors, and ensuring that the board functions effectively. The Chief Executive Officer (CEO) is head of the executive management team, and all executive management, including the executive directors, are accountable to the CEO.

Best practice in corporate governance is therefore for the chairman to control the board and the CEO to control the company. However, if the same individual combines these two roles, there would be a high risk of the company being dominated by one individual.

The scale of this risk, and the potential consequences for the company, are possibly difficult to assess. However, there have been reported cases of companies coming under the control of an over-powerful chairman/CEO, with harmful consequences for shareholders.

In the UK, the Combined Code also recommends that the chairman of the board should not be a former CEO, because this would create a risk that the new CEO would be subject to the chairman's influence on executive matters, and that the chairman would try to persuade the new CEO to run the company in the same way as the chairman did in the past.

(b) A Non-Executive Director (NED) has several roles.

(i) NEDs are expected to bring a variety of skills and experience to the board of directors from outside the company to complement the experience and skills of the executive directors. They should therefore bring greater balance and a broader outlook to the discussions of the board. In general terms, the NEDs should help to prevent the domination of the board by a single individual chairman or CEO.

(ii) They should contribute to the decisions of the board of directors. The board should reserve certain decisions to itself, and should not delegate the decision-making authority to only executive management. NEDs should contribute fully to the decision-making processes of the board, for example making decisions about the company's strategy.

(iii)   NEDs also perform a policing and monitoring role. Under the leadership of the senior independent director, NEDs in UK listed companies are expected to monitor the performance of the chairman. The NEDs are also expected to meet at least once each year, with no executive directors present.

(iv)   The audit committee, consisting entirely of independent NEDs, is required to monitor the integrity of the financial statements and the independence of the external auditors.

(v)   The remuneration committee, also consisting entirely of independent NEDs, is responsible for negotiating the remuneration of their executive director colleagues.

(vi)   Independent NEDs should make up a majority of the members of the nominations committee, which is responsible for recommending board appointments to the main board.

(vii)   There should be a senior independent director, whose functions include acting as an alternative channel of communication for the shareholders in the event that their communications with the chairman are ineffective and unsatisfactory.

(viii)   Some NEDs are not independent, and represent the interests of a major shareholder. These NEDs are therefore expected to express the views of the major shareholder at board meetings. However, all directors are expected to carry out their fiduciary duties, and consider the interests of the company when expressing their views.

In their role as contributors to decision-making about the company's strategy, NEDs work together with their executive director colleagues. All directors, executive and NED, have fiduciary duties to the company and a duty of skill and care. All directors are in principle equally liable for the consequences of decisions taken by the board.

However, in their roles on the audit committee and the remunerations committee, and in their role as monitor of the chairman's performance, and in the potential role of the senior independent director as a channel for shareholders to express complaints, NEDs act as a policeman or monitor of the executive management and the chairman.

These two broad roles of colleague and policeman might be difficult to reconcile, and this can create a tension for the NEDs in carrying out their responsibilities.

(c)   There is a risk that the directors of a company will run the company in their own personal interests, without sufficient regard to the interests of the shareholders.

It is generally accepted that executive directors will respond to incentives in their remuneration package to improve the company's performance. In theory, a remuneration package should therefore be structured in such a way that directors are suitably rewarded for company performance that benefits shareholders. With a well-structured package, there should be shared interests of shareholders and directors in improving performance in both the long-term and short-term.

On the other hand there is a risk that the remuneration package of an executive director will provide an incentive to the director to achieve performance targets that are not in the company's best interests.

The principles that should be applied by a remuneration committee in negotiating a remuneration package for an executive director are as follows:

(i)   The remuneration package should consist of a combination of basic salary and incentive payments. A good basic salary is considered necessary to attract individuals of a suitable calibre.

(ii)   The proportion of a remuneration package that is basic salary and the proportion that consists of incentives and rewards is a matter for negotiation, but the incentives element should be significant.

(iii)   There should be a combination of long-term and short-term incentives. Executive directors should be rewarded for achieving performance levels that benefit the company both in the long-term and the short term. It is usual to reward directors with cash bonuses for achieving annual performance targets, and with shares or share options that reward the director over time for growth in the company's share price.

(iv)   The remuneration package will probably also contain a pension element, with the company making contributions into a personal pension scheme for the director, or guaranteeing a minimum pension on retirement. An attractive pension package is often regarded as a necessary feature of remuneration to attract suitable talent, but it can also be a means of persuading a talented executive to remain with the company.

(v)   The remuneration committee should also consider the possibility that the executive director will perform badly, and might be asked to resign from the company. In these circumstances, there is a risk that the 'dismissed' director will receive a high payment on leaving the company, in settlement of the company's contractual obligations. Such settlements, if excessive, might be criticised as 'rewards for failure' and damage the company's reputation with investors. The remuneration committee should therefore negotiate terms with a director that seek to limit any such payments in the event of dismissal: for example, the director should have a right in his or her contract to a notice period not exceeding one year (or even less) – as recommended in most cases by the UK Combined Code. In addition, the remuneration committee should seek to negotiate terms such as the payment in lieu of notice to be made in instalments over a one-year period, and to be forfeited if the individual finds similar new employment with another company during the notice period.

The NEDs on the remuneration committee are faced with the problem that they are not remuneration experts, and many remuneration committees in the UK hire the services of external remuneration consultants. The committee should be aware, however, that remuneration consultants might recommend comparatively high remuneration packages with complex conditions and terms. A principle for the committee should therefore be to consider the advice of remuneration consultants, but to make decisions on remuneration that appear to be in the company's best interests – which might be something different.

31   METTO MINING

Key answer tips

Using Carrol's work will provide structure to part (a) of the question, both in terms of levels of social responsibility and responses to the conflict.

In part (c) you are only asked to briefly explain, so not much detail is required for the four marks available.

(a) **Corporate social responsibility**

Carrol identifies four ascending levels of corporate social responsibility. Lower levels should generally be addressed first although true responsibility can only be demonstrated with reference to all four.

Since an organisation exists in order to meet the *economic* needs of its shareholders this provides the foundation to the model. These economic needs can be seen in the need to generate profits and through them dividends and share price growth over time. It might also be the case that economically the company should produce products of worth to society in a cost effective manner. In the scenario institutional investors' needs for an adequate return would be associated with this level of responsibility.

Legal responsibility relates to the need to operate within national and international frameworks and standards. The company has a legal responsibility to act in shareholders' interests creating a cross over between this and the foundation level. More importantly to the scenario the company is failing to adhere to the legal standard within the host country for health and safety. This should have serious repercussions although the willingness of the state to act in this matter is called into question.

Ethical requirements call for the company to operate with a level of integrity. This would include showing due concern for stakeholders, honesty and integrity in dealings and a level of social and environmental concern. The company is failing to meet these obligations. The changing position of the ethics manager suggests the company could have taken action to better protect its workforce. This disregard as to the needs of others is both an ethical and a legal issue. Further, action taken to silence protests does not suggest openness and fairness in dealings with stakeholders. Finally, their lack of support for the changes proposed by the Institutional shareholder cannot be considered an appropriate ethical response.

Philanthropic needs relate to charitable work and so could be associated with the recommendations put forward by Julie Walker. Although this might demonstrate social responsibility at an ethical level it does not really satisfy the demands of Carrol's model since the action is taken under duress and not in a way that would not directly benefit the company. Charitable acts should not be self serving and here they probably would.

Responses to ethical conflict

The company's initial stance is a reactive denial of responsibility. This is one of a number of positions it may take.

Once it appears that a *reactive* stance is not sufficient it shifts to a *defensive* stance by attempting to blame the problem on suppliers. This externalisation of blame is very common and is a slight improvement on simply saying the explosions were unavoidable, at least someone is responsible.

Internalisation of responsibility has not occurred here. If it does then the company might attempt to *accommodate* stakeholders' wishes by making charitable donations and improving safety standards in line with legal requirements.

The final stance sees the organisation move a more *proactive* approach to social responsibility. This would involve identifying stakeholder needs in a formal risk management process and seeking to meet needs as part of a structured strategy, acting in a positive way to promote corporate citizenship.

(b) **Corporate citizenship**

Corporate citizenship identifies a number of rights associated with a person's position as a member of society. These rights relate to a social right to basic levels of education and health, civil rights including the right to freedom of speech and movement and political rights to vote or attain political office.

Accompanying the bestowing of benefit through these rights is a responsibility to uphold rights of others in society. In this way the person has a responsibility to pay taxes in order to support a public education system, responsibility to allow others freedom to speak and responsibility to support democracy, possibly by ensuring the individual exercises their voting prerogative when required.

In as much as companies are artificial people they too have rights and responsibilities. It is in the latter area that the company has failed to meet its obligation. It denies the right of others to protest against its action, does not do what it can to provide them with social wellbeing through a safe work environment and possibly places undue pressure on the local government so circumventing the democratic wishes of the people for fair government.

These are serious allegations and should be known and answered by the ethics manager. Unfortunately the board has remained silent on these issues, again calling into question their belief in supporting a basic level of morality in their business activities.

(c) **Stakeholder classifications**

There are a number of ways in which stakeholders can be classified:

Primary and secondary

This could relate to the perceived level of importance of stakeholders. In this respect shareholders would be narrow and suppliers would be wide or more distant in the thinking of directors. Classifications such as this do not necessarily suggest a disregard for given groups but do suggest a level of investment in supporting a fruitful relationship. The company's accusations against its suppliers follow as a result of classifications such as this.

Narrow and wide

This could be interpreted in the same way as primary and secondary or considered in terms of the impact of stakeholders on the organisation. This might mean that the government is a narrow target being able to stop mining operations if it desires. Wider classifications include a replaceable low paid work force who have little individual power to force change.

Active and passive

The collective will of activists and employees protesting together is a much more potent force rather than the passive acceptance by those not demonstrating for change. The government is at present passive since it does not comment on any mining activities carried out by the company.

Voluntary and involuntary

The Institutional Shareholder has a voluntary relationship and may withdraw from that relationship at any time. The workforce to a degree might be considered involuntary given that employment opportunities are likely to be few forcing people to consider dangerous and difficult work in mines.

(d)   **Responsibilities of property and ownership**

Julie Walker identifies the need for share ownership to be coupled with a responsibility to act. This statement attempts to convey that share ownership is asset ownership no different from owning a motor car or house. This being the case the owner must take responsibility for the upkeep, use and disposal of the asset. In the same way shareholders cannot deny their responsibilities simply because the agency relationship creates distance and intangibility in assessing the degree to which true ownership exists.

Many shareholders believe that share ownership does not convey any responsibility on the share holder to act in a responsible way for the actions of the company. In turn directors state that the company is not theirs to use as they will since it belongs to shareholders. The vacuum that this thinking creates leads to a general lack of care and ethical behaviour that leads to disasters such as those identified in the scenario.

INTERNAL CONTROL AND REVIEW

32   REVIEW OF INTERNAL CONTROL

Key answer tips

As this question asks about best practice in corporate governance, this is an indication that the company is subject to a system of corporate governance similar to that in the UK rather than a rules-based system like the US.

It is a good idea to base the answer on a code of governance with which you are familiar – in this case the answer uses the UK model.

(a)   **Answer to question 1**

On the assumption that Gash is a listed company based in a country with a principles-based corporate governance system similar to that in the UK, the annual review of internal control should apply to the entire system of internal control, not just to internal control for financial reporting. The internal control subject to review will therefore be all operations/management systems and the efficiency and effectiveness of systems and operations; financial controls and compliance controls (= controls to ensure that the company complies with relevant laws and regulations).

In other countries, notably the US, the annual review of internal control required by corporate governance law is restricted to financial controls and financial reporting.

Answer to question 2

(i)   Senior management are responsible for implementing the internal control system. They should provide the culture or control environment for the organisation, giving a lead to all other employees. They are also responsible for establishing the systems for identifying and assessing risks, for deciding and implementing the internal controls for managing the risks, and for establishing a system for control reporting and a system for monitoring the effectiveness of controls. All these are executive tasks and are therefore the responsibility of executive managers.

The executive management is also accountable to the board of directors for their management of the internal control system.

(ii)   According to the Combined Code in the UK, the audit committee should have the task of reviewing the effectiveness of the system of financial controls annually. In addition, unless a separate committee of independent non-executive directors is given the task, the audit committee should also review the effectiveness of the entire system of internal control for the company (operational and compliance controls as well as the financial controls) and the risk management system. The purpose of this review should be to check that the control system appears to be functioning adequately, or to identify any weaknesses in the system (which should then be discussed with the executive managers and possibly the external auditors). The audit committee should report its findings to the board of directors.

(iii)   The board of directors is required by the Combined Code in the UK to report to the shareholders (in the annual report) that they have reviewed the effectiveness of the system of internal control.

The UK Combined Code does not require the board of directors to **evaluate** the effectiveness of controls, and the Turnbull Guidelines do not make this requirement either. The board is simply required to inform shareholders that they have made the review, but without giving their assessment.

(b)   If the audit committee is responsible for the review of controls, it is important to remember that the committee consists of non-executive directors, and the time the committee members have available is therefore restricted. The review should be carried out in a way that makes the most effective use of the committee's time.

The review should be structured, and should consider the important elements of the control systems. A useful framework might be the COSO framework for internal control, which states that an internal control system has five elements:

(i)   a suitable control environment and control culture;

(ii)   a system of risk identification and assessment;

(iii)   devising and applying suitable internal controls;

(iv)   communicating and providing control information (and other relevant information);

(v)   carrying out reviews of the control system and the controls.

An effective internal control system must function in each of these five areas. A review should therefore consider all five areas.

The most efficient method of carrying out the review is probably to study documents and hold meetings with key members of the management team, including the chief executive, finance director, chairman of the risk management committee and head of internal audit. Key documents would include minutes of the risk committee meetings, reports by the internal audit team and recommendations for improving controls provided by the external auditors (as part of the annual audit).

The control environment and culture can possibly be reviewed simply by discussing controls with senior management, and assessing the opinions and views that they express.

The system of risk identification can be reviewed by discussing risk assessment with the manager responsible (for example, the chairman of the risk committee) and by reading reports of the risk committee meetings. Any issues that arise from reading these reports can be discussed with the relevant executive manager.

The committee members need to understand the key risks that have been identified by management, in operational, financial and compliance areas. They then need to establish whether the system of devising and implementing controls is effective. To carry out this review, it might be useful to discuss controls with the finance director (financial controls) and the head of internal audit (all controls). If there are internal audit reports recommending improvements in controls, the committee should establish whether the recommendations have been implemented (and if not, why not).

The effectiveness of communicating relevant information might be reviewed by discussing with the CEO how managers are expected to respond to control reports, and how control reports are used. It might also be appropriate to identify any new regulations introduced during the year, to find out how quickly the information about the regulations and procedures to comply with the regulations was distributed to staff.

The effectiveness of monitoring controls should be discussed with senior management. Recommendations of the external auditors and the effectiveness of internal audit should be discussed.

Since senior executive managers are accountable to the board of directors for the system of internal control, it would also be appropriate to require the CEO to make presentations to the board, or prepare occasional board reports, that provide a review of the control system from the viewpoint of the management.

(c)   The potential ethical problem for the internal auditors is that in carrying out their audit work, they might conclude that the finance director is at fault, for example for failing to apply sufficiently strong controls or for failing to communicate control information. From a professional point of view, the internal auditor would be required to criticise his or her boss. From a personal and career perspective, an auditor might not want to make any such criticism.

The ACCA Code of Ethics and Conduct applies to all ACCA members, who might include not only the internal auditors, but also the finance director.

The fundamental principles could be helpful because if they are applied, they should help to remove personal animosities from the situation, that can affect the judgment of individuals.

The principles include the requirement for accountants to conduct themselves with integrity and objectivity. They should also apply professional and technical standards in their work. If these principles are applied, the internal auditor should be able to discuss any weaknesses in the control system with the manager responsible, even if this individual is his or her boss. By acting in an open and honest manner, without any personal bias being shown, and by taking an objective view of the situation, the auditor should try to establish a platform for a professional discussion of the audit findings. Where relevant, if professional and technical standards are applied, the auditor can demonstrate the objectivity and rationality of his or her approach.

If the finance director is an ACCA member, the Code of Ethics and Conduct requires him or her to act in a similar manner. Problems presented by the internal auditors should be considered objectively, without feeling a need to deny responsibility and escape blame.

The Code of Ethics and Conduct can also help in this type of situation because it provides an external guide to professional conduct that both parties can refer to and recognise.

33 SPQ

Key answer tips

This question provides a mix between theory (parts (a), (c) and part of (d)), and some application. The information on the computer system is not complete, so some speculation is needed in part (b) while much is made of the ethical issue for part (d). Be careful to allocate time in accordance with the mark allocation, and do not get carried away in explaining ethics in part (d).

(a)   Regarding internal control, internal auditors will review the system of internal control within an organisation. They will test the effectiveness of the controls as an independent third party and then provide a report on their work. Internal auditors do not establish the operational controls they test as this would impair the independence of their review.

Regarding risk management, internal auditors will again review the system for identifying and responding to risks in an organisation. They will focus on high risk areas specifically, and, where controls are found to be weak, they will again prepare an appropriate report, making recommendations for control improvements.

To be clear, internal auditors are specialists in risk management and internal controls – but those risks are managed by individual line managers. Internal auditors ensure that risks have been identified, analysed and managed, giving advice on appropriate controls when asked.

Internal auditors may also advise the board of various internal controls and risk management, including areas such as:

- how to identify risks;

- how to establish a culture to manage risks within an organisation;

- reporting on how effective management are at managing risk in the organisation; and

- ensuring that appropriate legislation has been complied with.

(b)   *Risk: hacking and fraudulent access to computer systems*

SPQ's computer systems appear to have been accessed by unauthorised third parties with the aim of obtaining goods without paying for them. It is not clear how access occurred, although it is possible that other systems are also vulnerable.

Control recommendations

- Monitor access requests from 'customers' to identify where multiple requests are made from the same computer. Where this occurs, check transactions to ensure that they do not 'disappear'.

- Review firewall controls to ensure these are effective.

- Monitor system access from internal sources, using a control log, to identify whether staff in the IT department are placing fraudulent orders.

Risk: non-payment of deliveries

It appears that deliveries of goods have been made without the customer being invoiced for the goods or cash being received. The risk is that sales in SPQ are understated.

Control recommendation

Only despatch goods where payment has been received in full. This may require amendment to computer programs to ensure that this control is active.

Risk: transactions deleted from customer database

It is possible that the customer database is not complete given that transactions appear to have been deleted after delivery of goods. The risk is therefore that SPQ's accounting records are not being maintained correctly.

Control recommendations

Check the integrity of the details in the database using run-to-run totals or similar methods of reconciling transactions on a daily basis.

Monitor access to the database ensuring that all internal amendments are routed through the database administrator. Control logs can again be used for this purpose.

Risk: ineffective internal audit reports

There is a risk that internal audit reports do not identify the extent of risks identified in SPQ as managers are requesting that the report is modified. There is also the risk that the audit reports may not be actioned anyway as the internal auditor reports to the CEO rather than to a person independent of the operational running of the company.

Control recommendation

The internal auditor should report to an independent person, such as the chair of the audit committee. The latter will be able to ensure that all internal audit reports are actioned appropriately.

(c)　*Issues to be considered in planning an audit of activities*

Previous internal audit reports. These will identify the results of previous audits for each activity and therefore indicate the extent of work expected for the next audit.

Changes made to the system. Where significant changes have been made then the audit will take longer as amendments will have to be documented and tested. The level of testing will also increase as less reliance can be placed on the results of previous audits.

Review of the work carried out by external auditors. Where external auditors have audited a system and found no errors, then the internal audit department can take some confidence from these results and decrease the extent of its testing.

Discussion with local managers. This will help identify any concerns with the system and therefore affect the extent of work undertaken by the internal auditor.

Obtain information on known risks. In SPQ, the internal audit department was directed to audit the system by the chief accountant, who may have realised the risk of error. Identifying known risks will help internal audit focus work on those areas to determine the extent of risk and errors.

Confirm the audit objectives. Audit work should always be carried out with specific objectives in mind.

(d)　***Ethical principles***

Integrity

The internal auditor should be straightforward and honest. He should not supply any information which is known to be misleading, false or deceptive. This means that the internal auditor should not give in to pressure to amend the report unless factual errors are identified in it.

Objectivity

This is a combination of impartiality, intellectual honesty and freedom from conflicts of interest. It means that the internal auditor should not allow the influence of others to override his decisions. Again this means that the report should not be amended, simply because managers suggest it will be unpopular.

Professional competence and duty of care

As a new appointee, the internal auditor will have confirmed that he has the appropriate skills and knowledge to perform his job and therefore that reporting will be carried out with reasonable skill and diligence. To amend the report would suggest that reasonable skill and care will not have been used, as the report would be inaccurate.

Professional behaviour

The internal auditor has to act in a manner which is consistent with the good reputation of the Institute. To amend a report would effectively involve being conservative with the truth, which an ACCA member should avoid.

Resolution of ethical conflict

Ethical conflicts should be resolved by:

- following the organisation's grievance procedures;

- discussing the matter with a superior (unless that person is involved with the ethical situation), and then subsequent levels of management;

- where necessary, discussing it with the member's professional body;

- where the conflict has not been resolved, the member may have to consider resignation.

34 INTERNAL CONTROL ASSESSMENT

(a) Internal management control refers to the procedures and policies in place to ensure that company objectives are achieved. Controls attempt to ensure that risks, those factors which stop the achievement of company objectives are minimised.

The Auditing Practices Board in the UK provides guidance to auditors with specific reference to the implementation of International Standards on Auditing. The APB identifies that the purpose of the internal control system is to ensure, 'as far as practicable:

- the orderly and efficient conduct of its business, including adherence to internal policies

- the safeguarding of assets

- the prevention and detection of fraud and error

- the accuracy and completeness of the accounting records

- the timely preparation of financial information.'

Internal control is a process, rather than a structure. It is a continuing series of activities, planned, implemented and monitored by the board of directors and management at all levels within an organisation. However it provides only reasonable assurance, not absolute assurance, with regard to achievement of the organisation's objectives.

The objectives of internal control relate to the effectiveness and efficiency of operations. Internal control is therefore also concerned with the achievement of performance objectives, such as profitability, as well as the management and control of risks in order to restrict the likelihood of adverse events or results

(b) (i) **The control environment**

The board of directors is ultimately responsible for ensuring that the system of internal control is adequate and effective. The directors must therefore ensure that senior executive management monitor the internal control system effectively.

Senior executive management is responsible for setting internal control policies and monitoring the adequacy and effectiveness of the internal control system.

Responsibility for establishing specific internal control policies and procedures is typically delegated to the heads of business units. However, senior management remains responsible for ensuring that the policies and procedures that are applied are adequate and effective.

The board of directors and senior management are both responsible for promoting ethical standards and establishing an appropriate culture within the organisation, in which employees are fully aware of the importance of internal controls.

(ii) **Risk recognition and assessment**

An effective internal control system requires that all the significant risks facing the organisation should be recognised and continually assessed. Internal controls might need revising when new risks arise or existing risks change, to ensure that controls remain effective.

Within the context of risk management, it is tempting to think of risk recognition and assessment as an activity undertaken at a strategic level by the board of directors and senior management. From an internal control perspective, however, the need for risk recognition and assessment goes much further down the organisation's management structure. There is a need to continually review the risks to the achievement of the organisation's performance, information and compliance objectives.

The risk assessment should be conducted for each business within the organisation, and should consider, for example:

- internal factors, such as the complexity of the organisation, organisational changes, staff turnover levels, and the quality of staff

- external factors, such as changes in the industry and economic conditions, technological changes, and so on.

The risk assessment process should also distinguish between:

- risks that are controllable: management should decide whether to accept the risk, or to take measures to control or reduce the risk

- risks that are not controllable: management should decide whether to accept the risk, or whether to withdraw partially or entirely from the business activity, so as to avoid the risk.

(iii) **Control activities and segregation of duties**

Control activities should be an integral part of the organisation's daily activities. These should include top level reviews, procedural controls within each department or section, checking for compliance with risk exposure limits, a system of approvals and authorisations, a system of verifications and reconciliations and physical controls.

There should also be an appropriate segregation of duties, so that work done by one person acts as a check on the work of another. This will reduce the possibility of error and fraud.

There are two elements in control activities:

- establishing control policies and procedures

- ensuring that these policies and procedures are properly applied.

(iv) **Information and communication**

There should be an adequate information system, supplying internal financial, operational and compliance data and relevant external data. The information should be reliable, timely, accessible and provided in a consistent format (to make it more understandable).

Internal information is part of a record-keeping process, and there should be established policies for record retention.

Where there is significant risk from the possibility of a disruption to the business in the event of an unexpected disaster, there should be contingency plans for the transfer of information processing to an off-site facility. Business continuity plans (or 'business resumption plans') should be tested periodically to ensure their effectiveness.

There should be effective channels of communication within the organisation, so that all staff receive the information that is relevant to the performance of their tasks and duties.

(v) **Monitoring control activities and correcting deficiencies**

The effectiveness of the internal control system should be monitored on an ongoing basis. Monitoring of key risks should be a part of the daily activities of the organisation, as well as a task for periodic internal audits.

There should be an effective and comprehensive review of the internal control system by a competent internal audit team. The internal auditors should report to the audit committee or the board of directors, as well as to senior management.

Deficiencies in internal control should be reported in a timely manner and addressed promptly. Where these deficiencies are material, they should be reported to senior management and the board of directors.

34   YAHTY *Walk in the footsteps of a top tutor*

Key answer tips

Don't miss out on the easy mark for the format of the answer stated at the beginning of the requirements.

Part (c) of this answer is very long and includes more detail than you would be expected to provide to achieve a good mark. However even if not covering them in quite so much detail you will need to identify the major areas of weakness which need to be addressed.

The highlighted words are key phrases that markers are looking for.

REPORT

To: Board of YAHTY

From: An accountant

Subject: Internal control systems

Date: DD MM 200X

The purpose of this report is to discuss internal control systems and the responsibilities of directors towards these.

(a)   This answer is illustrated with references to the Turnbull guidance on Internal Control.

The Turnbull guidance on Internal Control is provided in the UK Combined Code. There is no specific statement concerning what internal controls should be present in an organisation. Rather, organisations are encouraged to implement a sound system of internal control and risk management as part of a system of good corporate governance.

The guidance provides three specific suggestions:

- Internal control should be embedded within the processes of an organisation, enabling objectives to be pursued and met.

- The internal control system should remain relevant over time as the business environment changes.

- Each company must apply a system of internal control that takes account of its particular situation and circumstances, and allows for reporting of control failures and weaknesses.

The internal control system will therefore include:

- Control activities.

- Information and communication processes.

- Processes for monitoring the effectiveness of the internal control system.

In summary, the internal control system is provided to reduce risks in a company, not eliminate them completely. Elimination may not be cost effective, and it is by taking some risk that many companies obtain profits.

(b) **Duties of directors in relation to internal controls**

The UK Combined Code requires the board of directors to:

Maintain a sound system of internal control, which is embedded in the operations of the company and forms a part of its culture. The directors do not necessarily implement the control system; this action will be delegated to more junior managers.

At least once each year, carry out a review of the effectiveness of the system of internal control, and report to shareholders that they have done so in the company's annual report and accounts. This action shows that the directors are aware of their responsibilities and also should provide reassurance to investors that the company is being managed effectively. This annual review should cover all controls (financial, operational and compliance) and risk management.

The Turnbull Guidance comments that, in carrying out this review, the board should have a risk management policy to identify risks and take appropriate action in relation to each risk. Specifically that policy needs to identify:

- the nature and extent of the risks facing the company

- the extent and categories of risk which it regards as acceptable for the company to bear

- the likelihood that these risks will materialise

- the company's ability to reduce the frequency or incidence of any risks and to reduce the impact on the business of any risks that do materialise

- the costs of operating particular controls relative to the benefits obtained from managing the risk.

(c) **Comments on internal control system in YAHTY organisation**

Advice provided by investment accountants

Each investment accountant can provide/recommend the individual investment services for their clients. Whilst some accountants may be skilled and have appropriate knowledge, this may not be the case for all accountants. The internal control system appears to be weak in two respects:

- firstly, training of accountants, and

- secondly, ensuring funds are invested to produce a high return, not simply to meet the general investment requirements of clients.

The control of the senior accountant providing investment advice if required is ineffective for two reasons:

- Firstly, the span of control is excessive; with 35 investment accountants having 200 clients each, this could relate to over 7,000 different clients to provide advice to. Given a 200-day working year, this equates to about 12 minutes for each client pa. Control cannot be exercised on a timely basis.

- Secondly, there appears to be no necessity for any client account to be reviewed anyway. The senior accountant only acts on a request basis.

These control weaknesses could result in individual client accounts providing a financial performance well below optimum.

Controls that should be implemented include:

- decreasing the span of control by employing more senior accountants

- standard review of a percentage of client accounts each year

- more detailed investigations where any investment account shows poor investment decisions.

Payment authorisations

Each investment accountant is allowed to make fund transfers relating to investments for their clients. This is appropriate as the accountant will understand the specific client requests and therefore be able to ensure that investments are being made in the appropriate funds.

However, only transfers above €100,000 require a second signatory. This amount is potentially excessive, given that the average fund value is €500,000 and most transfers are below €50,000 anyway. The authorisation limit means that almost all transfers are not checked. Control weaknesses include:

- The investment accountant could make an inappropriate investment decision.

- Funds could be transferred to the investment accountant's own bank account. This could occur because the list of investments is not linked to the bank account – so the list can be manually amended by the accountant to exclude specific investments.

Controls that should be implemented include:

- Lowering the authorisation limit for second signatories to €25,000.

- Providing for a random check on other transactions to ensure they are valid and relate to appropriate funds.

- Linking the list of investments to the payment systems in the company. When a payment is made the list is updated, thus precluding manual updating by the accountant.

Storage of documents

YAHTY is quite correct to retain evidence of the funds transfers carried out by the investment accountants. This will be needed in case of dispute regarding the amount of transfer or the funds transferred to.

However, there is a control weakness in keeping the transfer documents in date order. While this assists initial filing, document retrieval may be extremely difficult. The normal method of searching for a document is likely to be by client name; the date of the transaction may not be immediately available. Working through all documents relating to one date will also be time consuming.

To improve the control, the ordering of the documents should be changed to storage by client name. Investment accountants may undertake this task if necessary as they will be raising the documents.

Alternatively, control would be improved by using pre-numbered documents and retaining the document number on individual client accounts on the computer system. Filing of documents by document number would then provide a quick and efficient filing and retrieval system.

Closing of client accounts

The closure of a client account provides the good control of a list of investments supported by the appropriate documentation. The weakness in the control is confirming the completeness of the list of funds being transferred. If a fund is omitted from the list, there does not appear to be any way to identify this omission. This is a similar issue to the manual updating of the list of investments already noted above.

The control of the senior accountant reviewing the list of investments and agreeing the source documents will be ineffective in identifying omissions. Similar controls are again required for the payment authorisations mentioned above.

36   GERANIUM

(a)   Geranium's board of directors are responsible for the system of internal control and for reviewing its effectiveness in producing a set of financial statements that are true and fair. An internal control system is designed to manage rather than eliminate the risk of failure in order to achieve business objectives, and can only provide reasonable and not absolute assurance against material misstatement or loss.

The financial statements of Geranium will not be perfect in that small errors may have occurred and may not have been noticed. The board, audit committee, external and internal auditors are primarily interested in correcting large errors in the accounts that might mislead any potential investors in Geranium.

The board should maintain a sound system of internal control to safeguard shareholders' investment and Geranium's assets, and should establish formal and transparent arrangements for considering how they should apply financial reporting standards and internal control principles, and for maintaining an appropriate relationship with its auditors.

The board or the audit committee need to satisfy themselves that there is a proper system and allocation of responsibilities for the day-to-day monitoring of financial controls, but they will not do the monitoring themselves. They will use the auditors to perform any necessary work, and expect them to report back their findings and any recommendations.

The audit committee, with respect to the internal auditors, should:

- review and approve the scope of work of the internal audit department.

- ensure that the internal auditors have access to the information they need and the resources (staff, experience and budget) necessary to carry out their duties.

- approve the appointment or termination of the head of internal audit.

- meet the external and internal auditors at least annually, without management being present, to discuss the scope of the work of the auditors and any issues arising from the audit.

The audit committee, with respect to the external auditors and the board, should:

- review the external auditors' findings and should in particular discuss major issues that arose during the audit and have subsequently been resolved, and those issues that remain unresolved.

- review key accounting and audit judgments, and review levels of error identified during the audit, obtaining explanations from management and the external auditors as to any errors that remain unadjusted.

When reviewing management reports on internal control, the board should consider:

- the significant risks, and assess how they were identified, evaluated and managed.

- the effectiveness of the internal controls in managing the significant risks.

- whether necessary actions are being taken promptly to remedy any weaknesses, and whether the findings indicate a need for more exhaustive monitoring of the system of internal control. This work might be undertaken by internal or external auditors.

(b)   Financial controls should provide reasonable assurance of the safeguarding of Geranium's assets; the maintenance of proper accounting records and the reliability of financial information. Financial control dominates the thinking of accountants because of their association with financial reporting and audit.

Budgets are one of the most used forms of financial control. They will hold Geranium's managers accountable for achieving financial targets, and these managers must explain any variances between actual and budgeted performance. Targets usually include increasing revenues, reducing costs, increasing profits and increasing returns on investment (ROI). However, this can lead to dysfunctional behaviour where a manager in charge of part of the budget will, for example, delay capital expenditure on an expensive piece of gardening equipment so that he or she meets their ROI target in the short term.

Non-financial performance management requires accountants to have a better understanding of control system design (to reduce the incidence of fraud, for example); target setting; connecting control systems with business strategy (making sure that the systems we have in place help us achieve our objective of, say, increased profits); and focusing on the external environment within which the business operates.

Non-financial controls influence behaviour to ensure that it is legally correct, co-ordinated and consistent throughout the organisation and is fair and equitable. These controls include:

- formal and informal structures such as an organisation chart so that staff know who they are accountable to, and for. For example, the manager of the garden centre might have two assistant managers who look after different areas – indoor and outdoor plants – and each has their own specialist staff in these areas.

- rules, policies and procedures, such as dress codes (garden centre uniforms) and working hours, or disciplinary procedures for when a member of staff has not followed the rules.

- physical controls such as the need for secure, high fencing around the garden centres so that theft is minimised.

- incentives and rewards for employees who have met targets or excelled in, say, customer service. This could be in the form of Profit Related Pay or an Employee of the Month award.

- personnel controls including the need for continuous training on plant care and customer service.

37 AUDITOR INDEPENDENCE

Key answer tips

Although the first two parts of this question are theoretical, part (c) asks you to discuss the validity of the second part of the statement. This requires you to go beyond your theoretical knowledge and consider arguments to support or dispute the statement.

(a) According to the King Report on Corporate Governance from RSA: 'Internal audit is an independent objective assurance activity. It brings a disciplined approach to evaluate risk management, control and governance.'

In order to carry out the activity of internal audit objectively and to be free to provide an objective assessment of the control systems and their weaknesses, the internal auditor must be independent of the executive management of the business and must not be involved in the activities or systems being audited. Internal auditors must be able to give their opinion without being affected by any pressures which compromise their professional judgment or prevent them questioning the activities being audited. The auditor must be free to act with integrity and protected from undue influence by the chief executive and finance director.

It is also important there is an appearance of independence to an external observer and that there is nothing which could lead a third party to question the independence of the auditor.

To ensure that the internal audit function provides an objective evaluation there should be measures in place to protect the independence of the internal audit department. In addition to a lack of involvement in the activities being audited, independence requires that:

- The internal auditor should follow acceptable ethical and work standards.

- The head of internal audit should report directly to a senior director or the audit committee.

- The head of internal audit should have direct access to the chairman of the board of directors, and to the audit committee, and should be accountable to the audit committee (Smith Guidance).

- The audit committee should approve the appointment and termination of appointment of the head of internal audit.

(b) There are a number of potential threats to the independence of auditors. Most of the analyses of these threats have been carried out in the context of external audit – however the majority also apply to internal audit.

The following threats have been identified by professional accounting bodies:

Self-interest threat

This threat exists when an auditor or an audit firm has an interest in the audit client. This interest is often financial. For example, if the auditor owns shares in the client company this could encourage the auditor to produce a favourable report which is not supported by the evidence found in order to avoid a potential adverse effect on the share price.

Self-review threat

This threat exists when an audit firm or team member is asked to review an area for which the firm or individual was previously responsible. It is difficult for the auditor to be objective in such circumstances. An example of this threat is where the auditor has previously prepared original data used to generate financial statements or preparing other records that are the subject matter of the audit engagement.

Advocacy threat

This threat occurs when the audit firm, or a member of the audit team, promotes, or may be perceived to promote, an audit client's position or opinion. For example, the audit firm may act as an advocate on behalf of an audit client in litigation or in resolving disputes with third parties.

Familiarity threat

This threat exists when an audit firm or a member of the audit team becomes too sympathetic to the client's interests because of a close relationship with an audit client, its directors, officers or employees. An example of this is a member of the audit team having a close family member who is a director, officer or other employee of the audit client and is in a position to exert direct and significant influence over the subject. The acceptance of gifts or hospitality, unless the value is clearly insignificant from the audit client is another source of this threat.

Intimidation threat

The intimidation threat occurs when a member of the audit team may be deterred from acting objectively and exercising professional scepticism by threats, actual or perceived, from the directors, officers or employees of an audit client. Common examples of this are the threat of replacement over a disagreement regarding the application of an accounting principle or pressure to reduce inappropriately the extent of work performed in order to reduce the fees for the audit.

In addition to the threats described above, internal auditors are particularly vulnerable to ethical threats when they are asked to behave in a way which conflicts with ethical standards and guidelines. As an employee of the same business, internal auditors can be subject to more personal threats related to their employment if they do not comply. There is also a greater possibility of divided loyalties.

(c)   It could be argued that an auditor can never be completely independent, and that it is unlikely that anyone will ever be completely free from all economic, financial or personal relationships. For example, the fact that an auditor is paid a fee by the client means that there will always be a financial relationship between the auditor and the client.

In addition, the auditor has to develop a good working relationship with the client, which means that over the time of an audit the threat of familiarity could increase.

There is likely to be some degree of threat to the auditor's independence in any situation, and to avoid it completely might make it impossible for companies to gain access to the expertise which auditors are able to provide.

On this basis it is likely to be impossible to avoid threats to independence completely. However an auditor with high professional and ethical standards should be able to be objective without the complete absence of threats to his or her independence.

Given that the possibility of threats to independence will always exist to some degree, it is the response to them which is of key importance. The measures included in governance codes related to auditor independence which were identified in part (a) are there to minimise the threat and provide safeguards to ensure that even where the threat exists auditors are able to act independently.

38   FIS

Key answer tips

The first part of the question implies that there are inefficiencies in the information system, so a careful read through the scenario information will hopefully identify some of those inefficiencies.

However, having identified the inefficiencies, you also need to explain why they may cause problems for the fund managers. So again, relate your answer to the scenario to provide this information. For example, if information is only received every hour, state that this may be a problem and then show why the nature of the job may require more frequent information.

Finally, recommending a process for improving the situation means you need to explain how the MIS could be improved. These improvements may be related back to the scenario information – so check this information again. Alternatively, you may need to recommend enhancements to the system; in this case make sure that the enhancements are practical and not too expensive.

(1) Inefficient processes for capturing knowledge

The MIS appears to provide a very basic system for capturing basic information about each investment such as the shares held and their location etc. However, information that is of real use to the managers, including details of price movements on shares and other information which may affect the share price, is more difficult to obtain and is supplied by a variety of different systems. There is also no guarantee that all the data has been captured or that where similar information has been produced at different times information is not duplicated or even contradictory.

Information for fund managers needs to be amalgamated into one system, as proposed by the Board. This will remove the problems of timeliness and difficulty of comparing information from one source.

(2) Failure to appropriate knowledge already available

Additional knowledge may be available to the fund managers, but this is maintained in the new business section of the organisation. It is not clear whether information from this MIS will actually assist the fund managers, but given that the new business representatives are making similar decisions to assist potential clients, then the information is likely to be useful.

(3) Difficulty of measuring intangible benefits

The directors may well be correct in their assessment that the tangible benefits of the new system do not outweigh the costs. However, the CBA is incomplete because it does not take into account the intangible benefits that are likely to arise from the system. For example, better investment decisions may result in higher returns, or at least lower losses for client funds. However, these benefits do not actually affect FIS in tangible terms, and so will be excluded from the CBA. There are though distinct intangible benefits in terms of a higher return for clients and more favourable publicity by providing clients with a better service.

The CBA analysis for the new MIS needs to be expanded to include intangible benefits.

(4) Information overload

The fund managers may be making poor decisions that may be related not simply to the old system, but also to the problem of having to obtain and reconcile information from too many sources. Fund managers may be suffering from information overload, that is they are receiving too much information from too many sources making it difficult or impossible to identify important information from routine data.

This situation can be remedied by providing one comprehensive system for managers. This will remove the issue of having too many different sources of information, although care will also be necessary to ensure that the new MIS focuses on the information needed for investment decisions, rather than provide a lot of detail about the funds themselves, which may not help in making these decisions.

39   RG

Key answer tips

Part (a) of this question encourages you to read the scenario information to find weaknesses in the information provided to the directors. The three points provide the detail needed to make these comments – so think about what information the directors would like, and then see where the information provided does not meet these expectations. Other statements such as without reference to past production data also imply some weakness. In this example, think how a budget would normally be produced, and the weakness becomes apparent. Improving the information in part (ii) then becomes relatively easy. There are two comments to make in this section; firstly to state how the weakness will be overcome, and secondly stating the other information that the directors may need. In other words the MIS does not provide all of the required outputs and so the missing information must be identified and commented on.

Part (b) is more theoretical; it doesn't really need the scenario to provide an answer. If you are short of ideas, consider what the MIS is doing; namely providing summary historical information to the directors. Therefore, the MIS is unlikely to be able to provide much information about the future, or changes in trends.

(a)   (i)   The directors want information which helps their strategic control of the business. Information used at the strategic level normally has the following characteristics:

- It is highly summarised.

- It does not need to be as accurate as operational information.

- It will often be used in making poorly-structured, non-programmable decisions.

- The information will often be forward-looking.

- Non-routine information and reports will often be required.

- It will contain a high amount of probabilistic information (estimates).

The output from the current system has the following weaknesses:

Summary business plan

This would appear to be an unreliable document as it has been prepared by an inexperienced person who seems to have ignored the information content of past production data. The plan is forward looking, though two years would be an absolute minimum for most strategic planning.

Because historical data is not shown on the report, it will be difficult for the directors to assess the assumptions lying behind the report. This is very important when dealing with future estimates where judgement will play a large part and will be especially important here where the author of the report is inexperienced.

Stock balances

This report is much too detailed for the directors and should be presented in a much more summarised form. As it stands, the report would be of use to people much further down the hierarchy in the firm who are making day-to-day operational decisions.

Changes in demand

This may be too detailed, but the directors may well want to have access to this information on demand. Five years is probably going back too far as there will have been many market changes over that time and early trends may no longer be relevant.

The report seems to be poorly presented being purely numerical and not allowing the directors to compare different sections.

(ii) The information could be improved as follows:

Additional outputs

In addition to the existing reports the following could be useful in strategic planning:

- Financial model which allows the directors to see the effects of different inputs and assumptions.

- Summary accounting information. Though this is historical, future projections may depend on an analysis of past trends.

- Sales analyses by product, customer, type of customer, geographical area, sales rep.

Sales value, volume and gross profit percentages should be shown.

In addition, the existing reports could be improved as follows:

Summary business plan

This should:

- look further ahead

- show historical data

- show the assumptions on which the projections are based

- show income and expenditure on likely new product lines

- contain market and competitor information.

Stock balances

This should:

- be summarised much more

- highlight important data, such as large variances

- be arranged in ways which are of importance to the management of the business.

Summary of changes

- Information about all sections should be available on the same screen to allow comparisons to be made.

- Graphics would help the directors to identify important trends and significant events.

- It might be possible to omit data from over three years ago.

- Industry statistics, market growth and the changes in market share would be useful.

(b) The MIS will predominantly use data which is generated internally by the organisation, though some external data, such as market growth and size can be entered. The MIS system will be particularly poor at dealing with the following:

- Analysing strengths, weaknesses, opportunities and threats.

- Assessing customer satisfaction.

- Predicting changes in consumer taste.

- Predicting technological advances.

- Incorporating the effects of political, economic and social changes.

- Making use of information about competitors.

These limitations can be illustrated by considering the strategic decision about whether to expand abroad. It may be possible to look up some elementary data on a public database, but it is unlikely that such information will be incorporated into a formal MIS. Most of the work done on this decision will be once-only, ad hoc calculations. They may be performed on a spreadsheet, but they will be outside the routine reporting systems.

40   SUPERMARKET

(a)   **Failures in internal control**

Failures in internal control can be categorised using a recognised formal framework. COSO is such a structure, recommended in the Sarbanes-Oxley Act and commonly used in the UK and elsewhere.

There are both systematic failures and human errors in judgement that have combined to create the problems faced by the organisation. COSO identifies a *control environment* as the ethical, structural and cultural foundation to a control system. In this respect failure would relate to the ethical policy of the organisation in pursuing profits to the detriment of quality and public safety. This is also a cultural and leadership issue that goes through the spine of the organisation to the board and the CEO. The CEO must accept that he has a personal responsibility for the failure and should act accordingly.

Control activities within the value chain are also a cause of failure. This COSO category investigates the practical controls that exist as part of operations and seeks to identify problematic areas. Supplier selection processes and criteria are one such failure. The criteria seems to be driven by price above all other issues and will, almost inevitably lead to ever increasing problems in quality. The lack of government control in the region should also have highlighted the potential risks involved in sourcing from this location.

Another control activity is the goods receipt process at the stores. This seems ill equipped to carry out any form of quality control except that of a cursory nature. Quality control without fully examining food stuffs will be inappropriate unless it relies on previous quality control carried out at some point higher in the value chain. Since this does not exist it suggests a system wide or systematic failure through the company.

Control reporting or *information and communication* is a third category in the COSO framework. There are two examples of failure in relation to this. Firstly, the failure of store managers to report upwards the problems they were finding with the foodstuffs delivered to them. This failure has continued for some time and so suggests senior management with the power to correct the fault were unaware of it. Secondly, the protracted failure of senior managers to take action down the chain for the last six months is clearly unacceptable and suggests another control environment or ethical failure.

The final category of COSO is *monitoring*. This relates to the audit function or the control over the control. Failure seems to relate to the local auditor who has possibly colluded with the factory managers in order to bypass hygiene regulation and standards. Independence of such individuals must be assured as part of future recommendations to the company.

Improvements

The most important improvement is the need to balance cost against control and risk reduction. This need must begin at the board level with a reassessment of objectives and standards for operations. The threat to the public health cannot be ignored on commercial and ethical grounds.

There may be no need to search for alternative suppliers if quality standards can be improved although it is more likely that current suppliers are tainted with the stain of the scandal and so really should be replaced. Supplier selection processes need to be tightened, using suitable board level non-executive (NED) expertise to assist. Experts within proposed countries of origin may also be employed to identify potential suppliers and assist in future local audits.

The seeming complacency of local store managers must be eradicated. Much more stringent control over quality must take place at each and every step in the supply chain ending with a detailed procedural check carried out by local store manager prior to food stuffs being paced in the shelves. The usual controls over sell by dates and stock rotation should be in place.

Lines of communication including the creation of whistleblower channels to the audit committee should be put in place in order to ensure the swift and effective communication of sensitive and commercially damaging data to the appropriate authorities.

Finally, it is important for this organisation to ensure that it is responsive to external stakeholder issues. There seems to be a failure to consider the needs of suppliers and certainly, through the store managers comment regarding the minor number of complaints, customer safety. Human life is of paramount importance and it is staggering that such comments are accepted by senior management as being appropriate. The reference to the environmental group and government action reinforces the need to consider all stakeholders that impact on the organisations part of a formal review of internal control.

The conclusion must relate to the responsibility of the board in implementing these changes swiftly and effectively.

(b) **Review of internal control**

A formal staged process for the review of internal control might embrace the following.

1. Identification

This relates to the classification and examination of major risks faced by the organisation. It might centre on a stakeholder analysis to identify potential government action and customer response as well as on tangible risks such as the risk of quality failure in the supply chain.

2. Estimation

This relates to examining the likely impact of risk emergence or failures. The estimation might be a financial analysis of impact and the cost of problem rectification.

3. Development

Strategies to deal with a crisis of avert a crisis will be discussed and selected. Risk management might suggest the classic TARA (transfer, avoid, reduce, accept) classification of possible measures or a more specific company driven framework could be used.

4. Evaluation

The stakeholder impact and strategy costs should be matched before a final decision is made. Intangible estimates such as shareholder action or loss of good will may also form part of the decision making process.

5. Implementation

This could involve project planning and monitoring. Actual implementation is below board level but identification of reporting lines and how the board will monitor success will be important in any change process.

6. Review

This could include a number of elements in terms of the need to review the success of implemented strategies or the need to review the quality of the above process on a regular (annual) basis and the need to subsequently continually adapt and improve over time.

7. Disclosure

Good governance highlights the need to disclose the fact that such a process exists and its nature and content. This is a minimum standard expected of any large organisation such as the supermarket in the scenario.

41 CC & J

Key answer tips

Ensure that you manage your time appropriately to answer all parts of this question. Parts (c) and (d) require more application than theory, so may require a little longer to tackle.

(a) **Threats to auditor independence**

The threats to auditor independence may be categorised as self interest, self review, advocacy, familiarity and intimidation threats or considered through a practical reflection on the detail of the scenario.

The most obvious problem is the level of familiarity that existed between the auditor and Banco. The auditor has overstepped his professional relationship with the company and as such his ability to exclude personal considerations from professional decision making has been severely compromised. His attendance at family gatherings affects his ability to deal with the executive and his inclusion in the shooting trip has a similarly detrimental effect on his relationship with other members of the audit committee, even if they are not effective in their position. Strict guidelines in relation to this area may have assisted had they been issued through head office.

A related point is how independence weakens over time. The relationship between the partner and the firm has existed for many years and this in itself suggests objective decision making may be compromised. The company should have a clear policy regarding auditor rotation, as required by governance regimes and auditing standards.

The contractual relationship between the two companies is another problematic area. Reliance due to size of revenues generated from single client is one area of concern. This can be coupled with the amount of non audit work carried out and the level of profits gained through this. Such financial interest reduces the ability of the auditor to operate without concern as to financial consequence. The limited size of the audit fee may in itself compromise the ability to carry out a full audit with the allowable budget.

Fees should be set with reference to head office management and policy determined as to whether any non audit work can be carried out. It is well known that Sarbanes-Oxley specifically prohibits non audit work for financial auditors demonstrating the importance of the issue in global governance.

The existence of competitors and the strength of competition for lucrative work may affect the willingness of the auditor to make decisions that negatively affect client relationships. This is difficult to deal with except through reliance on the professionalism of the individual partner. It is clear in the case that such professionalism is in short supply at CC & J. This in turn brings into question the quality of recruitment and training practices at the firm. Head office cannot ignore their own culpability in what has happened. The seeming isolation of the individual involved and the lack of head office involvement in policy making is at the heart of the problems that have occurred.

(b) **Composition of audit committee**

The audit committee generally consists of three individuals as noted in the scenario. However, all three should be non-executives, independent of the executive and reporting directly to the chairman and shareholders.

This independence rules out the involvement of the CFO in any capacity since he cannot be at once the controller and the controlled. It is surprising, if not shocking, that the CFO has the role of chairman of the audit committee since this would not be accepted by any governance regime. Being a large company this should have come to the notice of the regulatory body and been dealt with immediately.

The independence of the audit committee does not mean complete separation from involvement in the company as is described here. They need to be separate and yet deeply involved, aware of financial position and accounting treatments. This suggests the need for financial expertise as a prerequisite to membership. In general guidance suggests that at least one member should be a financial professional, in reality all should have some understanding of audit issues and finance regulation.

Independence must be protected in the same way that auditor independence must be assured. This is not to suggest that the audit committee does not have any social involvement with officers of the company although their involvement in a company excursion seems to over step what would be considered to be appropriate. At the other end of the spectrum it is almost unbelievable that they do not meet regularly with the auditor and only consider company operations on an annual basis. If they were to be effective then a balance should have been struck and their role clearly defined.

The lack of an effective audit committee in itself threatens the independence of auditors and so could have been discussed in part a) of this question. Advice from relevant governance codes such as the combined code would have outlined their responsibilities including the need to operate as an interface between the auditor and the company (discussed next).

(c) **Audit committee operation as an interface**

The audit committee operates as an interface or point of connection between a variety of stakeholders, all involved in ensuring control exists and that the company continues to operate in shareholders' interests.

External auditors should report to the committee who in turn inform the board and shareholders of major issues arising from the audit. This creates an independent reporting line outside of communication directly to the CFO and so increases the likelihood of financial impropriety coming to light.

The same form of communication is available to internal auditors although the frequency of contact may be greater and the issues raised more diverse in line with the broad scope of internal auditors roles within the company. This form of interface can then extend to a direct channel of communication for all staff to use should ethical or professional dilemmas be unearthed. In this way the interface becomes a whistleblower channel for fast communication of important issues to those responsible in part for strategic control.

The audit committee reports to the board of directors regarding its own work and the work of those discussed above. This form of interface reduces the volume of issues identified for board consideration, filtering down workload to only major concerns.

Finally the audit committee through disclosure in the annual report operates as a direct interface between the company and its shareholders providing them with detail regarding the status of control and how risks are being managed.

(d)   **Characteristics of good quality information required by audit committee**

In all of the above communication processes there is a need for good quality information in order to reduce redundancy and ensure clarity in reporting. Characteristics include the need for information to be limited to that which is relevant to the committee given its defined remit. Reporting should be an accurate, factual account of the issue being raised especially in relation to financial matters. It should be concise with due consideration to clarity given the limitations of time and committee understanding of detailed financial concerns.

In addition, timeliness with respect to committee meetings and confidentiality, especially in relation to whistleblower issues, must be assured. Beyond this, consideration must be given to the cost of producing excessive data and the cost in terms of committee time in absorbing such information. Above all, reports must be useful and used to support their deliberations.

IDENTIFYING AND ASSESSING RISK

42   LANDMASS

Key answer tips

The syllabus does not specify which corporate governance codes you need to be familiar with. However if you do know the details of the UK's Combined Code this should give you an understanding of the typical requirements of such systems for part (b).

(a)   Risks should be categorised by companies according to the circumstances in which the company operates and according to how it perceives its risks.

(i)   A distinction might be made between business risks and governance risks. Business risks relate to the risks of failing to achieve objectives in business operations. Governance risks would relate to the risks of failing to comply with best practice in corporate governance, a failure of internal controls, or a failure to comply with legislation or regulations.

(ii)   Broad categories of risk should be divided into sub-categories: for example, business risks might be categorised into strategy risks, competition risks and environmental risks (political risks, legislation risks, economic risks, technology risks, and so on).

(iii) If a company consists of several independent investment centres, each investment centre might be responsible for its own risk classification and risk management.

(iv) There might be established classifications of risk within a particular industry. For example, in banking, risks are classified for risk assessment and capital management purposes into credit risk, traded market risk, operational risk and other risks.

In most situations, however, companies should carry out regular assessments of the risks that they face, using risk categories that seem appropriate to their individual circumstances.

(b) This answer assumes that the corporate governance guidelines which Landmass will be subject to are similar to those in the UK's Combined Code.

When Landmass becomes a listed company, it will be expected to comply with corporate governance guidelines. The board of directors will be required to carry out an annual review of the system of internal control and risk management, and report to the shareholders that they have done so.

In order to do this, a formal system of risk management should be put in place. An appropriate approach would be to establish one or more risk management committees. The risk management committee(s) should be responsible for the supervision of risk management within the company. The role of a risk management committee might be to:

- identify and assess risks regularly, and provide information to the board of directors and executive management;

- formulate risk management policies, for submission to the board of directors for approval;

- communicate with executive management, to ensure that risks are taken into consideration in decision-making.

Since many of the specific business risks and internal control risks will differ for each of the three business areas of Landmass, it might be appropriate to establish risk committees at a divisional level. However, other risks might apply to the group as a whole (for example, risks arising from changes in the value of land, or changes in legislation relating to property rights) and it might therefore be appropriate to have a risk committee at group level, to consider broader strategic risks facing the company.

The management of risk, and the implementation of risk controls, is the responsibility of the management who make decisions for the company. This responsibility might remain at board level (for example, in assessing strategic risk, or making decisions about acquisitions or major capital investments), or might be delegated to senior management.

A risk management committee should assess business risks and strategic risks, but there will also be a requirement to assess the system of internal control in the company. In the UK, guidelines for the review of internal control systems were provided in the Turnbull guidelines, which were based on the review structure proposed by COSO. It is recommended that the management and review of internal control should be based on five elements:

(i) creating a suitable control culture and risk management environment within the organisation;

(ii) the regular review of risks, including procedures for identifying, assessing and prioritising risks;

(iii) selecting suitable internal controls to contain or prevent the risks;

(iv) communicating information about risks and risk controls throughout the organisation to the individuals affected by them;

(v) monitoring the effectiveness of controls, with a view to rectifying weaknesses in control that might be discovered.

This continual review of internal control could be made a responsibility of the risk management committee(s).

The board of directors should assess the adequacy of internal control and risk management systems each year. In addition, the company might be required to publish an operating and financial review (OFR) each year in which the significant risks facing the company are explained to the shareholders, together with information on how the company is managing these risks. The board of directors should therefore also consider a system for reporting on risks, based on the information provided by its risk committee(s).

It might also be appropriate to consider the role of an internal audit department within a risk management system. If a company has an internal audit department, the audit staff can provide a means of monitoring risks and controls, and reporting their findings to operational managers, possibly the finance director (or the person to whom the internal audit department reports) and the risk committee(s).

43   STREAK

(a)   Internal controls are an essential element in any system of internal control. Controls are needed to help to ensure that:

- the organisation's operational systems function effectively and efficiently;

- the accounting records are accurate and the financial statements show a true and fair view;

- the assets of the organisation are being safeguarded;

- fraud can be detected or prevented;

- the organisation complies with all the necessary laws, regulations and codes.

Internal controls are intended to reduce the risks of any of the above not happening.

Examples of internal controls include accounting and arithmetic controls (for example, control totals), procedural controls, the segregation of duties, management and supervision controls, controls applied by the organisation structure and physical controls (such as restricted access to secure places).

Controls might be ineffective. They might also become ineffective over time, as operating conditions change and as new risks arise. Within an internal control system:

- executive management has the responsibility for designing and implementing internal controls, possibly with advice from the external auditors: having established a system of controls, it should be a part of the normal responsibilities of the managers responsible to review the controls to check that they appear to remain efficient and effective;

- the external auditors will expect to review internal controls relating to the accounting system, as a part of their professional audit responsibilities;

- it is an appropriate element of an internal control system that there should be a regular independent review of risks and controls: a responsibility of an internal audit department might be to check on the efficiency and effectiveness of controls in different systems within the organisation, and report their findings to senior management and their recommendations to the line managers responsible.

Streak is a listed company, and so is likely to be required to comply with stock exchange or government requirements on corporate governance or explain its non-compliance in the annual report and accounts. For example, a requirement of the UK's Combined Code is that the board of directors should review the internal control system and satisfy themselves each year that an appropriate control system is in place – and report to the shareholders that they have done so. If the internal controls are investigated regularly by internal auditors, this should provide the board with substantial evidence for making their report to the shareholders.

(b)   It is assumed that the planned audit is not necessarily directed towards an audit of the accounting system for the film-making division.

When planning an audit, it is essential to establish the audit objectives. In this case, the objectives might be to identify key risks within the division, and carry out an investigation to establish whether suitable controls are in place, or whether losses have occurred or might occur as a result of weak controls.

Alternatively, a value for money audit might be carried out, to investigate the efficiency and effectiveness of operations within the division, and also whether the costs of the division are kept under control (the 'economy' of operations).

The risks within the system of capital expenditure might be:

- whether the divisional management conducts proper financial evaluations of proposed capital expenditures, using DCF-related techniques and testing for risk using techniques such as sensitivity analysis;

- whether the total capital expenditure is kept within budget;

- whether there is an effective system of controls over expenditure after a project has been authorised by senior management, to ensure that all individual items of spending are authorised at an appropriate management level, and that all money is spent as intended on the capital investment (and not on other items of expenditure);

- whether all expenditure is properly recorded in the accounts: auditing the accounts of the division should be a recurring and regular feature of audit work, by either the internal or external auditors;

- whether all assets, particularly expensive assets, are properly safeguarded (e.g. held securely and appropriately insured against loss or damage);

- whether post-audit checks are carried out by the division's management, as part of the internal control system, to assess the actual costs and benefits from a capital expenditure, and compare these with the expected costs and benefits when the expenditure was first authorised.

The audit plan should depend on which of these risks will be the focus of the audit. However, one approach might be to take a sample of capital expenditure projects, and investigate these projects to ensure that:

- the project was properly authorised after suitable financial evaluation;

- the individual expenditures for the project can be identified within the accounting system (probably the management accounts), to ensure that they have been properly authorised, and that the expenditures can be traced through to the accounting system.

In addition, a check should be made between the authorised total expenditure for each project and the actual expenditure recorded. If there are significant differences between approved expenditure and actual expenditure, further investigations should be carried out to discover the reasons for the spending 'shortfall'. The aim would be to check the allegation that approved capital expenditure is not being spent for other purposes.

A check should also be carried out on the post-audit work of the division, to establish the effectiveness of the division's system for monitoring its capital expenditures, to ensure that actual costs and benefits turn out as planned.

44 CALL CENTRE

(a) A full solution is not given here, because a suitable answer is to reproduce the five elements of an internal control system identified by COSO:

- control environment
- risk assessment
- control activities (internal controls)
- information and communication
- monitoring.

(b) The controls within the call centre should relate to the major risks that have been identified. The main risks might be:

- Dealing with customer queries or complaints incorrectly, and against the customer's interests (for example, failing to cancel interest charges when a complaint is justified).

- Dealing with customer queries or complaints inefficiently.

- By error or intentionally, reducing the balance on the customer's account by too much.

- Not being able to trace the details of a customer's previous call, in cases where the customer calls again to continue with a complaint.

- Unauthorised access to customer account details.

Suitable controls that should be in place might be as follows:

- All employees in the call centre should understand the importance of handling customer queries efficiently and correctly (i.e. treating the customer fairly, and resolving queries effectively).

- Organisation controls. There should be clear rules about how customer queries should be handled, and when they should be referred to a more senior person. If letters are sent to customers, there should be rules about who has the authority to sign the letters in the company's name.

- Operators should be supervised, to ensure that they are dealing with calls properly. Supervisors might listen in to calls at random, to carry out checks.

- The rules about authorisation of refunds to customers and the cancellation of interest charges should be applied properly. Authorisations to refund money should be signed at an appropriate level of seniority within the centre.

- Suitable individuals should be recruited as operators. For example, they should have a suitable 'manner' and 'voice' on the telephone.

- There should be a training system in place for training new junior operators and for grooming junior operators for a more senior position.

- Operators should have ready access to a set of operating rules and procedures.

- There should be an audit trail for calls, and all telephone calls should be recorded. Recorded calls should be retained for a suitable period of time.

- There should be controls over physical access to the call centre operations room, to prevent unauthorised access. The efficiency of the operators should be monitored by means of performance targets or efficiency standards. Performance reports should be sent regularly to the call centre manager.

- There might be some segregation of duties, to ensure that the individual who gives refunds to customers is not also responsible for updating the customer's account. This might provide a check on errors. (It is not clear in this situation whether the possibility of fraud exists, except through unauthorised access to customer account records.)

45   REGIONAL POLICE FORCE

(a)   There are several significant risks to the achievement of the corporate objectives of the regional police force.

- The police force has several different stated objectives, which means that there will have to be some prioritisation of objectives, given limited resources to carry out the police work. For example, how should decisions be taken about allocating resources to tasks that reduce crime and those that promote community safety (such as road traffic safety or anti-terrorist measures).

- The objective of reducing crime and disorder is a very broad one, given that there are many different types of crime and lawlessness. Priorities will have to be assigned to the reduction in different types of crime, and efforts to deal with some types of crime will not receive adequate police resources.

- There might also be a temptation for the police force to divert resources away from 'normal' police work to money-earning activities such as policing football matches. There is a risk that money-earning activities will divert too many resources away from normal police work, and the amounts of money earned will be insufficient.

- Since the police force is a public body, there is a high risk of political interference. Political decisions are taken about specific priorities for dealing with crime, setting targets for achievement, and allocating money from taxation. Political decisions might increase or decrease the funds available to the police.

- There might be some conflict between the objectives of the police force. For example, if tough police measures are taken to reduce rates of crime or to deal with public disorder, public confidence in the police force might be adversely affected if the police tactics are too aggressive. Excessive violence in dealing with political demonstrations is a particular source of risk to public confidence.

- Risks to the achievement of the corporate objectives might also arise from a lack of public support. The police force are accountable to the general public as well as to politicians, and success in dealing with crime and improving community safety depends heavily on public support for the police – for example in reporting crimes and being willing to give evidence in criminal trials.

(b)   The risks in a regional structure for the police force are as follows:

- The regional management will want to set its own targets for the achievement of corporate objectives, but these might conflict with national targets set by government.

- A regional police authority might formulate its own strategies for dealing with crime that are different from the strategies adopted by other regional authorities. As a result, different crimes might be dealt with in completely different ways in different regions. The resulting lack of consistency in policing around the country could have an adverse effect on public opinion and public confidence in the police force.

- Crime is not restricted to regional boundaries, and regional forces rely on co-operation from other regional forces to carry out their work. Operational difficulties might arise that reduce the efficiency and effectiveness of inter-regional co-operation.

- Some crimes are of such potential importance, and operate on a national or international basis, that they need to be dealt with on a national or international basis, and not at regional level. Without national and international structures and organisation, much police work would be ineffective.

- Information will have to be shared between regions. There might be some risk that information held in one region might not be properly accessible to another region.

(c)   In broad terms, the internal controls that should apply within a police force are similar to the internal controls that should operate in any large organisation. The aim of internal controls should be to ensure that the policies of the organisation are properly applied and that operations are conducted efficiently and effectively.

- There must be procedural controls, to ensure that activities are carried out in accordance with policy and legal requirements. Police work is subject to extensive procedural controls.

- There should be adequate management and supervisory controls. Supervisors should monitor the work of their subordinates, and should be accountable to their own superiors for the actions of the individuals in their charge.

- There should be controls over recruitment and training (personnel controls), to ensure that appropriate individuals are employed and that these individuals are given sufficient training to do their work properly.

- Organisational controls should ensure that there is sufficient accountability for police work that is carried out. Although there will be accountability through normal reporting lines in the organisational hierarchy, the work of a police force should also be subject to external assessment, for example from public or political bodies.

- There must be procedures for the authorisation and approval of police activity, including the commitment of expenditure to activities. Decisions to commit resources and spending to various activities should be taken at an appropriate level within the management hierarchy.

Key answer tips

The categories of risk used here in part (a) may include one or two which you have not specifically studied – however you should be able to use your general knowledge and information in the question to suggest examples.

The requirement to part (b) is precise in focusing solely on risks arising from the decision to sell all-inclusive deals. You will get no marks for including more general risks.

Ensure that you correctly identify the verb used in the question and the depth of answer required for it, since part (c) only requires a list of tasks. No further explanation of these is required, so no marks will be earned for it.

The highlighted words are key phrases that markers are looking for.

(a)   The following risks are faced by the GHI Group:

Financial risks

(i)   GHI is based in its home country, but organises holidays abroad. Its revenues will be in its home currency, but it will have to pay its suppliers of overseas accommodation and transport services in countries which do not use the Euro in their local currencies. The group is therefore exposed to currency risk given the mismatch of currencies between revenues and costs. It will be possible to charge customers in local currency for services they buy while on holiday (e.g. excursions, wines and spirits at meals, etc), so some matching of revenues and costs is possible, but there will still be a large mismatch. The risk is that, if the Euro depreciates against the foreign currencies, then more pounds will have to be paid to overseas suppliers, and the profitability of the holiday products may be undermined.

(ii)   There will be a cash flow *risk* arising from the uncertainty about how many people will actually take the holiday that they originally book. The traditional pattern is for holidaymakers to pay a modest deposit when they book a holiday, with the balance payable (say) a month before the departure date. The company must contractually book a room in a hotel once the initial booking is made, and will be liable to pay the hotel, but in practice a proportion of holidaymakers will be unable to take up their holiday due to illness, family bereavement, etc. They may forfeit the deposit they have paid, but the company must pay for the hotel rooms it has booked, and will lose the profits they had hoped to gain from selling excursions, etc. This uncertainty about the actual number of customers who will turn up leads to the cash flow risk of the company.

Political risks

(i)   The risk of terrorist acts in countries that are popular with GHI's customers may have a severe impact on sales. Overseas holidays are often a discretionary purchase so, if a bomb goes off in Egypt or Turkey or New York, then some holidaymakers will avoid that destination and choose either to holiday in their home country or perhaps just stay at home. It is difficult for a company such as GHI to predict when the next terrorist act will occur, but it is possible to buy insurance against the adverse effects that a major incident would cause the company.

(ii)   GHI is planning to buy two new hotels in the Eastern Mediterranean. The question does not state the countries in which these purchases are to be made, but there will be a discrimination risk that the local government authorities may disapprove of foreign owners of local assets and may make things difficult for the company. The nature of this risk may depend on the political relationship between the two governments.

Environmental risks

(i)   An increasing number of people are using the internet to book 'self-managed' holidays directly, rather than visiting a travel agent. This development in technology has created the risk to GHI that customers will no longer visit its retail travel outlets, and will no longer buy its packaged products. GHI must react quickly by offering its products on the internet at a competitive price, otherwise it will get left behind as the market develops.

(ii)   The growth in divorce rates and in people remaining single means that the traditional family 'bucket and spade' beach holiday with two parents and two children will become less of the norm. This social change means that GHI must offer products of interest to single people, older people and lone-parent families. The 'weekend break' trips to European cities are an example of products popular with the over 50s which will continue to grow in the future as the number of older people in society steadily increases.

Economic risks

(i)   GHI has decided to purchase two new hotels in the Eastern Mediterranean. These will be overseas assets whose cost is denominated in an overseas currency, therefore their translated value in the group's balance sheet will fluctuate from year to year. This translation risk could mean that the balance sheet appears weaker if the pound strengthens against the relevant overseas currency, which could have implications for the cost of borrowing charged by future providers of debt finance.

(ii)   GHI must decide on the currency in which it will pay its suppliers in overseas countries. It may be that anyone in the Americas or the Far East is happy to be paid in US dollars, while anyone in Europe or Africa can be paid in Euros. However, there is a currency selection risk in that, if GHI decides to pay African suppliers in Euros while its competitors pay their similar suppliers in dollars, say, then GHI's relative competitive position will depend on the dollar's performance against the Euro.

The risks given here are by no means the only risks you could have identified. And, it is equally possible to put some risks under different category headings. So don't worry about this, just ensure that you are discussing your risks in plenty of detail to earn the full marks.

(b)   GHI has decided to move from offering traditional 'room-only' or 'bed and breakfast' holidays to offering 'all-inclusive' holidays where the customer pays a larger sum up-front but all food and drink, sports facilities, entertainments, and so on in the hotel are then free. The risk is that:

(i)   customers may not be willing to pay the higher price; and

(ii)   the costs of the additional items may exceed the incremental revenues, so that GHI is worse off after the decision.

The willingness of customers to pay more for a product depends on the elasticity of demand for the product. The demand for package holidays is price elastic, in the sense that higher prices will reduce demand, given the competitive nature of the market. GHI must therefore send a clear message in its marketing literature about the premium quality nature of the holidays it is offering. Services such as free magazines and drinks on aeroplanes are cheap to organise, but may differentiate GHI's offering from the competition.

The risk is that customers will compare the more expensive GHI holiday with a cheaper holiday offered by a competitor, and decide that the extras offered by GHI are not worth the premium price. GHI can combat this risk by describing long lists of facilities that are included in the price, e.g. use of the hotel gym, swimming pool, tennis courts, etc. In reality the likelihood of a customer using all these facilities is low, but they will impress the potential customer in demonstrating the added value in an all-inclusive holiday.

Keeping tight control of costs is also important. The risk is that customers and staff will not place any value on goods and services that are handed out for free in the all-inclusive environment. Customers might take several different desserts from a free buffet, eat the one that tastes best, and throw the others away. Portion control must be stressed to staff in their training: all portions of food and drink should be the minimum possible to dissuade customers from throwing large amounts away. A training and audit regime for hotel staff should be implemented to monitor and control all portions offered to customers.

A final method of monitoring the success of the all-inclusive packages is to ask customers to fill out questionnaires at the end of their holiday, asking for their feedback. After all, there is no point marketing a premium product that customers are not happy with. Their suggestions for improvements should be taken very seriously and fed back as inputs into the planning process for the future.

(c) The role of the internal audit department is to provide assurance to senior management and the board of directors that business risks are being managed properly and that internal controls are operating as effectively as they were designed to. Thus, in the context of GHI's foreign property purchases, internal audit must first decide whether the controls over such property purchases are adequate, and secondly whether the controls have been carried out properly.

Relevant tasks for the internal audit department are as follows:

- Reviewing the procedures by which potential sites are identified. This could mean checking that a minimum number of overseas property agents were consulted (say, a minimum of three agents in each country), and ensuring that the agents' advice is communicated to the relevant people at GHI.

- Checking that company procedures are followed in respect of negotiation of prices to be paid for each hotel.

- Checking that professional advice is sought and followed in respect of the appropriate method of financing the purchase price, e.g. bank loans, share issue, etc. The treasury department at GHI head office should receive this advice and give their opinion on it.

- Checking that the treasury department paid the appropriate amount of foreign currency to the hotels' builders on time, and that foreign currency risks have been hedged in accordance with group policy.

- Checking that health and safety regulations are fully complied with, before customers are allowed in. This should include fire drills and the servicing of boilers, given the public's sensitivity to faulty boilers following a well-publicised tragedy in Corfu at the end of 2006.

- Creating a rolling timetable within the internal audit department to test all the operating sections of the new hotels over the next few months. The new hotels will then be fully integrated into all the other group assets that internal audit inspects.

 There are many other tasks that internal audit could carry out. The important thing here is to list out at least five items to reflect the five marks available.

CONTROLLING RISK

47 BTS COMPANY

(a) Risks must be continually monitored to ensure that they do not adversely affect the organisation. Risk monitoring takes place on three levels:

Strategic level

This is the monitoring of risks affecting the organisation as a whole. For example, threats such as new competitors and new technologies must be identified on a timely basis and the risk management strategy updated to reflect these changes.

Lack of monitoring at best will result in the organisation starting to fall behind competitors in terms of functionality or design of products. At worst, lack of monitoring may threaten the ongoing existence of the organisation as the organisation may find that its products are no longer saleable e.g. due to technological obsolescence.

Tactical level

This is monitoring of risks which affect tactical managers. Risks in this category may affect individual divisions or units of the organisation, or individual departments depending on how the organisation is structured.

For a divisional structure, lack of monitoring may affect continuity of supply or availability of distribution channels. Not recognising that a supplier is in liquidation will result in delay in obtaining alternative sources of material.

Risks at this level also include the resignation of key staff which may result in key processes not being completed, e.g. customers invoiced for goods received. Staff motivation should be monitored to give early warning of staff leaving.

Operational level

Monitoring of risks at the operational level includes the basic day-to-day running of the organisation. Lack of monitoring is unlikely to be a specific threat to the organisation initially, but continued errors or risks will add to reputation risk over time. For example, lack of specific items to sell because sales patterns have not been monitored will result in customers choosing alternatives, or moving to other suppliers in the short-term. However, continued lack of key goods will increase customer dissatisfaction potentially resulting in significant and ongoing decreases in sales.

(b) Risks that the BTS company should be aware of include:

Strategic – IT failure

The company is heavily dependent on its IT systems. Failure in this area would mean that the company cannot sell its products via the website, or indeed process orders or make payments to suppliers.

To mitigate this risk, BTS needs to ensure that mirrored servers are available (so if one breaks then the second server starts processing immediately from exactly the same place) There is also the need to ensure that appropriate disaster planning and backup facilities are implemented.

Strategic – distribution systems

BTS is also heavily dependent on the reliability of its distribution system to maintain customer confidence in the company. Given the increasing number of customer complaints, it appears that confidence in the FastCour firm is decreasing. However, at present there is no evaluation of alternative couriers or systems to use.

To mitigate this risk, the board should investigate alternative delivery solutions e.g. use of a different courier firm or even purchase of their own vans for delivery. If the service from the existing couriers continues to fall then switching delivery methods should be seriously considered.

Tactical – key staff

Production of chairs and sofas is under the supervision of two key members of staff, Mr. Smith and Mr Jones. While it is essential to have skilled members of staff available to maintain production efficiently, there is the risk that one or both of these staff members could leave the company. If this happens the ability of BTS to continue production at current levels could be jeopardised.

To mitigate this risk, the knowledge of the production controllers should be codified into a production manual which means it will be possible for another staff member to take over production duties. Mr. Jones and Mr. Smith must be made aware that this step is being taken, not because they are not trusted, but simply so BTS has a full record of all its activities.

Tactical – suppliers

BTS is very dependent on the Woody company for supply of wood for its products. However, the relationship with the supplier appears to be inappropriate – late payment and lack of warning regarding future orders means that Woody cannot plan supplies to assist BTS and may not be inclined to help anyway given the late payment. If Woody decide to stop supplying BTS then production would be adversely affected while a new wood supplier is located.

To mitigate this risk, BTS should attempt to enter into more of a partnership with Woody. Providing future wood requirements and paying on time would help Woody to look on BTS more favourably and help BTS guarantee supply of wood.

Operational – lack of fabric

Occasionally, BTS is unable to sell a specific chair or sofa because the customer's choice of fabric is unavailable. Lack of fabric is caused primarily by human error at BTS – the procurement manager forgets to re-order fabric. While lack of fabric on an occasional basis is not threatening for BTS, an increase in errors would mean loss of more orders which will start to affect sales significantly.

To mitigate this threat, BTS should either implement a computerised re-ordering system or possibly try and ensure that the procurement manager is trained in memory techniques or implements some other system to identify low fabric stock levels.

48   SOUTHERN CONTINENTS COMPANY *Walk in the footsteps of a top tutor*

Key answer tips

The first two parts of this question focus on risk management with the last part drawing on the governance area of the syllabus.

In answering the second part of part (a) you are required to address the risks that are stated in the case (all to be found in the first paragraph of information). References to risks other than these would not earn marks. The key to earning good marks in this section is to ensure that you provide clear reasons for the strategy that you have selected, since a number of possible strategies would be acceptable.

If you are unsure how to tackle part (b) a good starting point would be to explain the terms used in the question, such as 'risk awareness', 'embedded' and 'culture'. Do not write all that you know about how to embed risk awareness since this is not quite what the question is asking for.

Part (c) is in two sections, so make sure that you tackle both parts to earn your marks. Critically evaluate will require you to consider good and bad points about the package offered here.

The highlighted words are key phrases that markers are looking for.

(a)   **Risks at Southland and management strategies**

Risk management strategies

There are four strategies for managing risk and these can be undertaken in sequence. In the first instance, the organisation should ask whether the risk, once recognised, can be transferred or avoided.

Transference means passing the risk on to another party which, in practice means an insurer or a business partner in another part of the supply chain (such as a supplier or a customer).

Avoidance means asking whether or not the organisation needs to engage in the activity or area in which the risk is incurred.

If it is decided that the risk cannot be transferred nor avoided, it might be asked whether or not something can be done to *reduce* or mitigate the risk. This might mean, for example, reducing the expected return in order to diversify the risk or re-engineer a process to bring about the reduction.

Risk sharing involves finding a party that is willing to enter into a partnership so that the risks of a venture might be spread between the two parties. For example an investor might be found to provide partial funding for an overseas investment in exchange for a share of the returns.

Finally, an organisation might *accept* or *retain* the risk, believing there to be no other feasible option. Such retention should be accepted when the risk characteristics are clearly known (the possible hazard, the probability of the risk materialising and the return expected as a consequence of bearing the risk).

 You are only required to give four strategies here, so you can keep to those that fit into the TARA acronym.

Risks in the case and strategy

There are three risks to the Southland factory described in the case.

Risk to the *security of the factory* in Southland. This risk could be transferred. The transference of this risk would be through insurance where an insurance company will assume the potential liability on payment, by SCC, of an appropriate insurance premium.

Risk to the *supply of one of the key raw materials* that experienced fluctuations in world supply. This risk will probably have to be accepted although it may be possible, with redesigning processes, to reduce the risk.

If the raw material is strategically important (i.e. its use cannot be substituted or reduced), risk acceptance will be the only possible strategy. If products or process can be redesigned to substitute or replace its use in the factory, the supply risk can be reduced.

The *environmental risk* that concerned a possibility of a poisonous emission can be reduced by appropriate environmental controls in the factory. This may require some process changes such as inventory storage or amendments to internal systems to ensure that the sources of emissions can be carefully monitored.

(Tutorial note: the strategies for the individual risks identified in the case are not the only appropriate responses and other strategies are equally valid providing they are supported with adequate explanation)

It is acceptable to recommend acceptance for risks that are minor or hard to control. In the case of the possibility of poisonous emissions a recommendation of acceptance would be inappropriate – the business would not be allowed to continue with a possibility of harm to nearby residents.

(b) **Embedded risk**

Risk awareness is the knowledge of the nature, hazards and probabilities of risk in given situations. Whilst management will typically be more aware than others in the organisation of many risks, it is important to embed awareness at all levels so as to reduce the costs of risk to an organisation and its members (which might be measured in financial or non-financial terms). In practical terms, embedding means introducing a taken-for-grantedness of risk awareness into the culture of an organisation and its internal systems. Culture, defined in Handy's terms as 'the way we do things round here' underpins all risk management activity as it defines attitudes, actions and beliefs.

The embedding of risk awareness into culture and systems involves introducing risk controls into the process of work and the environment in which it takes place. Risk awareness and risk mitigation become as much a part of a process as the process itself so that people assume such measures to be non-negotiable components of their work experience. In such organisational cultures, risk management is unquestioned, taken for granted, built into the corporate mission and culture and may be used as part of the reward system.

(Tutorial note: other meaningful definitions of culture in an organisational context are equally acceptable)

(c) **Choo Wang's remuneration package**

Benefits of PRP

In general terms, performance-related pay serves to align directors' and shareholders' interests in that the performance-related element can be made to reflect those things held to be important to shareholders (such as financial targets). This, in turn, serves to *motivate directors*, especially if they are directly responsible for a cost or revenue/profit budget or centre. The possibility of additional income serves to motivate directors towards higher performance and this, in turn, can assist in *recruitment and retention*. Finally, performance-related pay can increase the board's *control over strategic planning and implementation* by aligning rewards against strategic objectives.

Critical evaluation of Choo Wang's package

Choo Wang's package appears to have a number of advantages and shortcomings. It was *strategically correct to include some element* of pay linked specifically to Southland success. This will *increase Choo's motivation* to make it successful and indeed, he has said as much – he appears to be highly motivated and aware that additional income rests upon its success. Against these advantages, it appears that the performance-related component does not take account of, or *discount in any way for, the risk* of the Southland investment. The bonus does not become payable on a sliding scale but only on a single payout basis when the factory reaches an 'ambitious' level of output. Accordingly, Choo has more incentive to be accepting of risk with decisions on the Southland investment than risk averse. This may be what was planned, but such a bias should be pointed out. Clearly, the company should accept some risk but recklessness should be discouraged. In conclusion, Choo's *PRP package could have been better designed*, especially if the Southland investment is seen as strategically risky.

Examiner's Report

Introduction

Question 2 was a 'risk' question with elements of executive pay introduced in part (c). The case concerned the risk committee at Southern Continents Company (SCC) considering the risks associated with a new manufacturing investment it had made.

The case identified three risks and **part (a)** asked candidates to describe four risk strategies and then to identify an appropriate strategy from those four for the management of each of the three risks. The first part of this was well done by most candidates by identifying and describing the four 'TARA' strategies of transference, avoidance, reduction and acceptance. The second part, which required candidates to apply the strategies to the risks in the case, was less well answered overall and should act as a reminder that application of answers to the case will often be an important source of marks in professional level papers.

Part (b) addressed material from study guide section D2b but seemed to catch many candidates by surprise. The point here was to explain that embedding risk involved establishing risk awareness and management in a company's culture, systems, procedures, protocols, reward and human resource systems, training, etc. To have risk embedded is similar to having quality embedded in that the tone is set at the top and is then supported throughout using the cultural and systemic architecture of the whole organisation.

Some candidates sought to use this answer to make recommendations to SCC of how to manage its risk with phrases such as 'SCC should...' or 'perhaps SCC might consider...'. Others interpreted the question to be asking what 'risk awareness' meant. Both of these approaches were incorrect. The question as it was set was to explain what embedding risk in culture meant (and nothing else).

Part (c) was a departure from the risk theme in an otherwise risk-based question and should serve to remind candidates that the questions in section B of paper P1 will often not be entirely located within a single area of the study guide. It took a particular theme from the case and asked candidates to explain the benefit of performance related pay and then to critically evaluate the pay package awarded to Choo Wang, the chief executive of SCC. This question therefore had two parts (based on the 'rule of and'): one based on what candidates will have learned from the course materials and one in which they were required to apply the learning to the scenario. Most candidates could explain some of the benefits of performance related pay but fewer were able to pass comment on Mr Wang's reward package.

	ACCA marking scheme	
		Marks
(a)	Risk strategies: Half mark for identification of each strategy up to a maximum of 2 marks. 1 mark for each strategy explained up to a maximum of 4. (Four from the five listed strategies needed to get maximum marks) Risks in case: 2 marks for each risk identified from case with an appropriate strategy identified and explained. (Up to a maximum of 6 marks)	12
(b)	1 mark for each relevant point made on 'embedding' up to a maximum of 4 marks. Up to 2 marks for recognition of the importance of culture in embedding risk.	5
(c)	1 mark for each relevant point made on benefits of PRP up to a maximum of 5. 1 mark for each relevant critical comment made on Choo's reward package up to a maximum of 5.	8
Total		25

49 TASS

(a) Risk management process

COSO provides an enterprise risk management process to accompany its framework for internal control. The organisation could adopt this in order to ensure risks have been adequately considered and strategy devised prior to embarking on its expansion programme.

The organisation needs to firstly ensure its *control environment* is geared up to the new challenges. This would include defining roles such as that of the risk manager and those who will spearhead the campaign. The company's internal culture with its track record of success ensures it is well placed to deal with the problems ahead and a robust ethical stance will allow it to deal with the inevitable issues arising from interaction with local government and other stakeholders.

Formalisation of corporate objectives including financial and market based goals provides a necessary benchmark for determining the scale and thrust of strategy as well as providing performance indicators of success. Objectives should be decomposed to a national and stores level and the accumulated through to the strategic level.

Event identification is a *risk categorisation* process built on experience in their home markets, reflection of problems experienced by competitors in the new markets and independent assessment by internal experts such as the risk manager and outside new market consultants. Some of the risks have been identified such as the risk of competitor action, supply chain concerns and customer acceptance.

Risk assessment is a formal process of determining the strength, scope and depth of these risks. It might be the case that covert corruption has been overstated or that simple measures can negate these issues. It might be the case that existing home market quality control systems can be exported and used without undue cost escalation in the new markets.

Risk response relates to the determination of broad strategies in order to deal with risks. The TARA framework could be used to identify which risks can be transferred such as asking suppliers to take on logistical concerns, which can be avoided in terms of countries or regions, which can be reduced through control systems and which should be simply be accepted as part of any globalisation strategy. The latter may relate to the CEO's viewpoint that accepts a level of risk as part of the need to sustain or improve profitability. It is likely that shareholders will feel the same way.

Risk management moves from risk awareness through to the implementation of strategy. Control activities need to be hierarchically developed in order to reduce risks and ensure success. This means assigning responsibility at the strategic and operational level and developing systems both to execute operations and monitor their success. Quality control has been singled out as one such area for consideration.

Information and communication systems must be developed in order to deal with the geography of the venture. Technology allows a virtual presence in the new markets for executive and the development of management information systems to monitor performance. Investment will be large and project controls necessary to ensure success.

Monitoring the execution of strategy is through these information systems. It also relates to the role of internal auditors and risk auditors in formally evaluating the quality of system used and the level of control exacted over each new venture. Monitoring and reporting are essential to reduce risk by retaining control.

A final step might be one of *evaluation, reflection and adaptation*. This adaptation could include the rolling out of successful market development further into new markets allowing the company to rapidly gain a foot hold on different continents.

(b)   **Role of a risk auditor**

The role of the risk auditor depends upon the existence of other risk related structures within the company. An organisation of this size will have a substantial finance function including internal auditors. This being the case the role of the risk auditor becomes more specialised and targeted.

If internal auditors are concerned with the back end of the risk management process in terms of monitoring the degree to which control systems are working effectively then the risk manager will concern herself with definition of risks and the development of systems and strategies to deal with those risk.

All of the stages relating to risk management shown above except possibly the monitoring process will therefore become the remit of the risk auditor. Her views in the scenario suggest that she has been active in risk identification and risk assessment although not so forthcoming in terms of risk strategies or solutions.

This definition of the role is only one interpretation of risk auditing. A separate view would be to liken the role to that of a risk manager. This would involve the risk identification, assessment and strategy determination issues as already identified.

It would also suggest a more senior role, possibly in a direct reporting line from internal auditors so as to cover all aspects of risk. This however seems unlikely.

A risk auditor is most likely to be a specialist internal auditor focused on monitoring compliance to detailed standards set by outside bodies. These would include ISO standards such as ISO9001 on quality management certification and ISO14001 on environmental management certification. Auditing and ensuring the maintenance of certification would form the main focus for their work.

Other standards might relate to health and safety, fire prevention or business ethics code maintenance. The concept of a risk auditor is flexible enough to involve anyone or all of these interpretations.

Risk audit is more commonly associated with the finance sector and banking where risk auditors consider the company's exposure to financial risk in the financial instruments it sells and uses. Hedging and portfolio management would be part of the work although this seems less of an issue for this retailer. The finance function would need to be quite sophisticated and diverse to warrant such a role in this capacity although it is not out of the question.

(c) **Embedding risk**

Turnbull and others talk of risk needing to be embedded in culture and embedded in systems. The latter relates to the need to take a proactive approach to risk management ensuring their threat is minimised within operations itself rather than relying on a reactive monitoring process that fails to deal with the threat materialising, rather seeking to understating why it has occurred and reduce its likelihood in the future.

Embedding risk in systems therefore relates to the design of systems, inclusive of the design of control systems but predominantly the design of the system used in the delivery of value adding services. Technology is often associated with this concept since the higher the level of automation the lower the level of human involvement and, arguably, the lower the likelihood of mistakes being made.

Embedding risk into systems in this organisation would include the need to develop sophisticated supply chain delivery and monitoring systems such as quality control, product production scheduling, transportation, refrigeration and warehousing systems. The scope of such an approach is as diverse as operations and the investment will be considerable. It is generally true that the quality of risk reduction is only as good as the weakest link in the value adding chain and so a comprehensive approach must be guaranteed.

50   RISK STRATEGY

(a) An organisation is likely to have a portfolio of projects, some incurring more risk than others, so that the overall risk appetite is met from that portfolio.

A high-risk appetite will indicate that the organisation will normally seek a higher number of higher-risk/return activities as the organisation is willing to accept more risk and its risk capacity has not been reached. However, a low-risk appetite indicates that a higher number of low-risk/lower-return activities will be preferred.

The way that an organisation manages risk will also affect its risk strategy. Using TARA as an example of risk management, the overall risk strategy of an organisation can be explained as follows:

- A strategy of primarily self-insurance may limit the organisation's strategy regarding undertaking risky projects. Self-insurance implies risk minimisation as an overall strategy.

- A risk strategy of risk transference may imply an overall strategy that incorporates a higher level of risk. However, risk will then be limited by the amount of insurance premiums. Where premiums become too high, the risk strategy determines that, overall, the organisation will seek less risky projects.

- A strategy of avoidance implies that the organisation wants to limit the total amount of risk.

- Finally, a strategy of risk reduction or mitigation may imply that the risk capacity of the firm is being reached and while additional risk can be accepted, the amount of risk that can be taken on is limited.

Risk capacity is also important when determining the desired method of expansion within an organisation. Where the organisation has a high risk capacity the overall risk strategy is likely to be directed to taking on higher risk projects. However, where the organisation's total risk capacity is being reached, then projects with a lower amount of risk will be expected.

(b) With respect to expansion into different markets and products, Ansoff's product/market matrix provides a summary of strategic options for an organisation. The matrix is shown below.

	Existing product	**New product**
Existing market	**Internal efficiency and market penetration 1**	**Product development 2**
New market	**Market development 3**	**Diversification 4**

The Ansoff matrix illustrates that an organisation can expand using existing or new products into existing or new markets. The level of risk associated with each strategy is:

- Option 1 – low risk as the product and the market are known. There is risk of attempting to sell a product in the marketplace when demand is falling (e.g. video players). Falling demand increases risk as staying in the market segment is not viable for the organisation. Exit strategies from this market/product are required.

- Option 2 – higher risk – although the market is known there is a risk that customers will not like the enhanced or new product (e.g. a mobile telephone that can double as an MP3 player).

- Option 3 – again higher risk – the product is known but the marketplace is not. The main risks relate to poor sales strategy or poor market research indicating that customers want the product when they do not (e.g. Asda (a large UK supermarket chain) retreating from Germany).

- Option 4 – highest risk option – both the market and the product are new combining the risks from Options 2 and 3. While the risk is highest here, so are potential returns if the new product can be successfully sold in the new market.

So where an organisation has reached its risk capacity, options 1 or 2 are likely to be chosen as product/market strategies. However, where more risk capacity is available, options 3 and 4 may be chosen.

(c) The risk strategy of any organisation will focus on ensuring that the organisation does not accept too much risk; in other words the organisation wants to continue in existence into the future. However, for a small company, there will be a higher risk of continuing to exist, simply because it will be selling a restricted product range or may not have access to funds to expand into other areas easily. So while the risk strategy may be to minimise risk, opportunities for actual risk minimisation will be limited.

For example, a fall in demand for the organisation's main product will have serious effects in terms of future security, but the company may not be able to affect demand significantly; as noted above, opportunities for risk minimisation will be limited.

Conversely, for a small company, risks may have to be taken in order to ensure that products are launched successfully into the marketplace. Without taking some risk in terms of investment or marketing activities, the newer small company will not be able to start trading.

So in summary, the small company may have to accept higher risk both in terms of product launch and inability to affect the market place in some way. While the organisation may want to limit risk, in fact it may have to accept a larger amount of risk due to its smaller size.

51 DOCTORS' PRACTICE

Key answer tips

Part (a) implies that the risks require little explanation, the requirement word is *identify*, which is a low level requirement. Your answer therefore needs to mention the main types of risk and then provide a brief example from the scenario.

(a) **Business risk**

Business risk relates to the activities carried out within an organisation, including business interruption, errors or omissions by employees, loss of key staff, etc. In the context of the doctors' practice, business risks include:

- Loss of key staff; with only eight staff, one or two partners leaving may mean the surgery will have insufficient staff to operate.

- Lack of drugs for the new surgery due to loss of suppliers or delays in supply.

- Blood and samples being lost in transfer to the local hospital prior to testing.

Financial risk

Financial risk relates to the financial operation of the business, including credit risk through to interest rate and cash flow risk. In the context of the doctors' practice, financial risks include:

- Insufficient cash resources to pay for the new surgery.

- Practice income not increasing by the estimated 20% leading to cash flow problems after the surgery is operational.

- Increasing interest rates on loans taken out to pay for the surgery which are unforeseen or not sufficiently well hedged.

Environmental risk

Environmental risk relates to changes in the political, economic, social and financial environment within which the company operates. In the context of the doctors' practice, environmental risks include:

- Changes in legislation making the operation of a local surgery illegal – all surgery to be carried out in local hospitals.

- Other doctors' practices opening their own surgeries, taking customers away from this practice.

- Outbreaks of new diseases (e.g. bird flu) which the surgery has insufficient inventories of drugs to treat.

Reputation risk

Reputation risk is caused by the organisation failing to address some other risk. In the context of the doctors' practice, this could be a result of:

- The surgery providing poor or ineffective treatment due to lack of staff training.

- Doctors giving incorrect advice because blood samples were not tested correctly or results were mixed up between different patients.

- Doctors issuing prescriptions with incorrect dosage.

- Drugs becoming contaminated due to poor storage conditions.

(b) Embedding risk management is the process of ensuring that risk management becomes an integral part of the systems and culture of the organisation. In this way, risk management is no longer seen as a separate activity but part of the way in which the organisation does business.

Embedding risk in control systems

The aim of embedding risk management in the control systems of the organisation is to ensure that the processes required for risk management are incorporated in the everyday activities of the business. For example, in response to the risk of prescribing an incorrect dosage, a system could be put in place replacing all handwritten prescriptions and generating prescriptions from a computer system which only allows a selection of predefined dosages for a particular drug.

The process of embedding risk management within an organisation's systems and procedures involves:

- Identifying the controls that are already operating within the organisation.

- Identifying the controls required for risk management

- Monitoring those controls to ensure that they work.

- Improving and refining the controls as required in order to incorporate risk management activities.

- Document evidence of monitoring and control operations

In addition, the system needs to be:

- supported by the board and communicated to all managers and employees within the organisation

- supported by experts in risk management

- incorporated into the whole organisation, i.e. not part of a separate department seen as 'responsible' for risk

- linked to strategic and operational objectives

- supported by existing processes such as strategy reviews,

- planning and budgeting, e.g. again not seen as an entirely separate process

- supported by existing committees, e.g. audit committee and board meetings rather than simply the remit of one 'risk management' committee

- given sufficient time by management to provide reports to the board.

Embedding risk in the culture of the organisation

Even if risk management controls are incorporated in the systems and activities of the organisation, risk management may still not be effective unless staff at all levels in the business recognise its importance and the need to carry out the activities required of them. This demands that risk management is embedded in the culture and values of the organisation so that it is seen as 'normal' for the organisation.

The first prerequisite for this is a high level of risk awareness. This means an understanding by all staff of the importance of risk and risk management, the way risks impact on the all aspects of the business and in particular on their department and activities, and their role in the management of risks faced by the organisation. It is essential for effective identification, assessment and monitoring of risks. A high level of risk awareness ensures that:

- All staff understand the risk management policy and processes and take responsibility for the management of risk in their particular area

- Staff are able to identify risks, particularly at the operational level which senior managers are not aware of

- The organisation identifies, assesses and monitors risks effectively across all functions and at all levels, strategic, technical and operational.

- The recognition and management of risk becomes part of the culture and everyday activities of the business.

Various cultural factors will affect the extent to which risk management can be embedded into an organisation:

- Whether the culture is open or closed

- the overall commitment to risk management policies at all levels in the organisation

- the attitude to internal controls

- governance.

There are various methods of including risk management in culture, some of which also form part of the process of embedding risk in the systems:

- aligning individual goals with those of the organisation

- including risk management responsibilities within job descriptions

- establishing reward systems that recognise that risks have to be taken in practice

- establishing metrics and performance indicators

- publishing success stories.

PROFESSIONAL VALUES AND ETHICS

52 VAN BUREN *Walk in the footsteps of a top tutor*

Key answer tips

This question mixes the area of internal review with that of ethics, in both a theoretical sense (part (c)) and practical sense (part (b)). Part (a) should be largely revision from previous studies on F8.

Part (b) requires careful application of knowledge to this scenario. In deriving duties of an employee it is helpful to think of what your own employer expects of you. You will need to be precise and specific in your description of the ethical tensions to earn the full marks available here.

Knowledge of the theories of ethics is key to part (c) though you will still need to apply them in the given situation. Structuring your answer keeping each part of the question separate will produce a more professional result.

The highlighted words are key phrases that markers are looking for.

(a) **Importance of independence**

The auditor must be materially independent of the client for the following reasons:

To increase credibility and to underpin confidence in the process. In an external audit, this will primarily be for the benefit of the shareholders and in an internal audit, it will often be for the audit committee that is, in turn, the recipient of the internal audit report.

To ensure the reliability of the audit report. Any evidence of lack of independence (or 'capture') has the potential to undermine all or part of the audit report thus rendering the exercise flawed.

To ensure the effectiveness of the investigation of the process being audited. An audit, by definition, is only effective as a means of interrogation if the parties are independent of each other.

Three threats to independence

There are three threats to independence described in the case.

The same audit partner (Zachary) was assigned to Van Buren in eight consecutive years. This is an association threat and is a contravention of some corporate governance codes. Both Sarbanes-Oxley and the Smith Guidance (contained in the UK Combined Code), for example, specify auditor rotation to avoid association threat.

Fillmore Pierce provides more than one service to the same client. One of the threats to independence identified between Arthur Andersen and Enron after the Enron collapse was an over-dependence on Enron by Andersen arising from the provision of several services to the same client. Good practice is not to offer additional services to audit clients to avoid the appearance of compromised independence. Some corporate governance codes formally prohibit this.

The audit partner (Zachary) is an old friend of the financial director of Van Buren (Frank). This 'familiarity' threat should be declared to Fillmore Pierce at the outset and it may disqualify Zachary from acting as audit partner on the Van Buren account.

(b) **(i)** **Contrasting roles**

Joint professional and organisational roles are common to most professionals (medical professionals, for example). Although the roles are rarely in conflict, in most cases it is assumed that any professional's primary duty is to the public interest rather than the organisation.

Organisational role

As a member of the staff of Fillmore Pierce, Anne is a part of the hierarchy of an organisation and answerable to her seniors. This means that under normal circumstances, she should comply with the requirements of her seniors. As an employee, Anne is ultimately accountable to the principals of the organisation (the partners in an audit firm or the shareholders in a company), and, she is subject to the cultural norms and reasonable expectations of work-group membership. It is expected that her behaviour at work will conform to the social and cultural norms of the organisation and that she will be efficient and hard working in her job.

Professional role

As an accountant, Anne is obliged to maintain the high professional and ethical standards of her profession. If her profession is underpinned by an ethical or professional code, she will need to comply with that in full. She needs to manage herself and co-ordinate her activities so as to meet professional standards. In this, she needs to ensure that she informs herself in current developments in her field and undertakes continuing professional development as required by her professional accounting body. She is and will remain accountable to her professional body in terms of continued registration and professional behaviour. In many cases, this accountability will be more important than an accountability to a given employer as it is the membership of the professional body that validates Anne's professional skills.

(ii) **Tensions in roles**

On one hand, Anne needs to cultivate and manage her relationship with her manager (Zachary) who seems convinced that Van Buren, and Frank in particular, are incapable of bad practice. He shows evidence of poor judgment and compromised independence. Anne must decide how to deal with Zachary's poor judgment.

On the other hand, Anne has a duty to both the public interest and the shareholders of Van Buren to ensure that the accounts do contain a 'true and fair view'. Under a materiality test, she may ultimately decide that the payment in question need not hold up the audit signoff but the poor client explanation (from Frank) is also a matter of concern to Anne as a professional accountant.

(c) **Absolutism and relativism**

Absolutism and relativism represent two extreme positions of ethical assumptions.

Definitions

An absolutist assumption is one that believes that there are 'eternal' rules that should guide all ethical and moral decision making in all situations. Accordingly, in any given situation, there is likely to be one right course of action regardless of the outcome. An absolutist believes that this should be chosen regardless of the consequences or the cost. A dogmatic approach to morality is an example of an absolutist approach to ethics. A dogmatic assumption is one that is accepted without discussion or debate.

Relativist assumptions are 'situational' in nature. Rather than arguing that there is a single right choice, a relativist will tend to adopt a pragmatic approach and decide, in the light of the situation being considered, which is the best outcome. This will involve a decision on what outcome is the most favourable and that is a matter of personal judgment.

Outcomes

If Anne were to adopt absolutist/dogmatic assumptions, she would be likely to decide that she would need to pursue what she perceives is the right course of action regardless of cost to herself or the relationship with the client or her manager. Given that she unearthed a suspect and unaccounted-for payment, and that she received an inadequate explanation from the client, she would probably recommend extension to the audit beyond the weekend.

If Ann were to adopt relativist or pragmatic assumptions, she would have a potentially much more complicated decision to make. She would have to decide whether it was more important, ethically, to yield to the pressure from Zachary in the interests of her short-term career interests or 'hold out' to protect the interests of the shareholders. Anne could recommend sign off and trust the FD's explanation but she is more likely to seek further evidence or assurance from the company before she does so.

Examiner's Report

Introduction

This was a popular question for candidates. It concerned an ethical dilemma facing a recently qualified accountant.

Part (a) asked candidates to explain the importance of auditor independence and then, using information from the case, to describe three threats to independence in the case. This task is a good example of the way that paper P1 links back to previous papers in the ACCA examination scheme, particularly F8. This task was performed well by many candidates.

Part (b) explored two themes related to professionalism and professional ethics. In the case, the recently qualified accountant faced a potential dilemma because both the client and her superior were putting pressure on her to ignore or overlook an irregular payment. Part (i) of part (b) was done reasonably well by many candidates but part (ii), which required candidates to explain the ethical tensions, was less well done.

All professionals, including professional accountants, face situations with ethical elements to them. Even when the decision has a regulatory or legal underpinning, as was the situation in the case, the professional still faces a choice to uphold the standards of the profession or to 'bend the rules' in the interests of an easier life in the short term. This was the nature of the ethical choice in this case.

Part (c) was challenging for some candidates. The terms absolutist/dogmatic and relativist/pragmatic are specifically highlighted in the study guide (section E1a) and so well-prepared candidates were fully aware of what the terms meant. In keeping with the nature of P1 questions, candidates were required to use and apply the theory rather than just repeat it. This is an important thing to note: candidates may be awarded some marks for explaining a theory but they will more often be expected to apply it to a case in some way (as in this case). Many candidates correctly recognised the links between absolutism and deontology and also between relativism and consequentialism.

			ACCA marking scheme	Marks
(a)			1 mark for each relevant point on importance of independence made and briefly described. Half mark for mention only. Up to a max of 3 1 mark for each threat to independence identified up to a max of 3 1 mark for each threat briefly described up to a max of 3	9
(b)	(i)		1 mark for each organisational duty identified and briefly described up to a max of 3 1 mark for each professional duty identified and briefly described up to a max of 3 1 mark for each contrast or comparison drawn up to a max of 2 (Maximum of 6 marks)	6
	(ii)		1 mark for each point made on inclination towards role as employee up to a max of 2 1 mark for each point made on inclination towards professional duty up to a max of 2	4
(c)			4 marks for evidence of understanding the two positions (whether as a definition or in other parts of the answer) 2 marks for explanation of how the positions affect the outcome Cross marks between these two to reflect adequacy of overall answer	6
Total				25

53 PHARMA

(a) **Definition of profession**

A profession is an occupation carried out by a privileged body of individuals. It is suggested that a profession has three characteristics.

The first is in the nature of *training* associated with the occupation. This should require a high level of formal qualification and be accompanied by the need to gain practical experience in the field. The nature of qualification may differ as will the balance between practical and academic rigor.

The second characteristic relates to the *privilege* bestowed on members of the profession. This may relate to the right given to doctors to prescribe medication or the right given to accountants to audit and prescribe change within the corporate body.

The final characteristic relates to the *price of privilege*. Any member of a profession must act in the interests of the society it is created to serve. This is known as acting in the public interest. As much as doctors work for the health of the social community so accountants work for the health of the business community.

Role of accountant in support of public interest

Within this distinction between doctors and accountants the role of the accountant and the problems in truly acting in the public interest can be examined.

In support of the business community the accountant has a valuable role to play. This includes monitoring companies and auditing accounts, reporting to regulatory bodies and providing market confidence in the well being of business entities. This general role assists fraudulent activities to be diagnosed and those perpetrating theft to be uncovered. The accountant becomes the watchdog of commerce ensuring rules are followed and regulation adhered too.

As an employee of a company the accountant has a related role to play extending into decision making and decision support of the executive through the provision of high quality information. The accountant is an advisor, a manger and a wealth creator through this process. He/she is also a communicator or agent for the owners in as much as it is a primary role to present accounting data in a form that is understandable to the business users. The accountant supports agency through transparency in disclosure and clarity in reporting.

Through the accountant's facilitation of commerce companies are able to raise funds, generate profits and pay taxes. These taxes support the wider community and so enable social functions to be funded for the benefit of all.

This final point is the only relationship the accountant has with the public in a general sense. The relationship is detached and dubious since a part of the accountant's role is to positively work against the payment of any monies to the wider community in the form of taxation.

This suggests that that focus for public interest is really restricted to the financial public meaning corporations and those that benefit through investment. Whilst it could be said that everyone's pension (assuming they will be entitled to one) benefits from the work of the business community the reality is that only a very small proportion of individuals gain from this form of output. The accountant working in the public interest seems limited in this sense.

Other issues seem to cloud the discussion further. People would not earn money to support themselves without business, economies would not grow and products demanded by customers would not exist. However, this strays from the question since it is not the existence of corporations or commerce that is called into question but rather the role of the accountant as a privileged member of society who does not actually work in the broader societal interest.

(b)   **Support of value laden role in society**

The wider value laden role relates to an extension to the accountant's current role in order to embrace the remit of the wider society. This suggests an expansion to the stakeholders influencing the accountant's role away from corporate masters towards public health, societal needs, governments, environmentalist, disadvantaged communities and in general the ethical role of a corporate citizen.

To respond to the diverse and broader need to accountant will need to develop systems that monitor and report on broader issues such as environmental impact, quality of life, species extinction and resource usage. Some systems already exist including environmental management and sustainability monitoring systems in larger companies. These need to be used in order to bring environmentalism into the decision making reference framework used by executives when determining strategy.

The key question behind the wide value laden role is the extent to which accountants believe this is necessary or achievable. Whilst most appreciate the need for change the egoistical nature of ethical decision making ensure accountants suppress concern for the common good beneath their allegiance to the corporate flag. This seems appropriate since organisations generally pay their wages in one form or another.

(c) **Confidentiality**

Confidentiality relates to the need for secrecy. The scenario uses the word in association with the need to keep its research a secret from its competitors in order to ensure they do not steal the company's ideas.

Confidentiality is a key principle defined in the IFAC code of ethics and here the association is generally between audit client and audit firm maintaining the confidentiality of findings on examination of the body corporate. Confidentiality leads to confidence in ensuring that any problems identified can be discussed and resolved in a private arena without the issue being disclosed, discussed or acted upon by external groups.

The existence of confidentiality is also an element of the agency relationship. Shareholders expect a degree of confidentiality to be shown by managers ensuring that they are the first to know about any issues that relate to their investment and its returns. This is naturally extended to the relationship between the accountant as employee and the executive of the company.

The concept is not without its detractors. The issue of whistleblowers sits very uncomfortably with the need for confidentiality as shown in this scenario. The need for confidentiality must be weighed against the public good and when the latter is found to be dominant the accountant must act and not remain silent.

The CEO's use of the concept is entirely inappropriate in the scenario. He likens confidentiality to the need for trade secrets and yet the essence of the secret being kept is that the product may kill children. It is certain that competitors would like to know this but equally certain they would not want to copy the product which is the interpretation given by the ethically misguided executive.

(d) **Courses of action in ethical dispute**

In a practical and personal way the Professor can be forgiven for taking no action. The sums of money involved and the effect on his personal career and therefore his family may be devastating if he decides to publish the report. It is worth bearing in mind that his findings may be flawed since the product would have been tested by government scientists prior to release.

If his report is correct, and he believes that it is, then despite the effect on his personal circumstances he may take a more utilitarian or egalitarian ethical stance where the needs of the many outweigh the needs of the one.

His first steps would be to seek advice from colleagues, both from an ethical perspective and to review the technical content of his findings. Professor Jones needs to be totally sure of his findings before publicising them.

If they are validated by colleagues then he would publish the document and accept the consequences that arise from that action.

54 DEONTOLOGICAL ETHICS

(a) **Deontological approach to ethics**

This is a non-consequentialist theory. Whether an action can be deemed right or wrong depends on the motivation or principle for taking that action. Actions can only be deemed 'right' or 'wrong' when the motivation or reason for taking an action is also known.

The deontological approach is based on the theory of Immanuel Kant. Humans are regarded as rational actors who can decide right and wrong for themselves. This decision making then determines the actions they will take.

The theory introduces the concept of the 'categorical imperative', i.e. a framework that can be applied to every moral issue. Humans are deemed to work within this framework in deciding what actions they should take.

The framework provides three maxims that are tests for any action. An action can only be morally 'right' if it survives all three tests or maxims. The maxims are as follows:

Maxim 1

Act only according to that maxim by which you can at the same time will that it should become a universal law.

This is the principle of **Consistency**. An action can only be right if everyone can follow the same underlying principle. The act of murder is immoral because if this action were determined moral then human life could not exist; that is if everyone murdered everyone else then there would be no one left alive! Similarly lying is immoral because if lying were moral then there would be no concept of 'truth'.

Maxim 2

Act so that you treat humanity, whether in your own person or in that of another, always as an end and never as a means only.

This is the principle of **Human dignity**. Everybody uses other humans in some way, e.g. to take orders and bring food in restaurants, to receive/deal with requests in call centres. This does not mean that the other human should be seen simply as a provider of those goods or services although it is easy to do so, it is 'their fault' that something has gone wrong. According to this maxim, their own needs and expectations are important and this must always be remembered; they are also human beings.

Maxim 3

Act only so that the will through its maxims could regard itself at the same time as universally lawgiving.

This is the principle of **Universality**. The test is whether an action is deemed to be moral or suitable when viewed by others, not by the person undertaking that action. The basic test is that if a person would be uncomfortable if their actions were reported in the press (even if no other people were harmed and all humans could accept the principle) then the action is likely to be of doubtful moral status. In other words, actions must be acceptable to everyone in what ever situation.

(b)   In this situation, toys have been produced in a country where the use of child labour is presumably either legal or accepted as part of the ethics of that society. Manufacturing is also carried out under poor working conditions, which appear to be the result of pressure to limit manufacturing costs. The result has been poor manufacturing quality and danger to health in the country where the toys were sold.

The use of child labour in one country must pass Kant's three categorical imperatives to be acceptable, both in the country of manufacture and in the country of sale.

The first principle is consistency. An action can only be right if everyone can follow the same underlying principle. In the country of sale the use of child labour is unacceptable; as child labour is unacceptable in one country then it is not possible to follow this principle in the manufacturing country. Both the toy re-seller and the purchaser of the toys are at fault. The re-seller should have insisted on the application of their ethics while the consumer could have not purchased the toys to indicate their disagreement with the use of child labour.

The second principle is human dignity. In other words, the needs and expectations of the child workers are important and this must always be remembered; they are also human beings. The use of child labour would appear to go against this principle. Children are being used to keep costs down in the manufacturing company, while being forced to work in poor working conditions. Presumably consumers in the country of sale would not like their children to work in these conditions as the needs of children in terms of security and expectations in terms of life expectancy are being compromised (do the child workers ever swallow magnets?). The use of child labour does not pass the second of Kant's tests.

The third principle is universality. The principle asks whether an action is deemed to be moral or suitable when viewed by others, not by the person undertaking that action. In other words, would the toy re-seller be comfortable with consumers knowing that child labour was used in the manufacture of the toys even though this was morally acceptable in the country of manufacture? The answer is presumably 'no' as consumers do not expect child labour to be used in their country. The fact that the re-seller kept this information secret also indicates that the use of child labour could be considered morally wrong.

From the view-point of the ethics in the country where the toys were sold, the use of child labour is wrong; it does not meet any of Kant's three maxims.

55 EEF AND TUCKER

(a) The Ethics Education Framework (EEF) is designed to provide a structure for the development of ethical education. It recognises that ethics education is actually a lifelong process and will continue through the career of an accountant or any other professional. The framework establishes a four-stage learning continuum which professionals will generally move through during their careers. The four stages are described below.

1   **Ethical knowledge**

Education focuses on communicating fundamental ethical knowledge about professional values, ethics and attitudes. The aim is to develop ethical intelligence by obtaining knowledge of the different ethical concepts and theories relating to the area of work.

The stage explains the fundamental theories and principles of ethics. Having obtained knowledge of these theories, the accountant will understand the ethical framework within which they operate.

To complete this stage, an ACCA member will have read the members handout on ethics and therefore understand in theoretical terms the ethical principles that they should follow.

2   **Ethical sensitivity**

Ethical sensitivity applies the basic ethical principles from stage 1 to the actual work of the accountant in the functional areas being worked on, e.g. auditing, taxation, consultancy, etc. The aim of the stage is to ensure that accountants can recognise ethical threats.

The stage is developed by providing case studies and other learning aids to show how and where ethical threats can arise. In other words the accountant is sensitised to ethical issues, i.e. the areas where ethical threats appear can be identified.

To complete this stage, the ACCA member will have worked through some case studies which identify ethical threats e.g. the offer by the client of the free use of the company's yacht may create a conflict of interest and independence issues on an audit. The ACCA online ethics module provides examples of identifying ethical problems.

3   **Ethical judgment**

This stage teaches the accountant how to integrate and apply ethical knowledge and sensitivity from stages 1 and 2 to form reasoned and well-informed decisions.

The stage therefore aims at assisting accountants in deciding ethical priorities and being able to apply a well-founded process for making ethical decisions. It is taught by applying ethical decision-making models to ethical dilemmas, showing how ethical judgment is being applied.

To complete this stage, the ACCA member will take the scenarios used in stage 2 further to identify methods of overcoming the ethical threat or dilemma. For example, the offer described above of use of the yacht should be declined.

4   **Ethical behaviour**

This stage is primarily concerned with explaining how an accountant should act ethically in all situations (i.e. not just the workplace but other situations where the profession of accountancy must be upheld).

The stage therefore explains that ethical behaviour is more that believing in ethical principles; it also involves acting on those principles. In terms of lifelong education, the accountant must therefore continue to be aware of ethical theory, ethical threats and continually seek to judge actions in the light of expected ethical behaviour. Teaching is primarily through case studies.

To complete this stage, the ACCA member will need to transfer the knowledge obtained in stages 1 to 3 into practice. For example, during actual audit work, ethical threats will be identified and the theoretical training in stages 1 to 3 applied. Refresher courses on ethical behaviour can be obtained if necessary using case studies or by re-visiting the online ethical module.

(b)   Tucker provides a 5-question model against which ethical decisions can be tested.

To be ethically correct, any decision should be:

- Profitable?

- Legal?

- Fair?

- Right?

- Sustainable or environmentally sound?

In this context, the decision by the training manager to decrease the training budget and focus more on personal training using a computer, can be assessed as follows:

Profitable

The decision will decrease the expenditure for the accountancy firm, so in this sense it is profitable. However, there may be a negative impact on staff perception on the importance and method of training. Additional costs may be incurred in recruiting new staff to replace any who decide to leave the company.

Legal

The decision is certainly legal in terms of meeting the training requirements of the firm and the institute. Training hours can be monitored by the software, ensuring that CPD requirements for checking training hours are met.

Fair

It is difficult to determine whether the move is fair. It is fair in terms that all staff will have access to the training as and when it is required. However, it may not be considered 'fair' in that training time will involve unpaid overtime; staff may resent this.

Right

It is 'right' that the accountancy firm provides appropriate training for its staff.

Sustainable or environmentally sound

The decision appears to be environmentally sound in that there will be decreased travel time and therefore less use of resources involved in travel (e.g. petrol).

56 PUBLIC INTEREST

(a) The public interest can be defined as that which supports the good of society as a whole (as opposed to what serves the interests of individual members of society or of specific interest groups within society).

Acting against the public interest therefore means acting against the good of society as a whole. Occasionally, it may also be necessary to serve the interests of individual members of society or interest groups rather than society as a whole. In this situation the public interest is served as those groups need to take priority over what the public may want as a whole.

Acting in the public interest can also be applied to the provision of information about accounting or the actions of organisations or other institutions. The accountant or other advisor or government deems that information should be made available even if the individual firm does not want disclosure.

Acting against the public interest therefore implies that information is not being made available by accountants to the public when that information should be made available. Similarly, there may be situations when disclosure would not be in the public interest, i.e. information should be kept confidential to avoid harm to society.

Public interest disclosure of information is expected within the ethical guidance provided by most accountancy bodies. Taking action against the public interest is not therefore something that accountants contemplate lightly as this would be breaching the ethical guidance from their professional body.

(b) **Illegal activities – toxic waste disposal – impact on stakeholders**

Not providing information on illegal actions of QPT allows actions to continue to the long-term detriment of stakeholders. In this situation, the share price of QPT is likely to fall when information about the illegal disposal of toxic waste is finally disclosed. There is also the risk that payments to creditors will be delayed, or even no payment made at all if QPT goes into liquidation as a result of having to pay large fines.

Lack of disclosure would decrease accountability to stakeholders in terms of information they need to make informed decisions regarding QPT now. If it is found out that the accountants knew about the illegal act and did nothing, then this will also start to bring the profession into disrepute.

Illegal activities – toxic waste disposal – impact on the general public

Non-disclosure of information on illegal toxic waste disposal could also potentially harm the general public as a whole. This will be the case if the waste enters the drinking water supply and members of the public are harmed by drinking the contaminated water. It would therefore be in the public interest to disclose this information.

The issue that QPT and/or their accountants need to be careful of is causing any form of panic due to release of this information. QPT may need to liaise with any public health department to ensure disclosure is handled carefully to minimise panic.

Money Laundering – legal duty to disclose

Again, it would be against the public interest not to disclose the information. Lack of disclosure would mean that the crime of money laundering can continue, and both the directors of QPT and the accountants will be in breach of money laundering regulations. The accountants are in breach because in many jurisdictions there is a duty to disclose knowledge of money laundering.

In some situations therefore there is a legal duty to disclose information. Non-disclosure is a criminal offence as well as being against the public interest.

Price sensitive information

As part of the audit, the accountant is currently aware of information on the overall result of QPT for the year. To release this information prior to publication of the financial statements would harm QPT and could harm the stock exchange and economy to a certain extent in QPT's country.

Disclosing price sensitive information in this situation would therefore be inappropriate because the public interest would be harmed in terms of potentially making the economy of QPT less stable.

57 INO COMPANY

(a) Corporate ethics relates to the application of ethical values to business behaviour. In the same way that individuals have ethical values and are expected to follow those values, so organisations are now also expected to have ethical values.

Corporate ethics relates to many different areas of the organisation's activities. For example ethics is relevant to the overall strategy determination of the organisation through to the treatment of individual workers.

Again, as with individual ethics, corporate ethics goes beyond legal requirements indicating a higher moral standard than simply 'following the law'. There will be situations where an organisation follows the law, but ethical action means doing something more than this. This indicates that ethical actions are to some extent discretionary, in that the organisation does not have to take ethical action. However, expectations on the organisation from other sources (e.g. customers, suppliers and employees) also indicate that ethical action is normally expected of a company.

Organisations are encouraged to report their ethical approach in a corporate and social responsibility (CSR) report. In many jurisdictions, this report is again not required by law or accounting standards, but is indicative of best practice. Lack of standards means that CSR reports are not necessarily comparable between organisations, limiting their usefulness. However, some organisations do provide comprehensive CSR reports (e.g. Marks & Spencer in the UK) providing detailed information on their ethical stance.

(b) **Customers / goods produced**

As with any other company, INO has a responsibility to produce quality goods and services for its customers at a reasonable price, allowing INO to make a reasonable profit for providing those goods and services. To this end, INO must attempt to build up customer trust and faith over time so customers will purchase and be satisfied with INO products.

The decision not to carry out rectification work on the N920 model may have little or no impact on INO as the risk of failure is extremely small. However, should failure occur and some cars overheat causing engine failure then the reputation of INO will be damaged (the company knew about the issue prior to failure) and faith in INO and its products will fall. Although there is no legal requirement to provide rectification, ethically INO must consider this to ensure customers are not injured driving INO vehicles.

INO should therefore provide for rectification work, even though the costs would appear to outweigh the benefits of this action.

Suppliers of tyres

Suppliers provide goods and services for a company. They will normally attempt to provide those goods and services to an appropriate quality in a timely fashion and in return expect to be paid on a timely basis.

INO does appear to pay its suppliers promptly, maintaining this element of any ethical contract. Similarly INO attempts to create partnership agreements with suppliers enabling both INO and the supplier to work to further their joint interests. However, the use of child labour in a foreign country by the UIN Company may not be seen as ethically correct. Not only is INO promoting potentially unethical (albeit legal) activities in that country, there is also an association risk. Most countries believe it is ethically incorrect to employ children and have enacted laws to confirm this view. INO may lose customers if information about the use of child labour appears in the public domain.

Given that INO and UIN do attempt to collaborate in the supply of tyres, INO should initially ask UIN whether the policy of using child labour can be amended. If this is not possible, then INO may consider choosing another supplier of tyres based on more ethical criteria.

Product development

INO produces motor vehicles. These products have a potentially damaging effect on the environment in terms of carbon and other emissions generated during their use. INO is therefore producing a product with a potentially damaging environmental effect.

However, INO does have an active R&D department which is researching into alternative fuels and other methods of decreasing the environmental impact of INO's products. These activities show appropriate environmental awareness on the part of INO.

To check the acceptability of the extent of R&D, INO can do two things:

- Firstly, INO can benchmark expenditure with other similar companies to ensure that the spend of €25 million is not a minimum amount.

- Secondly, a more judgmental view can be taken on the success of previous R&D projects and the effect increasing the R&D budget would have on the success of R&D and the timescales to project completion.

Just because INO is active in this area does not necessarily mean that sufficient is being done to reduce environmental damage from INO's products.

Shareholders

Shareholders are investors in the company. They will expect an appropriate and proper return on the money invested in INO. The board of INO will therefore be expected to provide information on the investment made by shareholders as well as a dividend showing the return on their investment. Good corporate governance principles would also indicate that shareholders will be involved in decision-making, especially where those shareholders are larger corporate investors.

The board of INO do not necessarily ascribe to all principles of good corporate governance so ethically they could be seen to be 'wanting' in this area. While dividends over the last few years have been above industry average, there has been no attempt to involve shareholders in decision making processes within INO. There could also be concern that dividends have been excessive, potentially jeopardising longer-term shareholder interests in favour of the short-term.

The board of INO need to take two actions:

- Firstly, find methods of involving shareholders more in the organisation, for example, by making an active part in the AGM.

- Secondly, providing more detailed profit and cash flow forecasts to determine whether larger dividend payments now limit opportunities for growth and investment in the future.

CSR reporting

The INO Company obviously works within society which implies some corporate and social responsibility to that society. Although not necessarily a legal requirement, many companies produce a Corporate and Social Responsibility report as a means of communicating this relationship to third parties.

At present, INO does not produce any CSR report which means the organisation is potentially missing out on positive publicity in this area. The ethical stance of the company is correct in carrying out CSR activities; it is the lack of reporting that is the issue here. However, the ability of INO to produce a CSR report is severely hindered by the lack of any CSR targets or reporting systems within the organisation. While INO does carry out some appropriate activities such as providing employees with a sports hall and ensuring that community projects are supported, there are no formal budgets for these activities or methods of evaluating the success of the investments.

INO therefore needs to set formal criteria for its CSR activities and then show in the CSR report how those targets have been met.

58 CODES OF ETHICS

(a) **Professional code of ethics**

Professional codes of ethics are implemented by most professional institutions (including all accountants' institutes) as a set of guidelines which members are required to follow. The elements of the codes are:

Introduction

The introduction provides the background to the code, stating who it affects, how the code is enforced and outlines disciplinary proceedings which will occur should the code be breached.

Fundamental principles

These are the key principles that must be followed by all members/students of the Institute. The principles may be stated in summary format leaving detailed application to the individual in the specific circumstances that they are in.

Conceptual framework

The framework explains how the principles are actually applied, recognising that the principles cannot cover all situations and so the 'spirit' of the principles must be complied with.

Detailed application

Examples of how the principles are applied in specific situations. However, where there is no specific example of how to apply the principles, the member needs to decide a specific course of action based on the general application of the principles.

(b)   The fundamental ethical principles of the ACCA apply to all members and student members; so there is no difference in the potential treatment of Mr. M or Lex in this respect.

Lex

There appears to be two sections of the code of ethics that Lex may have breached.

- Firstly, **Integrity** – members should be honest and straight-forward in all personal and business relationships.

- Secondly, **Confidentiality** – information on clients should not be disclosed without specific authority.

Lex may not have been acting with integrity by disclosing information about Mr. M and Mr MoneyPenny. While Lex was attempting to be helpful to you, that information was possibly not in the public domain which means it should not be disclosed. Also, personal issues should not be a reason for making business decisions. In other words, Mr M should not be influenced in trying to obtain cash from Mr MoneyPenny simply because he is a friend. In effect, confidentiality has been breached; Mr M may not be an external client but he is an internal client of Lex – that is someone he reports to and must therefore keep happy.

As you have now obtained the information, it is difficult to ignore it. However, it is unclear how the information can be used.

Informing Mr. M of the situation will only reflect poorly on Lex; as the most recent member of staff he was only attempting to help you. If Lex is reported then no other member of staff is likely to trust you again. Reporting to Mr. M could also result in disciplinary action for Lex, which again will lower the amount of trust he has with you. The most prudent action regarding Lex appears to be to do nothing.

Mr M

As noted above, Mr M appears to be basing business decisions on his friendship with other people. In this sense the following ethical principles may have been breached:

- Firstly, Integrity – members should be honest and straight-forward in all personal and business relationships.

- Secondly, Objectivity – members do not allow bias or conflict of interests in business judgements.

It certainly appears that Mr M has been less than objective. Without the friendship with Mr MoneyPenny, it appears that the customer would have been sued by now to recover the outstanding money. The action also appears to lower the integrity of Mr M because the level of trust you have in his actions will now be lower – you can no longer be sure of his motivations.

You now have a possible reason for Mr M not pursuing Mr MoneyPenny for the outstanding debt; although to be clear this is only hearsay and may yet be determined to be incorrect. To progress matters, you could ask Mr. M if there are any other reasons he can think of as to why the debt from Mr. MoneyPenny remains unpaid – this gives him the chance to explain that Mr MoneyPenny is a personal friend.

If Mr M denies knowledge of friendship, then there is simply his word against Lex's – it will be difficult to report the case to ACCA's ethics committee for lack of objectivity because there is no breach of principles that can be proven.

However, there is still the issue of the outstanding amount from Mr MoneyPenny. You can suggest that a provision is made, although again Mr M may reject this assertion. Other options available to you therefore include:

- Reporting directly to the board on the issue,

- Taking ethical advice from ACCA's ethics department.

As with the situation with Lex, it appears no further action can be taken due to lack of any firm evidence.

59 FIVE ETHICAL SITUATIONS

(a) There are a number of possible threats to fundamental ethical principles which lead to conflicts of interest affecting accountants in their work. Professional codes of ethics aim to enable the accountant to understand how to resolve these conflicts of interest.

Conflicts of interest and their resolution are explained in the conceptual framework to the code of ethics. A framework is needed because it is impossible to define every situation where threats to fundamental principles may occur or the mitigating action required. Different assignments may also create different threats and mitigating actions – again it is not possible to detail all the assignments an accountant undertakes. The framework helps to identify threats – using the fundamental ethical principles as guidance. This approach is preferable to following a set of rules which may not be applicable in a particular case.

Once a material threat has been identified, mitigating activities will be performed to ensure that compliance with fundamental principles is not compromised.

Where conflicts arise in the application of fundamental principles, the code of ethics provides guidance on how to resolve the conflict.

The conceptual framework:

- provides an initial set of assumptions, values and definitions which are agreed upon and shared by all those subject to the framework.

- is stated in relatively general terms so it is easy to understand and communicate.

- recognises that ethical issues may have no 'correct' answer

- provides the generalised guidelines and principles to apply to any situation.

(b) **Situation 1**

Ethical threat – dishonesty

Accountants need to be honest in stating their level of expertise – and not mislead employers by implying they have more expertise than they actually possess. In this situation, A is implying he was better at studying for his exams than his actual exam success rate. This may make the potential employer view A more favourably, or enable A to meet a recruitment criteria of 'first time passes only' for success in obtaining the job.

Ethical safeguards

It is difficult to stop provision of incorrect information in this instance. However, A should be following the fundamental ethical principle of integrity in applying for the job. Alternatively, the potential employer could ask all applicants to confirm that information provided is accurate as a condition of employment. Any errors or omissions found later could act as initial grounds for disciplinary action.

Situation 2

Ethical threat – overstatement of profits and salary

B's bonus is determined by the same accounts that B is working on. The threat is that B will overstate profits in some way to ensure that the bonus payable is as high as possible. Again, accountants should act with integrity and honestly, although these ideals conflict in this case with B's remuneration.

Ethical safeguards

The main safeguard will be to ensure that someone other than B determines the amount of B's bonus (and checks the accounts produced) – or that the bonus is not linked to the accounts that B is preparing. This removes the conflict of interest.

Situation 3

Ethical threat – receipt of bribes / gifts

D stands to gain 10% of a contract price by accepting the quote from F rather than another company. This means D's objectivity may be breached because he will be favourably impressed by the quote from F. There is also an issue of confidentiality because presumably D will want to keep the payment 'secret' from E Ltd so his employer does not know of the inducement.

Ethical safeguard

From D's point-of-view, the obvious ethical safeguard is not to accept the bribe. This removes the objectivity issue leaving D free to choose the best system rather than the one with the most financial advantage to him. Alternatively, D can inform the senior management and/or board of E Ltd, provide the relevant information on the three quotes, and let the board make the final decision. Should the board choose F then again D should not accept the bribe.

Situation 4

Ethical threat – Price fixing

In most situations, G would keep the affairs of his client confidential, and would be acting with integrity in taking this action. However, there is a conflict as H and I appear to have been acting illegally; increasing their profits at the expense of their customers. G can either choose to keep quiet about the situation or disclose the information to relevant third parties, effectively 'blowing the whistle' on H and I.

Ethical safeguards

G could report to the ethics committee or audit committee in H, should the company have either of these committees. As long as some appropriate action was taken, then this relieves G from external reporting obligations. External disclosure should only be made after taking into account various issues such as the gravity of the matter, the number of people affected and the likelihood of repetition. As many people are affected and repetition seems likely then external disclosure is likely to be appropriate.

Situation 5

Ethical threat – Incorrect financial information

Accountants need to be able to prepare information honestly and with objectivity. However, in this situation, J is being pressured into producing information which will be incorrect, simply to show K Ltd in a better light. The instruction provides a conflict with J's integrity because he wants to follow the instructions of L but may not be able to do so because this would be dishonest.

Ethical safeguards

J needs to consult with other people apart from L in an attempt to determine the correct course of action. J can consult with any committee charged with governance (e.g. the audit committee or ethics committee) or if necessary take advice from his professional body. If after these discussions, the situation cannot be resolved, J may have to consider resignation.

60   CARPETS AND FLOOR COVERINGS

Key answer tips

Part (a). Remember that the requirement here is to explain the difference – so each type of audit needs to be explained – but ensure that some 'contrast' is mentioned to show the examiner you have noticed the requirement verb.

(a)   A value for money audit is an audit of economy, efficiency and effectiveness (the '3Es'). The audit investigates an aspect of operations, such as the work done in a particular department, or the work carried out to perform a particular activity (in more than one department). The aim of the audit is to establish the objective or objectives of the operations, and consider:

- whether the objectives are being successfully achieved, and if not what the reasons might be;

- whether the operations are being performed in a cost-efficient manner, or whether there is unnecessary and wasteful spending on items of expense;

- whether operations are being performed efficiently.

A value for money (VFM) audit of the accounts department might therefore look at issues such as:

- staffing levels in the department, and whether these are too high (resulting in low productivity);

- whether customers pay on time, or whether the debt collection staff give customers too much time to pay, and whether bad debt levels are high. (Poor debt collection procedures and high bad debts would indicate a lack of effectiveness);

- whether the department has spent too much on its computer equipment (resulting in poor economy).

A VFM audit might also investigate part of the accounts department that are not subject to an 'accounting audit', such as the management accounts and the capital expenditure appraisal procedures. For example, a VFM audit might assess the value that is provided by the current management accounting control system (in terms of what it achieves, and whether it does its work efficiently and economically), and whether the benefits justify the costs incurred.

In contrast, an audit of the accounting system would be concerned with the reliability of the accounting records and whether the assets of the company are being properly safeguarded. The audits will therefore consider the reliability of internal controls, and whether the auditors can rely on the effectiveness of those controls. The focus is therefore entirely different. An audit of the accounts is not particularly concerned with efficiency or economy.

(b)   An audit needs to be conducted against a clear set of standards or targets. Since the company intends to publish an annual Social and Environmental Report, it has to decide the criteria against which its performance and policies should be measured.

The key issues should be established. The board of directors should have some idea of what these issues are, but guidance can be obtained if necessary from the company's shareholders, or from external agencies that have been established to assist companies to prepare Social and Environmental Reports (or Sustainability Reports). These sources include the UN's Global Research Initiative sustainability reporting guidelines.

The aspects of social and environmental responsibility that might need to be covered by the report – and audited – include environmental issues (pollution, waste, sustainable supplies of raw materials) and work-related issues (human rights, working conditions, pay, employee education, avoiding discrimination at work, and so on).

A social and environmental audit should be planned within the framework of the company's policies for social and environmental matters and targets for achievement. An audit can then assess whether the policies are being applied and whether progress is being made towards the stated targets (which could be either quantitative or qualitative targets).

From the information available, two social and environmental risks are apparent. It is not clear how serious they are, but if they could affect the short-term or long-term value of the company, they should be disclosed in the Social and Environmental Report. (In the UK, listed companies may be required in the future to disclose significant risks, including risks relating to social and environmental issues, in their annual Operating and Financial Review.) The two issues that seem apparent are:

Environmental issues relating to the disposal of old carpets and floor covering. BK currently burns some old materials and disposes of the rest using methods that are not stated. There is an immediate risk that BK is in breach of the law by burning the materials (air pollution and possibly other pollution) and might also be in breach of the laws on disposals of materials. Checking on compliance with the laws should be an element of a social and environmental audit. The company might also be affected by further legal restrictions on disposals (and recycling) of used items.

There are also human rights issues in connection with the possible use of child labour or slave labour by suppliers. Although BK is not directly responsible for the labour policies of its suppliers, a socially responsible policy would be to influence suppliers to adopt different labour policies or switch to different suppliers. If BK is using suppliers who use child labour or slave labour, there will be a risk to the company's reputation. This could have an impact on sales of the company's services.

(c)   From the information available about the dispute, it is not clear whether or not the internal auditor acted ethically.

The ACCA Code of Ethics and Conduct states that an accountant should act with integrity, and should be honest and straightforward in carrying out his or her work. There is a suggestion that this might not have been the case. The executive director accused the auditor of being 'deceitful'. It would also appear that the auditor did not discuss his findings or his concerns with the director or anyone else in the department subject to audit. This would have been inappropriate behaviour, because it would have lacked integrity. An internal auditor is required to look for weaknesses in systems, management and controls, but should discuss issues with the individuals concerned and be straightforward in doing so.

The Code also requires an accountant to act with objectivity, and to be intellectually honest and fair. It is not clear whether the auditor acted in this way, or whether perhaps a personal dislike of the director might have affected his opinions and biased his judgements.

The Code of Ethics and Conduct requires an accountant to show professional competence and due care in his work. The director has accused the auditor of not being qualified for the work. Without further information, this cannot be assessed any further.

It is also possible that the internal auditor was subjected to strong pressure from the director and others in the department to give a favourable audit report, when a more critical report would be appropriate. If this was the situation and the auditor was under pressure from the director, he would have been the victim of an ethical conflict of interest. The ACCA guidelines recommend that in such circumstances, the accountant should report the problem to his superior. However, since the target of the auditor's criticism was a director of the company, it is quite possible that his superior also felt a conflict of interest and inability to stand up to such a senior person.

When an accountant is unable to resolve a conflict of interest by referring the problem to a superior (or the superior's boss), there may be no alternative to resignation. It is possible that this is what happened in this particular case.

In conclusion, from the limited information available, it is not clear who was 'at fault', the director or the accountant (or both of them). However, with more information, it would be possible to judge the matter by reference to the ACCA Code of Ethics and Conduct.

61   COMPANY A AND COMPANY B

Key answer tips

A wide range of discussion on this topic is possible which means that alternative emphases are acceptable – the answer to part (b) below is not necessarily the only 'correct' solution. Remember to try and justify any points made to ensure that the examiner can see your thought process in making those points.

(a)   Economic activity has social and environmental effects and is only sustainable where its impact on society and the environment is also sustainable. The use of economic and social footprints is an attempt to evaluate the sustainability of an organisation's economic activity.

Measuring sustainability

Sustainability can be measured empirically using either the quotients approach which measures sustainability in terms of the amount of a resource available compared with the actual use of that resource, or subjectively by measuring the intentions of organisations to achieve certain goals or objectives.

The environmental footprint

The environmental footprint measures sustainability in terms of the resources used by economic activity. Where resource use exceeds provision, then the activity can be termed unsustainable.

The social footprint

The social footprint evaluates sustainability in three areas of capital, called 'Anthro capital', and organisations need to ensure that their economic activities are sustainable in each of these three areas:

- social capital – social networks and mutually-held knowledge for collectives to take effective action

- human capital – personal health, knowledge, skills, experience and other resources (including human rights and ethical entitlements)

- constructed capital – physical infrastructures in society such as roads, utilities, etc. that people build.

Organisations need to ensure that their economic activities are sustainable in each of these three areas. For example, regarding social capital, the government will set taxation rates, with those taxes being used to provide various services. Where the amount raised is less than the amount required for the provision of social capital, then the activities of society as a whole are unsustainable. The government will need to raise taxes meaning that companies will pay more tax. Sustainability is achieved where the social capital needs of society are being met. It can be argued that economic activity itself is unsustainable if education is insufficient to meet the needs of society.

The importance of the social footprint is that more capital can be generated if required, e.g. people can decide to improve their knowledge. The aim of economic activity may therefore be to generate sufficient social capital, or have a large enough social footprint, to ensure sustainability.

(b) The key financial objective of a company is normally considered to be the maximisation of shareholder wealth. However, most companies now have multiple objectives, some financial and some non-financial.

The objectives of Company A are out of line with those of most modern companies. Company A's focus is strongly on the maximisation of global shareholder wealth, yet companies have many other important stakeholders. These include: the managers and directors of the company, other employees, customers, suppliers, banks and other providers of non-equity finance, the government and society/the local community.

Shareholder wealth maximisation should be tempered by taking into account the needs of other stakeholders.

The balance between financial and non-financial objectives will differ between companies. Many companies specify non-financial objectives which might include growth of sales or market share, survival, technological leadership and product quality.

Increasingly companies are focussing attention on the needs of the community and the protection of the environment, both of which will tend to use cash resources and might reduce shareholder wealth. However, it is sometimes argued that if a company acts responsibly towards society and the environment this will create a good public image that ultimately leads to an increase in shareholder wealth. The impact of non-financial objectives on shareholder wealth is difficult to judge.

Company A intends to use sophisticated measures to maximise cash flow in each country where the company operates. Even if other stakeholders were to be ignored maximising cash flow in each country might not lead to the maximisation of group cash flow and shareholder wealth. If company A wishes to focus on cash flow maximisation it should be from the perspective of cash flows in its home currency, not many local currencies which could change in value relative to the home currency. The company's share price will depend on the expected cash flows in the currency in which its shares are denominated.

It is a difficult ethical question as to whether or not a company should outsource internationally. Many examples of this have occurred in recent years, particularly with respect to the manufacturing activities and call centres moving from developed countries to less developed countries where wage costs are much lower. When this occurs there will normally be redundancies in the developed countries. How much should a company consider this against increased profits, and possibly enhancement of the standard of living in less developed countries?

If company A wishes to focus on financial objectives it might be better to relate them to cash flows rather than profits.

Company B has adopted totally different objectives. There is no financial dimension to the stated objectives. It might be that the company expects financial success to result from these objectives, but that would not automatically occur.

The focus on customer satisfaction is increasingly common, and if successful should enhance sales. However, reducing price might satisfy customers yet it might also lead to cash flow problems and the destruction of value rather than its creation. High quality products are fine, as long as the quality is not at the expense of any profit. Increasing market share is also desirable, but needs to be accompanied by considerations of cash flow and potential wealth creation. Outstanding levels of sales and delivery service are sensible objectives, although again these need to be achieved in the context of managing the associated costs.

62   MATTI

Key answer tips

Part (a) – requires knowledge of Kohlberg. As this is an application question to a theory with many different elements, a columnar form of answer is likely to be appropriate. The theory can then be seen clearly beside the application of that theory. Remember to state clearly your reasoning for the examples provided for each level of Kohlberg.

Part (b) – this is one of the 'classic' cases used to explain the Kohlberg theory – amended slightly for this question. It is important to show clearly which CMD level Z and M are working at and again give reasons for your decision.

(a)

CMD Level	Example from
1.1 Pre-conventional – Obedience and punishment Right and wrong is defined according to expected rewards and/or punishment from figures in authority.	The accountant will follow the advice of the senior accountant and not place the provision into the accounts. This unethical decision will be taken because the accountant believes that he will be punished in some way if the provision is made. Being new to MATTI, he may also be unsure on how to follow the recommendations of his superior.

CMD Level	**Example from**

1.2 Pre-conventional – Instrumental purpose and exchange

Right is defined according to whether there is fairness in exchanges – individuals are concerned therefore with their own immediate interests.

The accountant will follow the advice of the senior accountant because he believes that in the future, the accountant will repay this favour in some way.

For example, the accountant may believe that he can be late for work one day, or leave early and that the senior accountant will accept this behaviour.

2.1 Conventional – Interpersonal accord and conformity

Actions are defined by what is expected of individuals by their peers and those close to them.

The accountant will follow the advice of the senior accountant because this is the way that all other staff act within the department.

Not to follow the suggestion would place peer pressure on the accountant to follow the senior accountant next time. Also, the accountant may not be accepted by his peers (this is a new company) and the accountant will not want to be 'rejected' by this group.

2.2 Conventional – Social accord and system maintenance

The consideration of the expectations of others is broadened to social accord in general terms rather than to immediate peers.

The provision is unlikely to be made, but the accountant is verging towards insisting on one being made.

The accountant will discuss the issue again with the senior accountant with an aim to understanding in more detail why a standard provision is not being made. He can suggest that in any other company the provision would be made.

3.1 Post-conventional – Social contract and individual rights

Right and wrong are determined by reference to basic rights, values and contracts of society.

The accountant believes it is right to make the provision and seeks some method of doing this.

For example, he may contact the audit committee and bring the matter to their attention, or even discuss the situation with the finance director. At this stage he will insist that the provision is made.

3.2 Post-conventional – Universal ethical principles

Individuals make decisions based on self-chosen ethical principles which they believe everyone should follow.

The accountant believes it is correct to make the provision and activity seeks methods of doing this.

If necessary, if the provision cannot be made then he may consider resignation rather than having his moral principles prejudiced by the ethical situation.

(b)   Z is clearly motivated by the need to improve his son's life. However, Z (presumably) also knows that stealing is wrong. Obtaining the drug without payment could be seen as unethical. In this situation, Z may also consider that it is a basic human right to have a good quality of life, and it is therefore incorrect for the health authority to deny the drug. The 'unethical' action of stealing is replaced by the need to justify his son's moral rights – it can be argued that Z is operating at level 3.1 of Kohlberg.

M is an employee of the hospital and therefore has to follow the rules and regulations of the hospital. If there really is insufficient funds to pay for the drug, then M must accept this, even though provision of the drug would improve the quality of life of Z's son. In this respect, M is following stage 1.2 or 2.1 of Kohlberg.

At stage 1.2 M is expecting an exchange from his employer, the hospital; following the hospital policy on drug provision means that he keeps his job.

At stage 2.1, M is acting in accordance with the expectations of his peers; all doctors presumably know that breaking hospital policy is not possible because the hospital will overspend on drug provision, putting jobs at risk as savings are made elsewhere.

63   SOCIAL ACCOUNTABILITY

Key answer tips

It is unlikely that you will be asked to explain all seven positions of social responsibility in a single question in the exam, but this question allows you to ensure that you can explain each position in a clear and structured manner.

(a)   In their book, *Accounting and accountability changes and challenges in corporate social and environmental reporting*, Gray, Owen and Adams suggest that all organisations should have some social responsibility. With social responsibility there is social accountability – that is organisations must account for their actions. Believing this means that there may be a difference between how the world is now and how it should be. The authors provide seven positions on social responsibility as alternative views on how the world should be, and it is the position taken which will determine the view on what actions need to be taken by businesses, governments and society. These positions are shown in the table below.

Position	Explanation
Pristine capitalist • The way the world works now is a good approximation of the way it should work. • The liberal democratic economy is accepted as correct. • Businesses have no moral obligations beyond their responsibilities to shareholders and trade creditors.	• The needs of shareholders are the most important consideration for organisations – and shareholders expect this. • Little or no concept of CSR. • Shareholders expect maximum returns – not providing these is agency theft (taking returns away from their rightful owners) • The authors see this as behind most of accounting theory and practice

Position	Explanation
Expedients • Long-term economic stability and welfare can only be achieved by accepting minimal social responsibilities	• Businesses need some minimal ethical guidance (may be legislative or self-imposed as enlightened self-interest). • Impact on society starts to become important and businesses cannot simply use resources without consideration of their impact on society.
Proponents of social contract • Companies and other organizations exist only at society's will and therefore must serve the requirements of society (to some extent). • Companies also behave in accordance with the ethical norms in society. Behaviour is modified as those norms change, e.g. to provide enhanced reporting because society suggests, and then the government requires, this.	• Existence of, and decisions made by, companies are justified if they serve the public interest. • The extent of responsibilities or accounting needed to disclose them is not clear.
Social ecologist • Overall concern for the environment and recognition that large organisations have caused environmental and social problems. • The same large organisations can be involved in reversing those problems, which is expected of those businesses.	• Economic systems should change, particularly in the area of resource use, pollution and waste control. • Only by making these amendments can quality of human life be improved, or at least remain constant.
Socialist • Capital should not be allowed to dominate social, economic and political life, and so change is required to decrease the influence of capital. • In the current system, capitalists do manipulate workers and other socially oppressed groups – change is therefore required.	• Economic systems and the creation of 'things' is a secondary objective rather than primary. • Mistrust of accounting and CSR systems, although there is not necessarily a clear view of how these should be amended/replaced.
Radical feminist • Economic, social, political and business systems reflect masculine concepts of aggression, achievement and conflict. • More feminine values of compassion, love and co-operation are missing from the business world. • Some radical re-adjustment is therefore needed in the ownership and structure of society in order to move to the feminist viewpoint.	• Lack of feminine views means that accounting and CSR systems are flawed. • Use of these constructs is not the correct way of organising essentially compassionate human beings.

Position	Explanation
Deep ecologist	
• Human beings do not have the right to existence or resources any more than other forms of life.	• Economic systems are completely incorrect, e.g. the decision to destroy wildlife habitats to build roads is not tenable and should not be considered.
• Businesses cannot therefore be trusted with something as important as the environment.	• As a minimum, economic activity should be sustainable.
• See position supported by lack of environmental awareness of many businesses	

(b)   Social auditing is a process that enables an organisation to assess and demonstrate its social, economic, and environmental benefits and limitations. It also measures the extent to which an organisation achieves the shared values and objectives set out in its mission statement.

The concept of social audit is to provide additional information on a company's activities over and above the financial accounts. A key feature of a social audit is the active involvement of external stakeholders, and in many situations the publication of a social audit by those external stakeholders. For example, one company, Social Audit Ltd, provides social audits on companies, sometimes without the active participation of the companies. In effect, the social audit is evaluating the organisation's social and environmental footprint within a given accounting period from the external perspective.

Typical sections of a social audit report include:

• an overview of the company including salient features of the financial accounts

• the company's stance regarding employees such as how pay and benefits are negotiated, provision of job security and policies on discrimination in the areas of sex, race and disabilities

• an overview of products with negative environmental impacts

• the environmental impact of the company itself in terms of pollution, emissions, recycling, etc. and health and safety policies

• the social impact of the company in terms of community support

• the response, if any, from the company.

Other social audit initiatives that may be more familiar include:

• the work of Greenpeace and Friends of the Earth in highlighting poor environmental polices

• independent review of products including their reliability and environmental impact in some situations (e.g. Which? Magazine in the UK)

• 'green' consumer audits – the provision of comparable information on companies in areas such as animal testing, involvements in arms manufacture or environmental impact with the objective of enabling the consumer to make informed choices on companies from which they wish to purchase.

Information provision can sometimes be used to try and promote change, e.g. potentially unethical/ethical policies in banks being highlighted (in the 1980s Barclays having potentially unethical polices but the Co-Op being seen as 'ethical'). Many companies (e.g. Traidcraft) now welcome social audits as a means of enhancing their ethical stance on trading.

Social auditing has been criticised on the following grounds.

- Information on the social audit is difficult to obtain, particularly where the target company is not co-operative.

- The objectives of the social audit itself are not always clear, so the completeness of information (or indeed the inherent bias because some information is missing) is difficult to determine.

- A lot of information is provided as un-manipulated data, and any commentary on that data could be interpreted as writer's bias.

- The report is not independently checked, decreasing its inherent value.

Section 5

PILOT PAPER EXAM QUESTIONS

1 CHEMCO

Chemco is a well-established listed European chemical company involved in research into, and the production of, a range of chemicals used in industries such as agrochemicals, oil and gas, paint, plastics and building materials. A strategic priority recognised by the Chemco board some time ago was to increase its international presence as a means of gaining international market share and servicing its increasingly geographically dispersed customer base. The Chemco board, which operated as a unitary structure, identified JPX as a possible acquisition target because of its good product 'fit' with Chemco and the fact that its geographical coverage would significantly strengthen Chemco's internationalisation strategy. Based outside Europe in a region of growth in the chemical industry, JPX was seen by analysts as a good opportunity for Chemco, especially as JPX's recent flotation had provided potential access to a controlling shareholding through the regional stock market where JPX operated.

When the board of Chemco met to discuss the proposed acquisition of JPX, a number of issues were tabled for discussion. Bill White, Chemco's chief executive, had overseen the research process that had identified JPX as a potential acquisition target. He was driving the process and wanted the Chemco board of directors to approve the next move, which was to begin the valuation process with a view to making an offer to JPX's shareholders. Bill said that the strategic benefits of this acquisition was in increasing overseas market share and gaining economies of scale.

While Chemco was a public company, JPX had been family owned and operated for most of its 35 year history. Seventy-five percent of the share capital was floated on its own country's stock exchange two years ago, but Leena Sharif, Chemco's company secretary suggested that the corporate governance requirements in JPX's country were not as rigorous as in many parts of the world. She also suggested that the family business culture was still present in JPX and pointed out that it operated a two-tier board with members of the family on the upper tier. At the last annual general meeting, observers noticed that the JPX board, mainly consisting of family members, had 'dominated discussions' and had discouraged the expression of views from the company's external shareholders. JPX had no non-executive directors and none of the board committee structure that many listed companies like Chemco had in place. Bill reported that although JPX's department heads were all directors, they were not invited to attend board meetings when strategy and management monitoring issues were being discussed. They were, he said, treated more like middle management by the upper tier of the JPX board and that important views may not be being heard when devising strategy. Leena suggested that these features made the JPX board's upper tier less externally accountable and less likely to take advice when making decisions. She said that board accountability was fundamental to public trust and that JPX's board might do well to recognise this, especially if the acquisition were to go ahead.

Chemco's finance director, Susan Brown advised caution over the whole acquisition proposal. She saw the proposal as being very risky. In addition to the uncertainties over exposure to foreign markets, she believed that Chemco would also have difficulties with integrating JPX into the Chemco culture and structure. While Chemco was fully compliant with corporate governance best practice, the country in which JPX was based had few corporate governance requirements. Manprit Randhawa, Chemco's operations director, asked Bill if he knew anything about JPX's risk exposure. Manprit suggested that the acquisition of JPX might expose Chemco to a number of risks that could not only affect the success of the proposed acquisition but also, potentially, Chemco itself. Bill replied that he would look at the risks in more detail if the Chemco board agreed to take the proposal forward to its next stage.

Finance director Susan Brown, had obtained the most recent annual report for JPX and highlighted what she considered to be an interesting, but unexplained, comment about 'negative local environmental impact' in its accounts. She asked chief executive Bill White if he could find out what the comment meant and whether JPX had any plans to make provision for any environmental impact. Bill White was able to report, based on his previous dealings with JPX, that it did not produce any voluntary environmental reporting. The Chemco board broadly supported the idea of environmental reporting although company secretary Leena Sharif recently told Bill White that she was unaware of the meaning of the terms 'environmental footprint' and 'environmental reporting' and so couldn't say whether she was supportive or not. It was agreed, however, that relevant information on JPX's environmental performance and risk would be necessary if the acquisition went ahead.

Required:

(a) Evaluate JPX's current corporate governance arrangements and explain why they are likely to be considered inadequate by the Chemco board. **(10 marks)**

(b) Manprit suggested that the acquisition of JPX might expose Chemco to a number of risks. Illustrating from the case as required, identify the risks that Chemco might incur in acquiring JPX and explain how risk can be assessed. **(15 marks)**

(c) Construct the case for JPX adopting a unitary board structure after the proposed acquisition. Your answer should include an explanation of the advantages of unitary boards and a convincing case FOR the JPX board changing to a unitary structure.

(10 marks)

(Including 2 professional marks)

(d) Explain FOUR roles of non-executive directors (NEDs) and assess the specific contributions that NEDs could make to improve the governance of the JPX board.

(7 marks)

(e) Write a memo to Leena Sharif defining 'environmental footprint' and briefly explaining the importance of environmental reporting for JPX. **(8 marks)**

(Including 2 professional marks)

(Total: 50 marks)

SECTION B – TWO QUESTIONS ONLY TO BE ATTEMPTED

2   ABC CO

In a recent case, it emerged that Frank Finn, a sales director at ABC Co, had been awarded a substantial over-inflation annual basic pay award with no apparent link to performance. When a major institutional shareholder, Swanland Investments, looked into the issue, it emerged that Mr Finn had a cross directorship with Joe Ng, an executive director of DEF Co. Mr Ng was a non-executive director of ABC and chairman of its remunerations committee. Swanland Investments argued at the annual general meeting that there was 'a problem with the independence' of Mr Ng and further, that Mr Finn's remuneration package as a sales director was considered to be poorly aligned to Swanland's interests because it was too much weighted by basic pay and contained inadequate levels of incentive.

Swanland Investments proposed that the composition of Mr Finn's remuneration package be reconsidered by the remunerations committee and that Mr Ng should not be present during the discussion. Another of the larger institutional shareholders, Hanoi House, objected to this, proposing instead that Mr Ng and Mr Finn both resign from their respective non-executive directorships as there was 'clear evidence of malpractice'. Swanland considered this too radical a step, as Mr Ng's input was, in its opinion, valuable on ABC's board.

Required:

(a)   Explain FOUR roles of a remunerations committee and how the cross directorship undermines these roles at ABC Co.   **(12 marks)**

(b)   Swanland Investments believed Mr Finn's remunerations package to be 'poorly aligned' to its interests. With reference to the different components of a director's remunerations package, explain how Mr Finn's remuneration might be more aligned to shareholders' interests at ABC Co.   **(8 marks)**

(c)   Evaluate the proposal from Hanoi House that both Mr Ng and Mr Finn be required to resign from their respective non-executive positions.   **(5 marks)**

(Total: 25 marks)

3   PROFESSIONAL CODES OF ETHICS

At a recent conference on corporate social responsibility, one speaker (Professor Cheung) argued that professional codes of ethics for accountants were not as useful as some have claimed because:

'they assume professional accountants to be rules-driven, when in fact most professionals are more driven by principles that guide and underpin all aspects of professional behaviour, including professional ethics.'

When quizzed from the audience about his views on the usefulness of professional codes of ethics, Professor Cheung suggested that the costs of writing, implementing, disseminating and monitoring ethical codes outweighed their usefulness. He said that as long as professional accountants personally observe the highest values of probity and integrity then there is no need for detailed codes of ethics.

Required:

(a)   Critically evaluate Professor Cheung's views on codes of professional ethics. Use examples of ethical codes, where appropriate, to illustrate your answer.   **(11 marks)**

(b)   With reference to Professor Cheung's comments, explain what is meant by 'integrity' and assess its importance as an underlying principle in corporate governance.

(7 marks)

(c)   Explain and contrast a deontological with a consequentialist based approach to business ethics.   **(7 marks)**

(Total: 25 marks)

4   FF CO

As part of a review of its internal control systems, the board of FF Co, a large textiles company, has sought your advice as a senior accountant in the company.

FF's stated objective has always been to adopt the highest standards of internal control because it believes that by doing so it will not only provide shareholders with confidence in its governance but also enhance its overall reputation with all stakeholders. In recent years, however, FF's reputation for internal control has been damaged somewhat by a qualified audit statement last year (over issues of compliance with financial standards) and an unfortunate internal incident the year prior to that. This incident concerned an employee, Miss Osula, expressing concern about the compliance of one of the company's products with an international standard on fire safety. She raised the issue with her immediate manager but he said, according to Miss Osula, that it wasn't his job to report her concerns to senior management. When she failed to obtain a response herself from senior management, she decided to report the lack of compliance to the press. This significantly embarrassed the company and led to a substantial deterioration in FF's reputation.

The specifics of the above case concerned a fabric produced by FF Co, which, in order to comply with an international fire safety standard, was required to resist fire for ten minutes when in contact with a direct flame. According to Miss Osula, who was a member of the quality control staff, FF was allowing material rated at only five minutes fire resistance to be sold labelled as ten minute rated. In her statement to the press, Miss Osula said that there was a culture of carelessness in FF and that this was only one example of the way the company approached issues such as international fire safety standards.

Required:

(a)   Describe how the internal control systems at FF Co differ from a 'sound' system of internal control, such as that set out in the Turnbull guidance, for example. **(10 marks)**

(b)   Define 'reputation risk' and evaluate the potential effects of FF's poor reputation on its financial situation.   **(8 marks)**

(c)   Explain, with reference to FF as appropriate, the ethical responsibilities of a professional accountant both as an employee and as a professional.   **(7 marks)**

(Total: 25 marks)

Section 6

ANSWERS TO PILOT PAPER EXAM QUESTIONS

1   CHEMCO

(a)   **JPX's current corporate governance arrangements**

Inadequacy of JPX's current corporate governance arrangements

The case highlights a number of ways in which the corporate governance at JPX is inadequate. JPX's history as a privately run family business may partly explain its apparent slowness to develop the corporate governance structures and systems expected in many parts of the world. There are five ways, from the case, that JPX can be said to be inadequate in its corporate governance although these are linked. There is overlap between the points made.

In the first instance, the case mentions that there were no non-executive directors (NEDs) on the JPX board. It follows that JPX would be without the necessary balance and external expertise that NEDs can provide. Second, there is evidence of a corporate culture at JPX dominated by the members of the family. The case study notes that they dominate the upper tier of the board. This may have been acceptable when JPX was a family owned company, but as a public company floated on a stock exchange and hence accountable to external shareholders, a wider participation in board membership is necessary. Third, the two-tier board, whilst not necessarily being a problem in itself (two-tier boards work well in many circumstances), raises concern because the department heads, who are on the lower tier of the board, are excluded from strategic discussions at board level. It is likely that as line managers in the business, the departmental heads would have vital inputs to make into such discussions, especially on such issues as the implementation of strategies. It is also likely that their opinions on the viabilities of different strategic options would be of value. Fourth, it could be argued that JPX's reporting is less than ideal with, for example, its oblique reference to a 'negative local environmental impact'. However, it might be noted that ambiguity in reporting is also evident in European and American reporting. Finally, having been subject to its own country's less rigorous corporate governance requirements for all of its previous history, it is likely that adjusting to the requirements of complying with the European-centred demands of Chemco will present a challenge.

(b)   **Risks of the proposed acquisition**

Risks that Chemco might incur in acquiring JPX

The case describes a number of risks that Chemco could become exposed to if the acquisition was successful. Explicitly, the case highlights a possible environmental risk (the 'negative local environmental impact') that may or may not be eventually valued as a provision (depending on whether or not it is likely to result in a liability). Other risks are likely to emerge as the proposed acquisition develops. Exchange rate risks apply to any business dealing with revenue or capital flows between two or more currency zones. The case explicitly describes Chemco and JPX existing in different regions of the world. Whilst exchange rate volatility can undermine confidence in cash flow projections, it should also be borne in mind that medium term increases or decreases in exchange values can materially affect the returns on an investment (in this case, Chemco's investment in JPX). There is some market risk in Chemco's valuation of JPX stock. This could be a substantial risk because of JPX's relatively recent flotation where the market price of JPX may not have yet found its intrinsic level. In addition, it is not certain that Chemco has full knowledge of the fair price to pay for each JPX share given the issues of dealing across national borders and in valuing stock in JPX's country. All mergers and acquisitions ('integrations') are exposed to synergy risks. Whilst it is expected and hoped that every merger or acquisition will result in synergies (perhaps from scale economies as the case mentions), in practice, many integrations fail to realise any. In extreme cases, the costs arising from integration can threaten the very survival of the companies involved. Finally, there are risks associated with the bringing-together of the two board structures. Specifically, structural and cultural changes will be required at JPX to bring it in line with Chemco's. The creation of a unitary board and the increased involvement of NEDs and departmental heads may be problematic, for example, Chemco's board is likely to insist on such changes post-acquisition.

Assessment of risk

The assessment of the risk exposure of any organisation has five components. Firstly, the identity (nature and extent) of the risks facing the company should be identified (such as considering the risks involved in acquiring JPX). This may involve consulting with relevant senior managers, consultants and other stakeholders. Second, the company should decide on the categories of risk that are regarded as acceptable for the company to bear. Of course any decision to discontinue exposure to a given risk will have implications for the activities of the company and this cost will need to be considered against the benefit of the reduced risk. Third, the assessment of risk should quantify, as far as possible, the likelihood (probability) of the identified risks materialising. Risks with a high probability of occurring will attract higher levels of management attention than those with lower probabilities. Fourth, an assessment of risk will entail an examination of the company's ability to reduce the impact on the business of risks that do materialise. Consultation with affected parties (e.g. departmental heads, stakeholders, etc.) is likely to be beneficial, as information on minimising negative impact may sometimes be a matter of technical detail. Fifth and finally, risk assessment involves an understanding of the costs of operating particular controls to review and manage the related risks. These costs will include information gathering costs, management overhead, external consultancy where appropriate, etc.

(c) **Unitary and two-tier board structures**

Advantages of unitary board structure in general

There are arguments for and against unitary and two-tier boards. Both have their 'place' depending on business cultures, size of business and a range of other factors. In general, however, the following arguments can be put for unitary boards.

One of the main features of a unitary board is that all directors, including managing directors, departmental (or divisional) directors and NEDs all have equal legal and executive status in law. This does not mean that all are equal in terms of the organisational hierarchy, but that all are responsible and can be held accountable for board decisions. This has a number of benefits. Firstly, NEDs are empowered, being accorded equal status to executive directors. NEDs can bring not only independent scrutiny to the board, but also experience and expertise that may be of invaluable help in devising strategy and the assessment of risk. Second, board accountability is enhanced by providing a greater protection against fraud and malpractice and by holding all directors equally accountable under a 'cabinet government' arrangement. These first two benefits provide a major underpinning to the confidence that markets have in listed companies. Third, unitary board arrangements reduce the likelihood of abuse of (self-serving) power by a small number of senior directors. Small 'exclusivist' boards such as have been evident in some corporate 'scandals' are discouraged by unitary board arrangements. Fourth, the fact that the board is likely to be larger than a given tier of a two-tier board means that more viewpoints are likely to be expressed in board deliberations and discussions. In addition to enriching the intellectual strength of the board, the inclusivity of the board should mean that strategies are more robustly scrutinised before being implemented.

Relevance to JPX in particular

If the JPX acquisition was to proceed, there would be a unitary board at Chemco overseeing a two-tier board at JPX. The first specific argument for JPX adopting a unitary board would be to bring it into line with Chemco's. Chemco clearly believes in unitary board arrangements and would presumably prefer to have the benefits of unitary boards in place so as to have as much confidence as possible in JPX's governance. This may be especially important if JPX is to remain an 'arms length' or decentralised part of Chemco's international operation. Second, there is an argument for making changes at JPX in order to signal a departure from the 'old' systems when JPX was independent of the 'new' systems under Chemco's ownership. A strong way of helping to 'unfreeze' previous ways of working is to make important symbolic changes and a rearrangement of the board structure would be a good example of this. Third, it is clear that the family members who currently run JPX have a disproportionate influence on the company and its strategy (the 'family business culture'). Widening the board would, over time, change the culture of the board and reduce that influence. Fourth, a unitary board structure would empower the departmental heads at JPX whose opinions and support are likely to be important in the transition period following the acquisition.

(d) **Non executive directors**

Four roles of non-executive directors

The Higgs Report (2003) in the United Kingdom helpfully described the function of non-executive directors (NEDs) in terms of four distinct roles. These were the strategy role, the scrutinising role, the risk advising role and the 'people' role. These roles may be undertaken as part of the general discussion occurring at board meetings or more formally, through the corporate governance committee structure.

The strategy role recognises that NEDs are full members of a unitary board and thus have the right and responsibility to contribute to the strategic success of the organisation for the benefit of shareholders. In this role they may challenge any aspect of strategy they see fit, and offer advice or input to help to develop successful strategy.

In the scrutinising role, NEDs are required to hold executive colleagues to account for decisions taken and results obtained. In this respect they are required to represent the shareholders' interests against the possibility that agency issues arise to reduce shareholder value.

The risk role involves NEDs ensuring the company has an adequate system of internal controls and systems of risk management in place. This is often informed by prescribed codes (such as Turnbull) but some industries, such as chemicals, have other systems in place, some of which fall under International Organisation for Standardisation (ISO) standards.

Finally, the 'people' role involves NEDs overseeing a range of responsibilities with regard to the management of the executive members of the board. This typically involves issues on appointments and remuneration, but might also involve contractual or disciplinary issues.

Specific benefits for JPX of having NEDs

The specific benefits that NEDs could bring to JPX concern the need for a balance against excessive family influence and the prior domination of the 'family business culture'. Chemco, as JPX's new majority shareholder, is unlikely to want to retain a 'cabal' of an upper tier at JPX and the recruitment of a number of NEDs will clearly help in that regard. Second, NEDs will perform an important role in representing external shareholders' interests (as well as internal shareholders). Specifically, shareholders will include Chemco. Third, Chemco's own board discussion included Bill White's view that the exclusion of departmental heads was resulting in important views not being heard when devising strategy. This is a major potential danger to JPX and NEDs could be appointed to the board in order to ensure that future board discussions include all affected parties including the previously disenfranchised department heads.

(e)   **Environmental reporting**

Memorandum

From:	Professional Accountant
To:	Leena Sharif
Date:	DD/MM/YYYY
Subject:	Environmental issues at Chemco and JPX

(1)   **Introduction**

I have been asked to write to you on two matters of potential importance to Chemco in respect of environmental issues. The first of these is to consider the meaning of the term, 'environmental footprint' and the second is to briefly review the arguments for inviting JPX (should the acquisition proceed) to introduce environmental reporting.

(2)   **'Environmental footprint'**

Explanation of 'environmental footprint'

The use of the term 'footprint' with regard to the environment is intended to convey a meaning similar to its use in everyday language. In the same way that humans and animals leave physical footprints that show where they have been, so organisations such as Chemco leave evidence of their operations in the environment. They operate at a net cost to the environment. The environmental footprint is an attempt to evaluate the size of Chemco's impact on the environment in three respects. Firstly, concerning the company's resource consumption where resources are defined in terms of inputs such as energy, feedstock, water, land use, etc. Second, concerning any harm to the environment brought about by pollution emissions. These include emissions of carbon and other chemicals, local emissions, spillages, etc. It is likely that as a chemical manufacturer, both of these impacts will be larger for Chemco than for some other types of business. Thirdly, the environmental footprint includes a measurement of the resource consumption and pollution emissions in terms of harm to the environment in either qualitative, quantitative or replacement terms.

(3)   **Environmental reporting at JPX**

Arguments for environmental reporting at JPX

There are number of arguments for environmental reporting in general and others that may be specifically relevant to JPX. In general terms and firstly, I'm sure as company secretary you will recognise the importance of observing the corporate governance and reporting principles of transparency, openness, responsibility and fairness wherever possible. We should invite JPX to adopt these values should the acquisition proceed. Any deliberate concealment would clearly be counter to these principles and so 'more' rather than 'less' reporting is always beneficial. Second, it is important to present a balanced and understandable assessment of the company's position and prospects to external stakeholders. Third, it is important that JPX recognises the existence and size of its environmental footprint, and reporting is a useful means if doing this. Fourth, and specifically with regard to JPX and other companies with a substantial potential environmental footprint, there is a need to explain environmental strategy to investors and other interested stakeholders (e.g. Chemco). Finally, there is a need to explain in more detail the 'negative local environmental impact' and an environmental report would be an ideal place for such an explanation.

Summary:

As JPX's 'environmental footprint' is potentially quite large, it is important that Chemco ensures as far as possible, that any such footprint left by JPX is known and measured. Additionally, in the interests of transparency, openness, responsibility and fairness, it is important that it is also fully reported upon for the information of both investors and other interested stakeholders.

ACCA marking scheme		Marks
(a)	Up to two marks per valid point made on the inadequacy of JPX'x governance	Max 10
(b)	One mark for identifying and describing each risk to Chemco in the JPX acquisition up to a maximum of six. Up to one mark per relevant point on assessing each risk and a further one mark for development of relevant points up to a maximum of ten.	Max 15
(c)	One mark for each relevant point made.	
	(i) Explanation of the advantages of unitary boards.	Max 4
	(ii) Case concerning the advantages of a unitary board at JPX	Max 5
	(iii) Clarity and persuasiveness of the argument for change in the JPX board.	Max 2
		Max 10
(d)	One mark for each explanation of the four roles of non-executive directors.	Max 4
	One mark for each specific benefit of NEDs to JPX	Max 4
		Max 7
(e)	Memo to Leena Sharif explaining environmental footprint – one mark for each relevant point made	Max 2
	Explain importance of environmental reporting – one mark for each relevant point made	Max 4
	Up to two marks for the form of the answer (memo in which content is laid out in an orderly and informative manner).	Max 8
Total		**50**

2 ABC CO

(a) **Remunerations committees and cross directorships**

Remunerations committees

Remunerations committees comprise an important part of the standard board committee structure of good corporate governance.

The major roles of a remuneration committee are as follows. Firstly, the committee is charged with determining remunerations policy on behalf of the board and the shareholders. In this regard, they are acting on behalf of shareholders but for the benefit of both shareholders and the other members of the board. Policies will typically concern the pay scales applied to directors' packages, the proportions of different types of reward within the overall package and the periods in which performance related elements become payable.

Secondly the committee ensures that each director is fairly but responsibly rewarded for their individual contribution in terms of levels of pay and the components of each director's package. It is likely that discussions of this type will take place for each individual director and will take into account issues including market conditions, retention needs, long-term strategy and market rates for a given job.

Third, the remunerations committee reports to the shareholders on the outcomes of their decisions, usually in the corporate governance section of the annual report (usually called Report of the Remunerations Committee). This report, which is auditor reviewed, contains a breakdown of each director's remuneration and a commentary on policies applied to executive and non-executive remuneration.

Finally, where appropriate and required by statute or voluntary code, the committee is required to be seen to be compliant with relevant laws or codes of best practice. This will mean that the remunerations committee will usually be made up of non-executive members of the board and will meet at regular intervals.

Cross directorships

Cross directorships represent a threat to the efficient working of remunerations committees. A cross directorship is said to exist when two (or more) directors sit on the boards of the other. In practice, such arrangements also involve some element of cross-shareholdings which further compromises the independence of the directors involved. In most cases, each director's 'second' board appointment is likely to be non-executive. Cross directorships undermine the roles of remunerations committees in that a director deciding the salary of a colleague who, in turn, may play a part in deciding his or her own salary, is a clear conflict of interests. Neither director involved in the arrangement is impartial and so a temptation would exist to act in a manner other than for the benefit of the shareholders of the company on whose remunerations committee they sit. It is for this reason the cross directorships and cross shareholding arrangements are explicitly forbidden by many corporate governance codes of best practice.

(b) **Mr Finn's remunerations package**

Different components of directors' rewards

The components of a director's total rewards package may include any or all of the following in combination. The basic salary is not linked to performance in the short run but year-to-year changes in it may be linked to some performance measures. It is intended to recognise the basic market value of a director. A number of benefits in kind may be used which will vary by position and type of organisation, but typically include company cars, health insurance, use of health or leisure facilities, subsidised or free use of company products (if appropriate), etc. Pension contributions are paid by most responsible employers, but separate directors' schemes may be made available at higher contribution rates than other employees. Finally, various types of incentives and performance related components may be used. Short to medium term incentives such as performance-related annual bonuses will encourage a relatively short term approach to meeting agreed targets whilst long term incentives including share options can be used for longer term performance measures.

Mr Finn's remuneration package

The case mentions that, 'Mr Finn's remuneration package as a sales director was considered to be poorly aligned to Swanland's interests because it was too much weighted by basic pay and contained inadequate levels of incentive.'

The alignment of director and shareholder interests occurs through a careful design of the performance related components of a director's overall rewards. The strategic emphases of the business can be built into these targets and Mr Finn's position as a sales director makes this possible through incentives based on revenue or profit targets. If current priorities are for the maximisation of relatively short-run returns, annual, semi-annual or even monthly performance-related bonuses could be used. More likely at board level, however, will be a need for longer-term alignments for medium to long-term value maximisation. While Mr Finn may be given annual or even quarterly or monthly bonus payments against budget, longer-term performance can be underpinned through share options with a relevant maturity date or end-of-service payouts with agreed targets. The balance of short and longer-term performance bonuses should be carefully designed for each director with metrics within the control of the director in question.

(c) **Evaluation of the proposal from Hanoi House**

The dilemma over what action to take in the light of Mr Ng and Mr Finn's cross directorship is a typical problem when deciding how to address issues of conflicts of interest. Should the situation be 'put right' at minimum cost, or should the parties in the arrangement be punished in some way as Hanoi House suggested? Swanland's more equivocal suggestion (that the remunerations committee reconsider Mr Finn's remuneration package without Mr Ng being present) may be more acceptable to some shareholders. This debate touches on the ethical issues of a pragmatic approach to some issues compared to a dogmatic approach.

For the proposal

Hanoi House's more radical proposal would have a number of potential advantages. Specifically, it could be argued that the resignation of both men from their respective NED positions would restore ABC shareholders' confidence in the remunerations committee. The appearance of probity is sometimes as important as the substance and resignations can sometimes serve to purge a problem to everybody's (except for the director in question's) benefit. The double resignation would signal a clean break in the apparently compromising relationship between Mr Finn and Mr Ng and, certainly as far as ABC was concerned, would resolve the problem decisively. It would signal the importance that ABC placed on compliance with corporate governance best practice and this, in turn, would be of comfort to shareholders and analysts concerned with the threat to the independence of ABC's remunerations committee.

Against the proposal

Hanoi House's proposal was seen as too radical for Swanland. Among its concerns was the belief that only Mr Ng's resignation from ABC's remunerations committee would be strictly necessary to diffuse the situation. Clearly Swanland saw no problem with Mr Finn's position on the ABC board in his executive capacity. Furthermore, it took a pragmatic view of Mr Ng's position as NED on ABC's board. It considered Mr Ng's input to be valuable on the ABC board and pointed out that this input would be lost if Hanoi House's proposal was put into practice. Hanoi House may therefore have been mindful of the assumed deficit of talent at senior strategic level in corporate management and accordingly, wished to retain both Mr Finn's and Mr Ng's expertise if at all possible.

ACCA marking scheme			Marks
(a) (i)		One mark for each valid point made up to a maximum of two for demonstrating an understanding of cross directorships.	Max 2
	(ii)	Award up to two marks for each valid point made on roles of remunerations committees	Max 8
	(iii)	Award up to two marks for each valid point on undermining the roles	Max 4
			Max 12
(b)		One mark for each component of a director's remuneration correctly identified.	Max 4
		One mark for each relevant point describing how Finn's remuneration might be more aligned to shareholders' interests.	Max 5
			Max 8
(c) (a)		One mark for each point evaluating the proposal from Hanoi House:	
		Arguments in favour	Max 3
		Arguments against	Max 3
			Max 5
Total			**25**

3 PROFESSIONAL CODES OF ETHICS

(a) **Professor Cheung's views on codes of professional ethics**

Professor Cheung adopts a sceptical stance with regard to codes of ethics. There are arguments both supporting and challenging his views.

Supporting Professor Cheung's opinion

Professional codes of ethics have a number of limitations, some of which Professor Cheung referred to. Because they contain descriptions of situations that accountants might encounter, they can convey the (false) impression that professional ethics can be reduced to a set of rules contained in a code (as pointed out by Professor Cheung). This would be a mistaken impression, of course, as the need for personal integrity is also emphasised. Ethical codes do not and cannot capture all ethical circumstances and dilemmas that a professional accountant will encounter in his or her career and this reinforces the need for accountants to understand the underlying ethical principles of probity, integrity, openness, transparency and fairness. Although codes such as IFAC's are intended to apply to an international 'audience', some may argue that regional variations in cultural, social and ethical norms mean that such codes cannot capture important differences in emphasis in some parts of the world. The moral 'right' can be prescribed in every situation.

Finally, professional codes of ethics are not technically enforceable in any legal manner although sanctions exist for gross breach of the code in some jurisdictions. Individual observance of ethical codes is effectively voluntary in most circumstances.

Against Professor Cheung's opinion

There are a number of arguments for codes of professional ethics that challenge Professor Cheung's views. Firstly, professional codes of ethics signal the importance, to accountants, of ethics and acting in the public interest in the professional accounting environment. They are reminded, unambiguously and in 'black and white' for example, that as with other professions, accounting exists to serve the public good and public support for the profession is likely to exist only as long as the public interest is supported over and above competing interests. The major international codes (such as IFAC) underpin national and regional cultures with internationally expected standards that, the codes insist, supersede any national ethical nuances. The IFAC (2003) code states (in clause 4), 'the accountancy profession throughout the world operates in an environment with different cultures and regulatory requirements. The basic intent of the Code, however, should always be respected.' The codes prescribe minimum standards of behaviour expected in given situations and give specific examples of potentially problematic areas in accounting practice. In such situations, the codes make the preferred course of action unambiguous.

A number of codes of ethics exist for professional accountants. Prominent among these is the IFAC code. This places the public interest at the heart of the ethical conduct of accountants. The ACCA code discusses ethics from within a principles-based perspective. Other countries' own professional accounting bodies have issued their own codes of ethics in the belief that they may better describe the ethical situations in those countries.

(b) **Integrity**

Meaning of 'integrity'

Integrity is generally understood to describe a person of high moral virtue. A person of integrity is one who observes a steadfast adherence to a strict moral or ethical code notwithstanding any other pressures on him or her to act otherwise. In professional life, integrity describes the personal ethical position of the highest standards of professionalism and probity. It is an underlying and underpinning principle of corporate governance and it is required that all those representing shareholder interests in agency relationships both possess and exercise absolute integrity at all times. To fail to do so is a breach of the agency trust relationship.

Importance of integrity in corporate governance

Integrity is important in corporate governance for several reasons. Codes of ethics do not capture all ethical situations and the importance of the virtue of the actor rather than the ethics of the action is therefore emphasised. Any profession (such as accounting) relies upon a public perception of competence and integrity and in this regard, accounting can perhaps be compared with medicine. As an underlying principle, integrity provides a basic ethical framework to guide an accountant's professional and personal life. Finally, integrity underpins the relationships that an accountant has with his or her clients, auditors and other colleagues. Trust is vital in the normal conduct of these relationships and integrity underpins this.

(c) **Deontology and consequentialism**

Deontological ethics

The deontological perspective can be broadly understood in terms of 'means' being more important than 'ends'. It is broadly based on Kantian (categorical imperative) ethics. The rightness of an action is judged by its intrinsic virtue and thus morality is seen as absolute and not situational. An action is right if it would, by its general adoption, be of net benefit to society. Lying, for example, is deemed to be ethically wrong because lying, if adopted in all situations, would lead to the deterioration of society.

Consequentialist ethics

The consequentialist or teleological perspective is based on utilitarian or egoist ethics meaning that the rightness of an action is judged by the quality of the outcome. From the egoist perspective, the quality of the outcome refers to the individual ('what is best for me?'). Utilitarianism measures the quality of outcome in terms of the greatest happiness of the greatest number ('what is best for the majority?'). Consequentialist ethics are therefore situational and contingent, and not absolute.

ACCA marking scheme		Marks
(a)	One mark for each valid point made supporting codes of professional ethics.	Max 6
	One mark for each valid point made on limitations of codes of professional ethics	Max 6
	Up to two marks for using an actual code of ethics by way of example.	Max 2
		Max 11
(b)	Definition of integrity – one mark for each relevant point	Max 4
	Importance of integrity – one mark for each relevant point	Max 4
		Max 7
(c)	Explanation of deontology – one mark for each valid point	Max 4
	Explanation of consequentialism – one mark for each valid point	Max 4
		Max 7
Total		**25**

4   FF CO

(a)   **FF Co and a 'sound' system of internal control**

Features of sound control systems

The Turnbull code employs the term 'sound' to indicate that it is insufficient to simply 'have' an internal control system. They can be effective and serve the aim of corporate governance or they can be ineffective and fail to support them. In order to reinforce 'soundness' or effectiveness, systems need to possess a number of features. The Turnbull guidance described three features of a 'sound' internal control system.

Firstly, the principles of internal control should be embedded within the organisation's structures, procedures and culture. Internal control should not be seen as a stand-alone set of activities and by embedding it into the fabric of the organisation's infrastructure, awareness of internal control issues becomes everybody's business and this contributes to effectiveness.

Secondly, internal control systems should be capable of responding quickly to evolving risks to the business arising from factors within the company and to changes in the business environment. The speed of reaction is an important feature of almost all control systems (for example a servo system for vehicle brakes or the thermostat on a heating system). Any change in the risk profile or environment of the organisation will necessitate a change in the system and a failure or slowness to respond may increase the vulnerability to internal or external trauma.

Thirdly, sound internal control systems include procedures for reporting immediately to appropriate levels of management any significant control failings or weaknesses that are identified, together with details of corrective action being undertaken. Information flows to relevant levels of management capable and empowered to act on the information are essential in internal control systems. Any failure, frustration, distortion or obfuscation of information flows can compromise the system. For this reason, formal and relatively rigorous information channels are often instituted in organisations seeking to maximise the effectiveness of their internal control systems.

Shortcomings at FF Co

The case highlights a number of ways in which the internal control at FF fell short of that expected of a 'sound' internal control system. First, and most importantly, the case suggests that the culture of FF did not support good internal control. Miss Osula made reference to, 'culture of carelessness in FF' and said that the issue over the fire safety standards, 'was only one example of the way the company approached issues such as international fire safety standards.' While having systems in place to support sound internal control, it is also important to have a culture that also places a high priority on it. Second, there is evidence of a lack of internal control and reporting procedures at FF. Not only was the incorrect fire-rating labelling not corrected by senior management, the attempt to bring the matter to the attention of management was also not well-received.

Third, there is evidence of structural/premeditated contravention of standards (and financial standards) at FF. In addition to the fire safety issue, the case makes reference to a qualified audit statement over issues of compliance with financial standards. There is ample evidence for shareholders to question the competence of management's ability to manage the internal control systems at FF.

(b) **Reputation risk**

Defining reputation risk

Reputation risk is one of the categories of risk used in organisations. It was identified as a risk category by Turnbull and a number of events in various parts of the world have highlighted the importance of this risk. Reputation risk concerns any kind of deterioration in the way in which the organisation is perceived, usually, but not exclusively, from the point of view of external stakeholders. The cause of such deterioration may be due to irregular behaviour, compliance failure or similar, but in any event, the effect is an aspect of corporate behaviour below that expected by one or more stakeholder. When the 'disappointed' stakeholder has contractual power over the organisation, the cost of the reputation risk may be material.

Effects of poor reputation on

There are several potential effects of reputation risk on an affected organisation. When more than one stakeholder group has reason to question the otherwise good reputation of an organisation, the effect can be a downward spiral leading to a general lack of confidence which, in turn, can have unfortunate financial effects. In particular, however, reputation risk is likely to affect one or more of the organisation's interactions with resource providers, product buyers, investors or auditors/regulators. Resource provision (linked to resource dependency theory) may affect recruitment, financing or the ability to obtain other inputs such as (in extremis) real estate, stock or intellectual capital. Within product markets, damage to reputation can reduce confidence among customers leading to reduced sales values and volumes and, in extreme cases, boycotts. Investor confidence is important in public companies where any reputation risk is likely to be reflected in market value. Finally, auditors, representing the interests of shareholders, would have reason to exercise increased scrutiny if, say, there are problems with issues of trust in a company. It would be a similar situation if the affected organisation were in an industry subject to high levels of regulation.

FF and reputation

At FF, the sources of the potential threat to its reputation arise from a failure to meet an external standard, an issue over product confidence and a qualified audit statement. The failure to meet an external standard concerned compliance with international fire safety standards. The issue over product confidence involved selling one product falsely rated higher than the reality. These would be likely to affect customer confidence and the attitude of any fire safety accrediting body. The qualified audit statement would be likely to intensify the attention to detail paid by auditors in subsequent years.

(c) **Ethical responsibilities of a professional accountant**

A professional accountant has two 'directions' of responsibility: one to his or her employer and another to the highest standards of professionalism.

Responsibilities to employer

An accountant's responsibilities to his or her employer extend to acting with diligence, probity and with the highest standards of care in all situations. In addition, however, an employer might reasonably expect the accountant to observe employee confidentiality as far as possible. In most situations, this will extend to absolute discretion of all sensitive matters both during and after the period of employment. The responsibilities also include the expectation that the accountant will act in shareholders' interests as far as possible and that he or she will show loyalty within the bounds of legal and ethical good practice.

Responsibilities as a professional

In addition to an accountant's responsibilities to his or her employer, there is a further set of expectations arising from his or her membership of the accounting profession. In the first instance, professional accountants are expected to observe the letter and spirit of the law in detail and of professional ethical codes where applicable (depending on country of residence, qualifying body, etc.). In any professional or ethical situation where codes do not clearly apply, a professional accountant should apply 'principles-based' ethical standards (such as integrity and probity) such that they would be happy to account for their behaviour if so required. Finally, and in common with members of other professions, accountants are required to act in the public interest that may, in extremis, involve reporting an errant employer to the relevant authorities. This may be the situation that an accountant may find him or herself in at FF. It would clearly be unacceptable to be involved in any form of deceit and it would be the accountant's duty to help to correct such malpractice if at all possible.

ACCA marking scheme			
			Marks
(a)	Description of 'sound' control systems – up to two marks for each valid point made		Max 6
	Explanation of shortcomings at FF plc – one mark for each valid point		Max 6
			Max 10
(b)	Definition of 'reputation risk' – one mark for each valid point made		Max 3
	Explanation of the financial effects of poor reputation – one mark for each valid point made		Max 4

	Recognition of the causes of FF's reputation problems – one mark for each valid point made	Max 2
		Max 8
(c)	Responsibilities to employer – one mark for each valid point made	Max 4
	Responsibilities to professionalism – one mark for each valid point made	Max 4
		Max 7
Total		**25**

Section 7

PILOT PAPER EXAM QUESTIONS – SUPPLEMENT

1   JH GRAPHICS

The board of JH Graphics, a design and artwork company, was debating an agenda item on the possible adoption of a corporate code of ethics. Jenny Harris, the chief executive and majority shareholder, was a leading supporter of the idea. She said that many of the large companies in the industry had adopted codes of ethics and that she thought it would signal the importance that JH Graphics placed on ethics. She also said that she was personally driven by high ethical values and that she wanted to express these through her work and through the company's activities and policies.

Alan Leroy, the creative director, explained that he would support the adoption of the code of ethics as long as it helped to support the company's long-term strategic objectives. He said that he could see no other reason as the company was 'not a charity' and had to maximise shareholder value above all other objectives. In particular, he was keen, as a shareholder himself, to know what the code would cost to draw up and how much it would cost to comply with it over and above existing costs.

Jenny argued that having a code would help to resolve some ethical issues, one of which, she suggested, was a problem the company was having over a particular image it had recently produced for a newspaper advertisement. The image was produced for an advertising client and although the client was pleased, it had offended a particular religious group because of its content and design.

When it was discovered who had produced the 'offending' image, some religious leaders criticised JH Graphics for being insensitive and offensive to their religion. For a brief time, the events were a major news story. As politicians, journalists and others debated the issues in the media, the board of JH Graphics was involved in intense discussions and faced with a dilemma as to whether or not to issue a public apology for the offence caused by the image and to ask the client to withdraw it.

Alan argued that having a code of ethics would not have helped in that situation, as the issue was so complicated. His view was that the company should not apologise for the image and that he didn't care very much that the image offended people. He said it was bringing the company free publicity and that was good for the business. Jenny said that she had sympathy for the viewpoint of the offended religious leaders. Although she disagreed with them, she understood the importance to some people of firmly-held beliefs. The board agreed that as there seemed to be arguments both ways, the decision on how the company should deal with the image should be Jenny's as chief executive.

Required:

(a)   Analyse Jenny's and Alan's motivations for adopting the code of ethics using the normative-instrumental forms of stakeholder theory.   **(8 marks)**

(b) Assess Jenny's decision on the possible apology for the 'offending' image from conventional and pre-conventional moral development perspectives. **(4 marks)**

(c) Explain and assess the factors that the board of JH Graphics might consider in deciding how to respond to the controversy over the offending image. **(10 marks)**

Positive & Negative

(d) Comment on the legitimacy of the religious group's claims on JH Graphics' activities. **(3 marks)**

(Total: 25 marks)

2   FRANKS & FISHER

Size ①

The board of Franks & Fisher, a large manufacturing company, decided to set up an internal control and audit function. The proposal was to appoint an internal auditor at mid-management level and also to establish a board level internal audit committee made up mainly of non-executive directors.

Proposal.

The initiative to do so was driven by a recent period of rapid growth. The company had taken on many more activities as a result of growth in its product range. The board decided that the increased size and complexity of its operations created the need for greater control over internal activities and that an internal audit function was a good way forward. The need was highlighted by a recent event where internal quality standards were not enforced, resulting in the stoppage of a production line for several hours. The production director angrily described the stoppage as 'entirely avoidable' and the finance director, Jason Kumas, said that the stoppage had been very costly.

Mr Kumas said that there were problems with internal control in a number of areas of the company's operations and that there was a great need for internal audit. He said that as the head of the company's accounting and finance function, the new internal auditor should report to him. The reasons for this, he said, were because as an accountant, he was already familiar with auditing procedure and the fact that he already had information on budgets and other 'control' information that the internal auditor would need.

Not on finance alone Internal audit covers - operation - compliance with laws.

It was decided that the new internal auditor needed to be a person of some experience and with enough personality not to be intimidated nor diverted by other department heads who might find the internal audits an inconvenience. One debate the board had was whether it would be better to recruit to the position from inside or outside the company. A second argument was over the limits of authority that the internal auditor might be given. It was pointed out that while the board considered the role of internal audit to be very important, it didn't want it to interfere with the activities of other departments to the point where their operational effectiveness was reduced.

Required:

Reason.

(a) Explain, with reference to the case, the factors that are typically considered when deciding to establish internal audit in an organisation. **(10 marks)**

Likely

(b) Construct the argument in favour of appointing the new internal auditor from outside the company rather than promoting internally. ↳ *Outsourcing* **(6 marks)**

(c) Critically evaluate Mr Kumas's belief that the internal auditor should report to him as finance director. **(4 marks)**

(d) Define 'objectivity' and describe characteristics that might demonstrate an internal auditor's professional objectivity. **(5 marks)**

(Total: 25 marks)

3   EASTERN PRODUCTS

Sonia Tan, a fund manager at institutional investor Sentosa House, was reviewing the annual report of one of the major companies in her portfolio. The company, Eastern Products, had recently undergone a number of board changes as a result of a lack of confidence in its management from its major institutional investors of which Sentosa House was one. The problems started two years ago when a new chairman at Eastern Products (Thomas Hoo) started to pursue what the institutional investors regarded as very risky strategies whilst at the same time failing to comply with a stock market requirement on the number of non-executive directors on the board.

Sonia rang Eastern's investor relations department to ask why it still was not in compliance with the requirements relating to non-executive directors. She was told that because Eastern was listed in a principles-based jurisdiction, the requirement was not compulsory. It was simply that Eastern chose not to comply with that particular requirement. When Sonia asked how its board committees could be made up with an insufficient number of non-executive directors, the investor relations manager said he didn't know and that Sonia should contact the chairman directly. She was also told that there was no longer a risk committee because the chairman saw no need for one.

Sonia telephoned Thomas Hoo, the chairman of Eastern Products. She began by reminding him that Sentosa House was one of Eastern's main shareholders and currently owned 13% of the company. She went on to explain that she had concerns over the governance of Eastern Products and that she would like Thomas to explain his non-compliance with some of the stock market's requirements and also why he was pursuing strategies viewed by many investors as very risky. Thomas reminded Sonia that Eastern had outperformed its sector in terms of earnings per share in both years since he had become chairman and that rather than question him, she should trust him to run the company as he saw fit. He thanked Sentosa House for its support and hung up the phone.

Required:

(a)   Explain what an 'agency cost' is and discuss the problems that might increase agency costs for Sentosa House in the case of Eastern Products.   **(7 marks)**

(b)   Describe, with reference to the case, the conditions under which it might be appropriate for an institutional investor to intervene in a company whose shares it holds.   **(10 marks)**

(c)   Evaluate the contribution that a risk committee made up of non-executive directors could make to Sonia's confidence in the management of Eastern Products.   **(4 marks)**

(d)   Assess the opinion given to Sonia that because Eastern Products was listed in a principles-based jurisdiction, compliance with the stock market's rules was 'not compulsory'.   **(4 marks)**

                                                                                                   (Total: 25 marks)

Section 8

ANSWERS TO PILOT PAPER EXAM QUESTIONS – SUPPLEMENT

1   JH GRAPHICS

(a)   The normative-instrumental distinction describes two different approaches or underlying ethical motivations. Often applied to the ways in which organisations behave towards stakeholders, it can be applied to any situation in which ethical motivations are relevant.

In the case, Jenny Harris is demonstrating a normative approach to adoption of the corporate code of ethics. It is evident from what she says that she is internally motivated. She described herself as personally driven by high ethical values and appears to see ethical behaviour as an end in itself. She tends not to take the business implications of the proposed code into account and thereby tends towards the altruistic rather than the strategic. Her attitude is informed primarily by internal motivation rather then the pursuit of external reward.

Alan, by contrast, demonstrates instrumental characteristics. He appears to be primarily motivated by business performance and sees the ethical code as a means to further other objectives (not as an end in itself). His attitude to the code of ethics is underpinned by questions about what can be gained, for the business, of the code's adoption. Accordingly, he is strategic rather than altruistic in his motivation.

(b)   This question draws upon two of Kohlberg's three levels of moral development. In particular, it asks how the decision on possible apology for and withdrawal of the image would vary depending on whether Jenny, as the chief executive of JH Graphics, makes conventional and pre-conventional ethical assumptions.

The conventional ethical level views the moral 'right' according to whether it is compliant with the existing legal and regulatory frameworks and/or norms of the society or culture in which the decision is taking place. If the image was generally acceptable and offensive only to the religious group in question, it can probably be assumed that it was otherwise culturally inoffensive. It was certainly not illegal as no laws were broken. From the conventional level, therefore, there is no case for withdrawing the image.

The preconventional moral development level views the moral right as that which attracts the least punishment and the most reward. Whereas in the case of personal morality, such rewards and punishments are likely to be made at the personal level, the issues involved are more complex for organisations. Preconventional morality might ask, for example, whether the company is likely to be rewarded or punished by keeping or withdrawing the image. In this context, rewards or punishments are likely to be viewed in economic terms or in terms of boycotts or increased business arising from the publicity.

(c) This is a complicated ethical situation and the board of JH Graphics will be considering several factors in attempting to come to a decision over what to do with the offending image.

One factor likely to be considered is the possible effects of the dispute on the reputation of company. It is not at all certain that the row will be damaging. In some industries, possibly including graphic design, to be seen to be capable of producing provocative and challenging imagery could be advantageous whereas in other situations it may be adverse.

The company will also be likely to take into account the level and direction of public/political opinion and support. The case mentions that the controversy was a major news story and it would be necessary to find out whether the independent coverage of the issue was generally critical or generally favourable of JH Graphics. If the majority of public opinion was against JH Graphics and supportive of the religious critics, that may be influential in JH Graphics considering the withdrawal of the image.

Consideration should also be given to the economic importance of the advertisement/ client to JH Graphics. The case says that the client is happy with the image (and presumably untroubled by the religious controversy) but from JH Graphics's point of view, the question concerns how much they could possibly lose if they unilaterally withdrew the rights to use the image and thereby upset the client.

The board would also be likely to consider the possible direct influence of offended religious groups on JH Graphics. The Mendelow map, which measures the influence of a stakeholder by considering its power and interest, may be helpful in determining how influential the religious group is likely to be on the wellbeing of JH Graphics. Is it, for example, large and potentially influential (e.g. in terms of mobilising opinion) or small and unlikely to have an effect?

The directors should also assess the value of all the unexpected publicity to JH Graphics? Mr Leroy is clearly of the view that is 'was bringing the company free publicity and that was good for the business'. Whilst such a profile raising controversy might be damaging to JH Graphics, it might also be advantageous, especially if being seen as being willing to 'push the boundaries' of taste and decency is a potential source of competitive advantage. The publicity received is obviously far more than the company could afford in terms of buying publicity but this needs to be weighed against whether the publicity is good for JH or adverse.

The national culture in which the decision is taking place could have an influence on the outcome. The intensity of the debate over the importance of not causing offence will vary depending upon the national culture, which can, in turn, be influenced and underpinned by historical and religious culture.

(d) This question touches on the debate over stakeholder recognition and the limits of corporate accountability and responsibility. It is in the nature of any stakeholder that they make a 'claim' upon the activities of the organisation. The debate is over whether that claim is recognised and whether, accordingly, the nature of the claim is taken into account in decision-making.

In this instance, it is relatively uncontroversial to recognise the religious group as a stakeholder (Freeman's definition defines a stakeholder as an entity that can 'affect or be affected by…'). The perceived legitimacy of the claim depends on where the limit of accountability is drawn and the reasonableness of the claim. There is a continuum of legitimacy with, perhaps, shareholders being 'entirely legitimate' in making a claim at one extreme and terrorists as 'entirely illegitimate' at the other. The legitimacy of the religious group's claim (they are unlikely to have a direct economic relationship with JH Graphics) depends upon where that line is drawn. It might also be pointed out that offence taken by a stakeholder doesn't necessarily imply a responsibility towards the stakeholder.

ACCA marking scheme		
		Marks
(a)	1 mark for each relevant point made on normative	Max 4
	1 mark for each relevant point made on instrumental	Max 4
		Max 8
(b)	1 mark for evidence of understanding the terms	Max 2
	1 mark for application of each to case	Max 2
		Max 4
(c)	2 marks for each relevant point made	Max 10
(d)	1 mark for each relevant point made	Max 3
Total		**25**

2   FRANKS & FISHER

(a) There is an obvious cost involved in setting up internal audit in an organisation and so it is typical to ask what factors signify the need for internal audit before one is established. Several factors influence the need for internal audit:

The scale, diversity and complexity of the company's activities. The larger, the more diverse and the more complex a range of activities is, the more there is to monitor (and the more opportunity there is for certain things to go wrong).

The number of employees. As a proxy for size, the number of employees signifies that larger organisations are more likely to need internal audit to underpin investor confidence than smaller concerns.

Cost-benefit considerations. Management must be certain of the benefits that will result from establishing internal audit and it must obviously be seen to outweigh the costs of doing so.

Changes in the organisational structures, reporting processes or underlying information systems. Any internal (or external) change is capable of changing the complexity of operations and, accordingly, the risk.

Changes in key risks could be internal or external in nature. The introduction of a new product, entering a new market, a change in any of the PEST/PESTEL factors or changes in the industry might trigger the need for internal audit.

Problems with existing internal control systems. Any problems with existing systems clearly signify the need for a tightening of systems and increased monitoring.

An increased number of unexplained or unacceptable events. System failures or similar events are a clear demonstration of internal control weakness.

The case on Franks & Fisher highlights three factors that would underpin its need to establish internal audit. There has been growth in number of products, activities and (presumably) processes in recent times, thereby complicating the internal environment and introducing more opportunity for internal control failure. There have been problems with internal control systems (the line stoppage and Mr Kumas's comment that, 'problems with internal control in a number of areas'). Finally, there was an unacceptable event (the line stoppage) that was attributed to poor internal control. Mr Kumas confirmed this with his opinion about a 'great need' for internal audit.

(b) In practice, a decision such as this one will depend on a number of factors including the supply of required skills in the internal and external job markets. In constructing the case for an external appointment, however, the following points can be made. Primarily, an external appointment would bring detachment and independence that would be less likely with an internal one. Firstly, then, an external appointment would help with independence and objectivity (avoiding the possibility of auditor capture). He or she would owe no personal loyalties nor 'favours' from previous positions. Similarly, he or she would have no personal grievances nor conflicts with other people from past disputes or arguments. Some benefit would be expected from the 'new broom' effect in that the appointment would see the company through fresh eyes. He or she would be unaware of vested interests. He or she would be likely to come in with new ideas and expertise gained from other situations. Finally, as with any external appointment, the possibility exists for the transfer of best practice in from outside – a net gain in knowledge for Franks & Fisher.

(c) The first thing to say is that Mr Kumas's belief is inappropriate and it would be unacceptable for the internal auditor to report to a divisional director who might be the subject of an internal audit. The reasons put forward in favour of his request are spurious. All of Mr Kumas's information and expertise would be available to the internal auditor in any event, with or without his oversight of the function. Reporting to Mr Kumas would be a clear threat to the independence of the internal auditor as he or she would not be objective in auditing the accounting and finance department. The advice from relevant codes and guidelines would also strongly counsel against Mr Kumas's proposal. The Cadbury code is typical where, point (g) under the 'role of the internal audit committee' emphasised the independence of the internal audit function from management. Mr Kumas's request should be refused.

(d) Objectivity is a state or quality that implies detachment, lack of bias, not influenced by personal feelings, prejudices or emotions. It is a very important quality in corporate governance generally and especially important in all audit situations where, regardless of personal feeling, the auditor must carry out his or her task objectively and with the purpose of the audit uppermost in mind. The IFAC Code of Ethics explains objectivity in the following terms (Introduction, clause 16): '… fair and should not allow prejudice or bias, conflict of interest or influence of others to override objectivity.'

It thus follows that characteristics that might demonstrate an internal auditor's professional objectivity will include fairness and even-handedness, freedom from bias or prejudice and the avoidance of conflicts of interest (e.g. by accepting gifts, threats to independence, etc.). The internal auditor should remember at all times that the purpose is to deliver a report on the systems being audited to his or her principal. In an external audit situation, the principal is ultimately the shareholder and in internal audit situations, it is the internal audit committee (and then ultimately, shareholders).

ACCA marking scheme		
		Marks
(a) 1 mark for each factor identified and briefly discussed		Max 7
1 mark for each factor applicable to Franks & Fisher		Max 3
		Max 10
(b) 1 mark for each relevant point identified and briefly described		Max 6
(c) 1 mark for each relevant point made		Max 4
(d) 2 marks for definition of objectivity		2
1 mark per relevant characteristic identified and briefly described		Max 3
		Max 5
Total		**25**

3   EASTERN PRODUCTS

(a)   An agency cost is a cost incurred by the shareholder in monitoring the activities of company agents (i.e. directors). Agency costs are normally considered as 'over and above' existing analysis costs and are the costs that arise because of compromised trust in agents (directors). In this case, the increased agency costs that arise are the increased monitoring and 'policing' costs that Sentosa House (Sonia) will incur because of the irregular behaviour described in the case.

The first problem identified is Eastern's non-compliance with relevant codes/ requirements in respect of non-executive directors and committee structure. There are an insufficient number of NEDs to form the normal committee structure for a public company which means that Sentosa may consider itself to have to monitor some of the risks to Eastern that otherwise the risk committee would undertake. The investor relations department shows evidence of being unhelpful and uninformed – an unfortunate combination of failings. The chairman appears to be arrogant and potentially untrustworthy (he saw no need for risk committee and dealt very abruptly with Sonia when she called). Finally, the company is pursuing risky strategies with no obvious explanation as to why such strategies are necessary.

In this situation, then, Sentosa House has the choice of selling its holding in Eastern or incurring increased monitoring costs to ensure that its own investors' interests, in turn, are adequately represented.

(b)   Intervention by an institutional investor in a company whose stock it holds is usually considered to be radical step and normally represents a step change in agency costs for the investor. This caveat notwithstanding, it is an important 'last resort' for institutional investors to have available to them as they seek to adequately represent the interests of their own investors.

There are a number of conditions under which it would be appropriate for institutional investors to intervene in a company whose shares it is holding.

The first condition is concerns about strategy in terms of products sold, markets serviced, expansions pursued or any other aspect of the company's overall strategic positioning.

Its operational performance may give rise, especially if there are one or more segments that have consistently underperformed without adequate explanation.

The third condition is when non-executive directors do not hold executive management to account. There may, for example, be evidence of unaccountable 'kitchen cabinets' or curious executive decisions that are not adequately challenged by non-executive directors.

Fourth, consistent or serious failure in internal controls would justify intervention, although this, in turn, may become evident through operational underperformance. Ongoing or unaddressed failures in, for example, quality assurance, health and safety, environmental emissions, budgetary control or information systems might justify intervention.

Failing to comply with the relevant code, laws or stock market rules is the next situation. If the company is listed in a rules-based jurisdiction, it is a matter of law but in a principles-based country, compliance is only 'optional' under the stock market's 'comply or explain' rules. Consistent or unexplained non-compliance is like to be penalised by the market

Sixth, inappropriate remuneration policies, if extreme or obviously self-serving, might attract intervention. Such a situation would normally also signify a failure of the remunerations committee which would make it a double cause for concern.

Finally, a poor approach to social responsibility is a condition for possible intervention, especially if there is publicly-available evidence that might adversely affect the reputation of the company.

With reference to the case, Eastern Products fails on several counts that might encourage institutional shareholder intervention. Firstly, its failure to comply with relevant code (particularly on number of non-executive directors and lack of risk committee). Second, the non-executive directors are not holding executives to account because there is an insufficient number of them. Third, there are concerns about strategy (which is considered to be very risky).

(c) Risk committees are considered best practice by most corporate governance regimes around the world for a number of reasons. Sonia has, for good reason, doubts over the competence and good faith of the management of Eastern Products and a risk committee made up of non-executive directors could help her confidence in a number of ways.

In the first instance, the information systems put in place to provide information for the risk committee. This would generate awareness of and facilitate review of all relevant risks for discussion by the risk committee, including those arising from the 'very risky' strategy.

It would review and assess the effectiveness of internal controls on risk. A committee made up of independent, non-executive directors would bring scrutiny to Thomas on two fronts. There is evidence that Thomas may be relatively inexperienced, having been in post for only two years, and the way that he dealt with Sonia's entirely legitimate enquiry shows some evidence of immaturity and/or impatience. Non executive presence would be able to challenge and act as a counterweight to this failing. Non-executive directors would also bring scrutiny of Thomas's leadership over strategy, especially (in the context of the risk committee) the wisdom of his 'very risky' strategies.

(d) The opinion shows confusion over the meaning of the term 'compulsory'. Whilst in a principles-based jurisdiction, compliance is not legally compulsory, it is required for the stock market listing. Accordingly, compliance is effectively compulsory if the company wishes to enjoy the benefits of its listing. Companies in principles-based jurisdictions are subject to 'comply or explain' in that non-compliance needs to be explained in terms of specific areas of non-compliance and the reason for noncompliance. Compliance is also necessary for market confidence in the Eastern Products stock in that the market would be likely to devalue a stock that was a consistent non-complier. Finally, shareholders and stock markets are entitled to challenge the explanation for non-compliance if they aren't satisfied with the explanation given in the annual report.

ACCA marking scheme		
		Marks
(a)	Definition of agency costs	2
	1 mark for each problem identified and briefly	
	discussed	Max 5
		Max 7
(b)	1 mark for each relevant point identified and briefly	
	described on conditions for intervention	Max 7
	1 mark for each relevant point made on Eastern	
	House	Max 3
		Max 10
(c)	1 mark for each relevant point made	Max 4
(d)	1 mark for each relevant point made	Max 4
Total		**25**